Crafting Truth

Crafting Truth

Short Studies in Creative Nonfiction

BRUCE BALLENGER
Boise State University

Longman
Boston Columbus Indianapolis New York San Francisco
Upper Saddle River Amsterdam Cape Town Dubai London Madrid
Milan Munich Paris Montréal Toronto Delhi Mexico City
São Paulo Sydney Hong Kong Seoul Singapore Taipei Tokyo

Executive Editor: Suzanne Phelps Chambers
Senior Marketing Manager: Sandra McGuire
Associate Development Editor: Erin Reilly
Production Coordinator: Scarlett Lindsay
Project Coordination, Interior Design,
    and Electronic Page Makeup: Integra Software Services, Inc.
Cover Design Manager: John Callahan
Cover Designer: Maria Ilardi
Cover Illustration/Photo: Spinning the Yarn, by Carl Wilhelm Hubner, © David
    David Gallery/SuperStock
Visual Researcher: Linda Sykes
Senior Manufacturing Buyer: Dennis J. Para
Printer and Binder: Courier Corporation—Stoughton
Cover Printer: Courier Corporation—Stoughton

For permission to use copyrighted material, grateful acknowledgment is made to the copyright holders on pp. 231–232, which are hereby made part of this copyright page.

Library of Congress Cataloging-in-Publication Data

Ballenger, Bruce P.
Crafting truth/Bruce Ballenger.—1st ed.
    p. cm.
Includes bibliographical references and index.
ISBN 978-0-205-58645-5
1. Authorship—Handbooks, manuals, etc.   I. Title.
PN145.B423 2011
808'.02—dc22

2010039767

2 3 4 5 6 7 8 9 10—V036—13 12 11

Longman
is an imprint of

www.pearsonhighered.com ISBN-10:   0-205-58645-7

ISBN-13: 978-0-205-58645-5

*For Karen, my first guide
into these territories.*

CONTENTS

ᘓᘓᘓ

Part 3
The Literary Journalists   115

Part 4

A Brief Anthology   163

PREFACE

We're all writing theorists, even if we never made writing a subject of study. We express these tacit theories about writing when we say things like, "The most important thing a writer should do is read a lot," or "How we create imaginative literature is a mystery that will never be understood," or "Great writers are born not made." These *are* theories, of course, which work from certain assumptions about language acquisition that may or may not be true, but because they seem commonsensical, these assumptions are rarely discussed. Before you begin working with *Crafting Truth: Short Studies in Creative Nonfiction,* I'd like you to know some of the theories behind this book. What are my beliefs about how nonfiction writers improve at their craft, and in what ways do these beliefs shape the book's approach?

First, though, here is one thing I *don't* believe: Writing talent is written into our genetic code. Perhaps genius is. I'm not sure. But I don't know any geniuses, and in 25 years of teaching writing, I haven't encountered any in the classroom. I also don't believe that writing is a mysterious process. Successful writers might think it is because they're spooked by the idea of analyzing a process that is working for them. Less successful writers might believe in the mystery of creation as a way to explain their failures; if writing is an unknowable craft, then what's the use of continuing the struggle? The academic discipline of composition and rhetoric has spent the last 60 years producing research on how writing ability develops—unraveling this "mystery." But while much of this process is clearly relevant to the development of creative writers, there isn't lots of practical information about how to encourage both imagination and craft. Naturally, that hasn't stopped anyone from publishing books like this one that seem to offer exactly that.

Generally speaking, most texts on creative nonfiction do one of two things: They offer a collection of published nonfiction by successful authors or they feature one of these authors explaining the craft in chapters on structure, scene, narrative method, and so on. Both of these approaches might be useful. Anthologies work from the theory that reading and analyzing a range of published pieces will help apprentice writers to identify techniques and then import these into their own work. Single-authored "how to" texts are based on the theory that knowledge of craft—acquiring information about how creative writing is done—will also transfer into the reader's own writing, perhaps providing new ideas about how a writing problem might be approached. There is, however, no evidence that either of these approaches work, even if they do "make sense."

I wish I could say that *Crafting Truth* is based on new research about how to help writers master creative nonfiction genres. But I cannot. The best I can do is tell you up front what the theories are behind the book's approach. Then you can decide whether they make as much sense to you as they do to me.

- *More than anything, writers improve by doing rather than just knowing.* Reading books about how to write essays, memoirs, or articles is undoubtedly useful, and there is no shortage of such good books. While, similarly, much of this book contains information about craft, it is very deliberately designed to encourage its users to *write* about what they read here. For example, every brief chapter concludes with a writing exercise that encourages readers to also be writers who apply what they've learned. Furthermore, I hope instructors will use the professional examples as occasions for analytical writing, helping their students to not just know about but to *understand* the narrative techniques of America's best nonfiction writers.

- *Analysis of many elements of craft is especially productive through close study of a relevant part of a larger text.* Writing students often don't do enough close reading, and the reason is simple—writing instructors often ask them to read a lot of material in one sitting: long essays or even books. Unlike conventional anthologies, most of *Crafting Truth* is organized around brief excerpts from larger works, chosen because they seem most fruitful for study. I'll admit that this approach is risky. Are these really the best excerpts from the respective works? When a part of a text is isolated from the rest of the work, is its essential context lost? These are important questions, but in my judgment much is still to be gained from reading just a small part of a larger work. You'll notice, however, that *Crafting Truth* does include an anthology of longer work, but that isn't the focus of the text.

- *There is value in analyzing how a variety of good writers handle the same narrative problems.* We are all well advised to spend time reading a body of work by a writer we admire. It is also wise to read the works from which the excerpts were taken; all of them, I think, represent landmark creative nonfiction. However, *Crafting Truth* offers its users an opportunity to efficiently examine the work of many published authors relatively quickly. In 20 minutes, for instance, you can see how

Truman Capote, James Baldwin, or Gretel Ehrlich each handles the crafting of scene or dialogue.

- *To fully appreciate how authors have constructed nonfiction narratives, it is important to study the larger work.* Students of writers like David Sedaris or Norman Mailer can learn much by reading excerpts from their best work, but the apprenticeship should extend to study of the works from which the passages in *Crafting Truth* are drawn. I have also included the longer work of a handful of additional contemporary creative nonfiction writers in an anthology in the back of the book. These selections provide great opportunities for applying what you learned from excerpts to more complete narratives.

You may know most of the published writers featured in *Crafting Truth.* You can probably think of more who might have been included. Creative nonfiction is arguably as old as the sixteenth-century French nobleman Michel de Montaigne, father of the personal essay—or older if you count St. Augustine's *Confessions*—and the so-called "fourth genre" has helped define this literary age. Creative nonfiction programs have proliferated in universities and colleges across the United States, including mine, and their courses rarely fail to enroll at full capacity. Literary journals and magazines are typically flooded with nonfiction submissions, and we are treated, almost daily, to essays on the radio. Before long, multimedia essays—pieces that use video, sound, and graphics—may become commonplace. Though the sections in *Crafting Truth* on memoir, literary journalism, and personal essay focus largely on what I consider canonical work in creative nonfiction, I've also tried to include examples of more-experimental material, like the radio essay or the fictional memoir.

More than anything, however, *Crafting Truth* is focused on how writers use words on a page—those orderly lines of text which, in the absence of other media, must stand alone. The qualities of a good story remain timeless, and the professional authors featured here are among the best nonfiction storytellers America has produced in the last 50 years. It is, admittedly, a narrow window through which to see the richness of creative nonfiction, which not only transcends this time but also this place. Creative nonfiction flourishes not only in English-speaking countries but also in Latin America and the East—and it has for a long time. Serious writers should make it their mission to experience all of these traditions. My ambition for *Crafting Truth*, however, is limited to this: to show you what a selection of contemporary American artists can do in four well-crafted paragraphs or less. It is a small window, but the view can be stunning.

~~~~~

Acknowledgments

This book began as a collaboration with students in my creative nonfiction classes. Our vision was that *Crafting Truth* would feature their responses to the work in the book and their ideas for writing exercises. We envisioned all kinds of ways these—and ultimately other—talented and largely (yet) unpublished writers could bring their voices to the text, and we all agreed that it would make the book unique. We thought students using the text would appreciate reading what other students had to say about craft. In this spirit, with the help of Patti Knox, a graduate of our MFA program, we launched a Web site to solicit student responses to the material in *Crafting Truth* from around the country, and we did a mass mailing to encourage submissions. Sadly, the effort generated little response. Distracted by other projects, it was several years before I could return to this book, and by then many of my original student collaborators had moved on, and I resumed writing *Crafting Truth* without them. But I still heard their voices puzzling over Mairs, marveling at Capote, and expressing reverence for Didion. Although this is not the book we planned to write together, *Crafting Truth* is inspired by my creative nonfiction students' insight into the genre and passion for their own experiments in truth-telling. I have been their student as much as I have been their teacher. Two students were especially important contributors to this project—Patti Knox and Andrea Oyarzabal. It was my good fortune that they happened into my classes at Boise State.

I'm grateful, too, for my editor's support. Suzanne Phelps Chambers was enthusiastic about *Crafting Truth* from the start, and she was incredibly patient with the project as it drifted past deadlines. Suzanne and Erin Reilly, my development editor at Pearson, were astute readers of reviews and revisions of the manuscript and offered great suggestions along the way. Sarah Burkhart has copyedited many of my books, including this one. I'm a writer who needs a good copyeditor, but I never imagined I would be blessed with one as good as Sarah.

Finally, I want to thank those reviewers, whose comments made a significant difference in the quality of this book: Bruce Alford, University of South Alabama; Lynn Bloom, University of Connecticut; Suzanne Greenberg, California State University–Long Beach; Libby Gruner, University of Richmond; Dawn Haines, University of New Hampshire; Holly Hassel, University of Wisconsin–Marathon County; Sonya Huber, Georgia Southern University; Kiese Laymon, Vassar College; Brandon R. Schrand, University of Idaho; Ira Sukrungruang, State University of New York–Oswego; Robert Vivian, Alma College; and Pauline Woodward, Endicott College.

BRUCE BALLENGER

Crafting Truth

INTRODUCTION

The Form and Theory of Creative Nonfiction

You already have spent your lifetime telling "true" stories, slapped together with the adhesive of two words: *and then.* "So the neighbor saw us parked on the street for about a half hour, and then called the cops. And then they looked under the seat of the truck, and they saw the open bottle of Bud. And then I offered to do a breath test, but the officer saw that I wasn't drunk. He could tell I was being honest, and then he brought me home. Sorry about the handcuffs; he said it was state law." The simplest (and sometimes the best) nonfiction stories are made this way, telling what happened from beginning to end, relying on the organizing power of chronology. But there are many other ways of telling a true story, and some of these begin in the middle—not at the end. Some linger on moments that would normally be just the flash of a highway sign while the teller speeds to his destination. Some stories compress or expand time—a single moment, maybe even five minutes, becomes an entire story that is as long as one that covers 30 years.

Crafting Truth is a book about why nonfiction writers might make decisions like these. It's a study of how writers' motives in telling stories lead them to shape one kind of narrative rather than another, particularly in the genres called "creative nonfiction." Of course, nonfiction genres run the gamut from writing we do in the workplace—memos and reports—to deeply personal explorations of sex abuse. Creative nonfiction is a subset of this large family, and this book focuses on the three most popular forms: essay, memoir, and literary journalism. Why these three? While they certainly differ, as you'll see, essays, memoirs, and literary journalism are all concerned with storytelling, and to a greater or lesser extent they are genres that draw from the same well as other imaginative literature. It's easy to confuse Truman Capote's *In Cold Blood* with a novel and a Lia Purpura essay with a poem. Both use the familiar devices of narrative storytelling: scene, character, dialogue, point of view, and often exquisite language. But creative nonfiction forms fundamentally differ from novels and poems in two ways: They don't just show but they tell, too, and the stories are "true."

1

On Missing the Target

It turns out that the best way to begin a story about telling true stories is at the beginning. Why might writers turn to an essay rather than a short story, or a memoir rather than a novel? A place to begin understanding this is to return to the title of one of George Orwell's famous essays, "Why I Write." Our interest here isn't Orwell, but another essayist, Joan Didion, who borrowed Orwell's title for a piece exploring the same theme. "I write entirely to find out what I'm thinking," wrote Didion, "what I'm looking at, what I see and what it means." Self-discovery is a motive many other writers share, most famously expressed by the novelist E. M. Forster when he said, "How do I know what I think until I see what I say?" To do this, however, they must accept something that apprentice writers rarely do: allow the work to defy intention. "Writers value the gun that does *not* hit the target at which it is aimed," wrote Pulitzer Prize–winning essayist Donald Murray.

This is quite an extraordinary idea, particularly for those of us who have been school writers most of our lives. The academic essay is most often an exercise in avoiding accidents: Decide on a thesis and use it to muscle the material into obedience; ignore what conflicts with what one already thinks; and march without digression toward a predetermined conclusion. There is nothing inherently wrong with such an approach. In school, the efficiency of knowing what ducks you will shoot, and in what order, makes a great deal of rhetorical sense. But creative nonfiction offers writers a different kind of invitation: the opportunity for surprises and discoveries that frequently occur when the writing takes wing in unexpected directions. You expect it to fly south and it flies east instead. Your job, simply, is to follow the writing to where it leads.

This motive—to discover what you didn't know you knew—might just as easily explain why a fiction writer or poet sits down to compose. What distinguishes the nonfiction writer's aims? For one thing, it's a great deal more personal. Nancy Mairs writes about suicide, rape, and her struggles with multiple sclerosis. While her intention is certainly to inform and enlighten, Mairs's motives as an essayist are drawn from a deeper well: "I have always had to tell myself the story of myself in order to sense a self at all." The narrator of nonfiction does not masquerade in the guise of someone else. While we might speculate about the relationship between author and narrator in a short story, in an essay there is no doubt. It is Nancy Mairs speaking when she confesses in her essay "Touching by Accident" that she considered killing herself with gas rather than Elavil but worried that the fumes might harm her cat, Bête Noire. Even though she rarely mentions herself, it is Joan Didion who is narrating the story of Lucille Miller burning her husband to death in a Volkswagen in "Some Dreamers of the Golden Dream." While the narrator may be, as Phillip Lopate put it, an "I-character"—someone who operates in a nonfiction narrative much as a character would in any story—there is no doubt that the slender "I" through which we see is the author whose name we know, who actually lives (or lived) somewhere and breathed this air.

The Collapse of the Narrator

It is this difference—the elimination of the usual gaps between the author of a story and its teller—that most distinguishes nonfiction from its cousins, fiction and poetry. The implications of this are significant. While all creative writers may celebrate surprise in their work, they may not be as intensely interested as creative nonfiction writers are in what *they* think or feel. E. B. White called the personal essay "the last resort of the egoist." Creative nonfiction, and the essay in particular, is a personal exploration in which the writer often lifts the curtain on the process of coming to know and makes it part of the story. The writer becomes a subject. While this can happen in other imaginative literature, creative nonfiction narratives are often balanced on the fulcrum of the author's self-knowledge.

This is not meant to suggest that all creative nonfiction writers choose the first person to tell their stories. Telling a nonfiction story in the third person is a question of craft: Where do writers want to direct their readers' gazes—on the narrator or the subject? Writers like Tracy Kidder, whose many works of nonfiction include *House* and the Pulitzer Prize–winning *The Soul of a New Machine*, noted that when he was young, he felt he had "a moral obligation to write in the first person" to confront the assumption that journalism could be objective. He realized later that he was much more likely to write honestly about subjects other than himself. Yet even in Kidder's work, his subjects and his readers know who is narrating. We immediately see through the illusion of omniscience in a way we might not in a novel. Because it's a work of nonfiction, readers easily imagine Kidder as an observer-participant in a scene, actively looking into the material at hand for the story he is telling.

The collapse of the customary gap between narrator and author also means that we read nonfiction narratives differently. We hold them to different standards. While we might tolerate unreliable narrators in fiction, we often tighten the restraints on nonfiction narrators. We want to like them despite their flaws. We must like them enough to want to know what they think and how they feel. We are drawn—or not—to the writers' quality of mind. We must also believe that nonfiction narrators will take us somewhere interesting. Creative nonfiction, like much writing, must ultimately answer a very simple question: *So what?* This is a particularly urgent question for essayists who dare to write about themselves. Why should anyone care that Scott Russell Sanders inherited a hammer from his father, the triggering subject of his much-anthologized essay "The Inheritance of Tools"? While readers might indulge ambiguity of purpose in a short story or poem, nonfiction narrators are expected to make explicit promises about the significance of their stories and to keep that promise. When they don't, we might find the work uninteresting, or worse, solipsistic.

Telling It Straight

Most of all, we expect nonfiction narrators to tell us the truth. "There is one thing the essayist cannot do," wrote White, "he cannot indulge himself in deceit or concealment, for he will be found out in no time." When we read a work of nonfiction, we expect that the events that are described actually happened and that the writers' responses to these events are honest. Few issues related to writing nonfiction have gotten more public attention than this. Even Oprah Winfrey weighed in on the topic when a few years ago, after recommending James Frey's "memoir," *A Million Little Pieces,* to her book club, she learned that some of his story was fictionalized. In a nationally televised confrontation with the author, Oprah said she felt "duped" and "betrayed" by Frey. Another best-selling memoir, *Running with Scissors* by Augusten Burroughs, was the subject of a lawsuit by a family who claimed the author's published account of his time with them was riddled with "fabrications" and "embellishments."

Burroughs's reaction to the allegations is telling. "This is my story," he told *Vanity Fair* magazine. "It's not my mother's story and it's not the family's story, and they may remember things differently and they may choose to not remember certain things, but I will never forget what happened to me, ever, and I have the scars from it and I wanted to rip those scars off of me." Memoirists and essayists agree on this: Memory is a fickle thing. All of us, writers or not, have the experience of telling a story in the presence of others who were involved and being told that it didn't happen that way at all. We remember some things and forget others. We tell stories with our own slants. But if the truth of what actually happened can be known, is the nonfiction writer obligated to get it right? For the journalist, the answer is simple. Accuracy is essential. But what about for the essayist or memoirist?

In "On Keeping a Notebook," Joan Didion wrote that she no longer worries about the distinction between "what happened and what merely might have happened," because the point of keeping a notebook is to remember "how it felt to be me." The same might be said of essays and memoirs; writers in these genres are certainly interested in getting at the *emotional truth* of things, a deeply subjective and deeply personal perspective of things remembered that may transform them into scenes few others who were there might recognize. But what distinguishes nonfiction from fiction is that characters in a nonfiction narrative, as Daniel Lehman observed, live both "inside and outside the story." They are not inventions but are (or were) real people. Sometimes these characters disagree with the telling, and even worse, are deeply wounded by what was said.

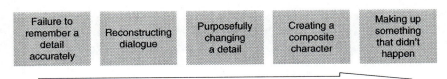

A Continuum of Lies: Where to Draw the Line?

Figure 1 Richard Hugo advises young poets that "the words should not serve the subject. The subject should serve the words. This may mean violating the facts.... You owe reality nothing and the truth about your feelings everything." Nonfiction obviously has a different relationship to reality. But what is it? What kinds of invention are acceptable and which are not? Imagine a continuum of lies, each more potentially egregious than the next. Where might you draw the line?

Yet creative nonfiction writers must have more latitude than the journalist, if for no other reason than the vagaries of memory. It is truly difficult, if not impossible, for instance, for a writer to accurately reconstruct dialogue from a conversation that took place 30 years ago unless she took notes; and most of us did not. Therefore, we might imagine a continuum of lies, some acceptable and others not, ranging from not remembering exactly to making up events that never occurred (see Figure 1). Ethically speaking, where should the creative nonfiction writer draw the line? For Tracy Kidder, whose work tends toward literary journalism, even if the characters in a story don't know or don't care whether it's truthfully told, the writer knows, and fabrications subvert the work. "I try to hew to what has begun to seem like a narrow definition of nonfiction.... I'm afraid that if I started making things up in a story that purported to be about real events and people, I'd stop believing it myself. And I imagine that such a loss of conviction would infect every sentence and make each one unbelievable."

The ethics of truth-telling for the creative nonfiction writer present this dilemma: *Which is the writer's most important obligation—to the reality of what happened or to telling a good story?* The novelist isn't troubled by this at all. Reality is in the service of imagination, and both are enlisted to tell a good story—and it's the story that matters. Creative nonfiction writers, on the other hand, begin with reality and are bound to find a story to tell within it. To knowingly fabricate what happened not only betrays the reader's trust, as Kidder reminds us; it also puts the writer's search for the truth of things at risk. All literature is arguably about trying to get to the truth of things. The writer's method of inquiry into truth is essentially inductive, looking closely at the particular and finding unexpected meaning in it. For Scott Russell Sanders it is a singular day when he hits his thumb with his father's hammer, and this ordinary event propels him into a meditation on the "cloud of knowing" that the hickory-handled tool contains. All creative writers deal in such telling details, but nonfiction writers must find them in the stuff of daily life, both moments remembered and moments observed. To knowingly invent such details—to make up the hammer—is to knowingly mislead the writer, as well as the reader.

Taking the Reflective Turn

The storyteller's art is to find a pattern in these telling details. All creative writers actively look for such patterns, trying to discover how the particulars might stand in for larger ideas about the way things are. The conventional advice to fiction writers is to avoid hammering home these discoveries to readers—to "show, don't tell"—and let the story speak for itself, however ambiguously. But nonfiction writers are much more committed to saying what they think, to both show *and* tell. "The essay is distinguished from the short story," said Scott Russell Sanders, "not by the presence or absence of literary devices, not by tone of theme or subject, but by the writer's stance toward the material. In composing an essay about what it was like to grow up on [a] military base, I *meant* something quite different from what I mean when concocting a story." This is one of the ironies of writing creative nonfiction: While writers often allow the work to initially defy intention, once it is discovered, nonfiction writers are determined that readers understand the meanings they dislodged in the telling of their stories.

Though nonfiction works vary in how much writers explain what they mean, reflection is an essential part of most creative nonfiction, particularly the essay and the memoir. Frequently, this is an account of not only what happened but what *happens,* much like the two narrative strands in the television programs *The Wonder Years, Grey's Anatomy,* and, if a dead narrator counts, *Desperate Housewives.* Whether this narrator is looking back or simply looking at more recent experiences, he brings understanding to an event that wasn't available at the time. In *The Wonder Years,* for instance, we experienced not only eighth-grader Kevin's awkward encounters with Winnie Cooper, the dark haired girl across the street, but also the reflections on the meanings of those experiences in the narrating voice of an adult Kevin. The personal essayist, in particular, is interested in this question: *What do I understand about this now that I didn't understand then?* These insights might constitute a narrative of thought in an essay that runs alongside the story of what happened. These reflections may be hinted at, expressed in a line, or examined in paragraphs of exposition, but they are rarely missing entirely from a work of creative nonfiction.

In the hands of an inexperienced writer, this reflection can be clumsy, and exposition in any story, including nonfiction, is often viewed suspiciously. Why is it necessary for writers to say what they think? Let the story speak for itself! In its least-appealing form, reflection is the paragraph at the end of a narrative that begins, "And now as I look back on this, I understand that true friends are hard to find." More often the turns to reflection might seem like unearned insight, added like a pinch of paprika to a soup because it helps finish off the look of the dish. In an essay or memoir, retrospection is not merely an ingredient in the narrative. It's what drives the process. The narrative is in the service of this groping toward some fresh understanding about the meanings of experience. It is in the reflective turns that the motives for writing memoirs or essays are satisfied—to enjoy the pleasures of discovering what you didn't know you knew.

It is helpful to imagine, Phillip Lopate has told us, that there are really two narrators in an essay or memoir—the "I-character" to whom things happened and the "intelligent narrator" who brings understandings about the significance of what happened that the "I-character" did not have then. As in the *The Wonder Years,* the intelligent narrator must be present throughout the work, not just at the end. In addition to the usual narrative pattern—this happened and then this happened—the arc away from the story to reflect on its significance represents another kind of narrative movement characteristic of nonfiction. We become as interested in this narrative of thought as we do in the events that unfold in the story, particularly if these insights are tethered tightly to the writer's experiences or observations. The essayist may even create the illusion that these thoughts seem to arise simultaneously with the telling itself (see the excerpt from Andre Dubus, on page 54).

Appreciating the essay and memoir has much to do with enjoying the pleasures of the writer's mind, following his or her often-meandering trails of thought through the story. "A personal essay is like the human voice talking," wrote Edward Hoagland, "its order, the mind's natural flow, instead of a systemized outline of ideas. Though more wayward or informal than an article or treatise, somewhere it contains a point which is its real center, even if the point couldn't be uttered in fewer words than the essayist has used." Reflection in an essay and memoir is a kind of messenger pigeon, sent by the writer to deliver the work's questions, ideas, tentative meanings; it rarely flies far from the story below or it risks drifting into abstraction and away from the writer's experience, which is the source of meaning.

Building It Scene by Scene

Literary journalism—a term that might describe not only Tracy Kidder's work but Truman Capote's "nonfiction novel," *In Cold Blood,* as well as similar books by Gay Talese, Norman Mailer, Jane Kramer, Barbara Ehrenreich, and Joe McGinniss—is a category of creative nonfiction that most resembles fiction. As Tracy Kidder observed earlier, literary journalists may not write in the first person, choosing narrators other than themselves and deflecting readers' gazes away from their personal reflections, which they may avoid entirely. One of these writers, Tom Wolfe, explained that the third-person point of view in which the writer "penetrates the thoughts of another person" is possible in nonfiction only through interview, but it is a perspective that is less limiting than first person and more likely to keep readers focused on the story.

Third-person point of view, Wolfe has told us, is one of four techniques the journalist borrows from literary realism. These techniques include what he calls "status details," or particulars that stand in for someone's social status or aspirations, as well as dialogue, which Wolfe believes best defines character. But the most fundamental of these devices is "scene-by-scene construction," the literary technique that is common to most forms of creative nonfiction, including essay and memoir. Scene can be understood as the most basic ingredient in nonfiction narrative, and it is a writer's skill at observing or remembering what exactly happened with a density of detail that often distinguishes the novice from the professional. To do this well requires a faith in the power of the particular. It is the kind of faith that all creative writers share—a recognition that even the most ordinary things can say more than they say. But for nonfiction writers, skillful rendering of scenes also demands an accountant's instinct for collecting and inventorying details.

Fiction writers, enjoying the luxury of invention, can mine their imaginations for material with which to craft a scene. Or if they draw on experience, they are not bound by time, borrowing here and there from multiple events to compose a single scene. The nonfiction writer, on the other hand, is constrained by the reality of what actually happened. What this means, practically speaking, is that the memoirist must attempt to reconstruct things—the color of the father's fedora, the brand of cigarette in his mouth, and the smell of his deerskin leather gloves—or the literary journalist must take copious notes, taking virtually no detail for granted. Who knows what materials might be needed to later craft the scene? "Writers," Henry James once said, "are people on whom nothing is lost," and this is especially true of the nonfiction writer who is charged, usually after the fact, with truthfully recreating reality.

The scene in nonfiction may in some ways closely resemble the scene in the short story or novel. It is frequently framed by time and place—something happened somewhere and then it was over—and is observed from a consistent perspective. In the essay and memoir, this is most often from the point of view of the narrator/writer, or in literary journalism, another character. In any scene, something happens. This may or may not be dramatic in the conventional sense, but it must always be relevant, either carrying some symbolic weight or providing background that will later carry some charge of meaning. Scenes in all imaginative literature also are rendered with great particularity, frequently drawing on all of the senses, though they may also include summaries or digressions; sometimes scenes might be interrupted only to be resumed later. Though fictional narrators rarely comment on the meaning of what happened in a scene, the essayist often does, and it is this reflection—which may be a line or paragraphs of exposition—that often distinguishes scenes in nonfiction from those in other genres.

For example, in Andre Dubus's lovely essay about his boyhood dreams of playing professional baseball, "Under the Lights," he crafted a scene in which Harry Strohm, the owner-manager of the local semiprofessional baseball team, joins Dubus's family for dinner after a game. After the meal, Dubus's father tells Harry that young Andre "wants to be a ballplayer." Remembering that Strohm had recently watched him mishandle a ground ball in a baseball clinic, Dubus was afraid of what the older man would say. "Harry turned his bright eyes on me," wrote Dubus, "and into the secret self, or selves, I believe I hid from everyone, especially my parents, and most of all, my father...."

> [A]mid the aroma of coffee and tobacco smoke at the table at Poorboy's, when he gazed at me with those eyes like embedded gems, brilliant and ancient, I saw in them myself that morning, bound by the strings of my fear.... Harry Strohm said nothing at the table; or if he did, I heard it as nothing. Perhaps he said quietly: That's good....
>
> I was wrong, and I did not know I was wrong until this very moment, as I write this. When Harry looked at me across the table, he was not looking at my body and into my soul and deciding I would never be a ballplayer, he was not focusing on my trifling error on that long day of the clinic. He was looking at my young hope and seeing his own that propelled him into and kept him in this vocation, this game he had played nearly all of his life.

While this scene contains many of the elements one might find in a work of fiction, it departs most noticeably when Dubus writes, "I did not know I was wrong until this very moment, as I write this." This begins a shift into retrospection that is more characteristic of the essay than of the short story. While some essays present scenes without commentary on their meaning (and some fictional narrators in short stories or novels reflect like essayists), it is more common that scenes in nonfiction are anchored firmly to explicit expressions about their significance. For the essayist and memoirist, the choice to craft a scene is not just to maintain the forward movement of the narrative; it is also an opportunity to mine the moment for meaning, to use it to satisfy the writer's hunger for self-discovery.

Creating Tension

For writers, this hunger to discover arises from a tension between what they think they know and what the writing is beginning to reveal, and these are the surprises that keep writers writing. This is also a tension that keeps readers reading. It is common knowledge that well-told stories demand some kind of narrative or dramatic tension, and this tension is created through the sense that there are opposing forces at work. The simple question, *What is going to happen next?* is triggered by the tension between what readers know and what they want to know, and this is the most familiar source of dramatic tension in storytelling. But because much creative nonfiction relies as much on exposition as it does on narrative, dramatic tension may simply not be enough. If not handled skillfully, manipulating a narrative in nonfiction to deliberately withhold information from readers, particularly when it implies that writers somehow don't know what's going to happen when it's obvious they really do know, can seem like a clever trick or a transparent device to make a story more interesting. Fortunately, nonfiction writers have other options to create tension.

Ultimately the work has to answer a simple question: *So what?* Or as Philip Gerard suggested, creative nonfiction must, directly or indirectly, make this clear: *What is at stake here?* Why might this story matter to the reader? What is at stake for the writer or the characters? Is there a larger truth that will somehow matter? Because much nonfiction, especially the personal essay, deals with experiences that are often quite ordinary—a visit to a summer lake, losing one's hat, watching a fight—the burden of these questions is particularly heavy. Tension is how the work tries to answer them. Fundamentally, every essay, memoir, or piece of literary journalism must seem purposeful. Readers must feel that writers are steering them

STRUCTURE AND TENSION

The effectiveness of the design of a nonfiction piece has a great deal to do with whether it has sufficient tension to keep a reader reading. There is a range of strategies for introducing tension into writing through structure. Here are some of them:

- *Withholding information.* This is a risky one. Whenever we deliberately don't say what readers expect us to say, writers risk seeming overtly manipulative. The worst example of this is what John McPhee calls the "blind lead"—the beginning that withholds information and promises something dramatic later, "blaring a great fanfare of trumpets and then a mouse comes out of its hole." But when it's artfully done, carefully holding off a reader by parceling out information can work to introduce tension.
- *Manipulating time.* The best place to begin a story may not be the beginning. Writers have power over time that they don't have in life. This power can be used to create tension by structuring past and present in ways that raise pressing questions. Why did that happen? What's the full story? What do these different moments have in common?
- *Juxtaposition.* The placement of ideas, moments,

toward some destination, or those readers will stop pedaling and get off the bike. After all, reading involves some work. Usually, purpose is signaled early in the work—the first few paragraphs of a short essay, the first page or two in a longer one, or perhaps an early chapter in a memoir. This destination must seem appealing, and tension is key.

Introducing tension in creative nonfiction is an exercise in defying readers' expectations. This can be accomplished in four ways: through dramatic tension (the most familiar kind), emotional tension, thematic tension, and, finally, the tension introduced through language.

- Dramatic tension, mentioned earlier, exploits readers' expectations about what will happen. *Will the story unfold in ways I expect?*

or information in proximity to each other can create tension, particularly when such an arrangement raises questions about their relationship. What could this scene possibly have to do with this one? Aren't these feelings contradictory?

- *Questions.* Writers often arrange material that raises questions in the reader's mind. But these may also be explicit. When the writer pauses to pose a question that arises from the material, she may do so to point directly to the tension that drives the piece or dictates its arrangement. These questions must, however, be well placed.

- Emotional tension arises from the gap between what readers' expect that writers should feel in a situation and what they report they really do feel. He was *glad* that his father was dead?

- Because so much creative nonfiction deals explicitly with ideas, the narrative of thought provides movement that conventional stories often lack, and this can provide thematic tension. Writers might offer an idea or a way of seeing the subject that is at odds with the way readers usually see it. For example, in "No Wonder They Call Me a Bitch," Ann Hodgman decides to take the claims of dog food companies seriously and find out whether Gravy Train really does make "thick, rich, real beef gravy." She spends a week eating it and other brands that make similar human rather than canine culinary appeals—something most of us would not consider doing to test the claims on a bag of dog food. Hodgman's funny essay is also a serious critique of such advertising pitches. Thematic tension might also arise when a writer juxtaposes two ideas that seem in opposition, and readers wonder how the apparent contradictions might be reconciled.

- Finally, we may be drawn to language. Writers might have a way of saying things that surprise us, things that imply a narrator with whom we are willing to spend some time. The great stylists—Norman Mailer,

Joan Didion, Tom Wolfe, Gay Talese, Hunter Thompson, and others—often exploit this tension, creating personas in their work that we might find appealing or repugnant or simply interesting. For example, here is the opening of Thompson's *Hell's Angels*:

> California, Labor Day weekend... early, with ocean fog still in the streets, outlaw motorcyclists wearing chains, shades and greasy Levi's roll out from damp garages, all-night diners and cast-off one-night pads in Frisco, Hollywood, Berdoo and East Oakland, heading for the Monterey peninsula, north of Big Sur.... The Menace is loose again, the Hell's Angels, the hundred-carat headline, running fast and loud on the early morning freeway, low in the saddle, nobody smiles, jamming crazy through traffic and ninety miles an hour down the center strip, missing by inches... like Genghis Khan on an iron horse, a monster steed with a fiery anus, flat out through the eye of a beer can and up your daughter's leg with no quarter asked and none given....

Thompson's voice here throws sparks, not only because he is writing about a group of irreverent, dangerous outlaws but also because he seems to share the irreverence. The language is electric—the bikers roll out, run "fast and loud," jam "crazy" through traffic, "flat out through the eye of a beer can"—and sometimes a little shocking—"fiery anus" and "up your daughter's leg." We are going on a ride not just with the motorcycle gang but with Thompson himself, and the language beckons us to go along.

Casting a Wide Net

When I was ten, I attended summer camp in northern Wisconsin, a few weeks in July that happened to coincide with a total solar eclipse. The year, I believe, was 1963, a few months before John Kennedy was slain in Dallas. I remembered the eclipse vividly, particularly the way that the shadows of the leaves on the tent canvas took on the curve of the eclipsing sun. For a few moments, it was a world of bent light before the darkness. In memory, and later in an essay about that time, this event took on symbolic significance. But was it 1963? And is it possible that I observed a partial eclipse, that the darkness wasn't as sudden and as black as I remembered it? It is the journalist's obligation to check such things, but depending on the essayist's position on truth-telling, the veracity of an account of an event that occurred almost 50 years ago may not demand research. What happened, or what *might* have happened, Joan Didion reminds us, may not be as important as "how it felt to be me."

But there are benefits to such research. I discovered, for example, that there was a total solar eclipse on July 20, 1963, that it lasted 1 minute and 39 seconds, and that it wasn't quite a complete eclipse in northern Wisconsin. Why does this information matter? The commitment to describe with some exactness where it was, what it looked like, how it smelled, how it felt, and what it was called is based on the belief that this is the kind of information that is mostly likely to get at the emotional reality of what happened. Novice essayists sometimes worry that this might detract from the universal qualities of the work, thinking that readers will see the particulars of the writer's experience as relevant only to the writer. Actually, the opposite is true. As E. B. White said, "If you want to write about mankind, write about a man." We are much more likely to recognize the universal in the particular and to find relevance in the concrete experiences of others. Fiction writers know this well, but they are also less committed than nonfiction writers to communicate certain meanings to readers. The trick is *how much* to explain. Tell too much and the narrative is overwhelmed by exposition, or tell too little and the story lacks weight.

The solution to this in any creative genre is to put one's faith in the power of the particular to provide the backbone for ideas. Most often, we think of these particulars as sensory details, and frequently these are the building blocks of scenes. But nonfiction writers should cast a wide net for material, and experience is just one source of concrete information. Research is another. Perhaps the school research paper is to blame, but frequently apprentice creative writers see research—reading and interviews—as irrelevant to crafting stories. Yet, especially in nonfiction, research is a rich vein of material because stories are built from the data of real life, and these stories might include historical events with which readers are familiar. Literary journalists know this, of course, but research can also be useful in memoirs and essays. Most importantly, listening to the voices of others helps writers think more deeply about the questions or ideas they're exploring in their work. This can lead writers in surprising directions. For instance, I once worked on an essay that explored how frequently told stories can, like photographs, harden memory in ways that resist new ways of seeing—a project that later inspired me to research "autobiographical memory," a new area of psychology scholarship. This, in turn, led to much richer and insightful reflection on my own impulse to tell certain stories about myself in certain ways.

There is a less obvious value to mining particulars from research. Knowing that the solar eclipse I remembered from summer camp happened on July 20, 1963, and lasted for 1 minute and 39 seconds helps bring it all back. That the darkness seemed to last longer in memory, and that it was blacker, helps me to understand more about how it felt that summer, and it provides new handholds for pulling myself deeper into the experiences I want to explore. Because they write about what is uncertain or even confusing, essayists look to particulars such as these to seize as they grope their way toward understanding.

Creative nonfiction writers who use research extensively in their work may do it for other reasons. John McPhee, writing *Survival of the Birch Bark*

Canoe, spent substantial time interviewing builder Henri Vaillancourt and reading up on historical construction methods. Susan Orlean, in *The Orchid Thief*, settled in for a few months with horticulturalist John Laroche and researched the natural history of Florida's Loxahatchee swamp. This research is an essential part of the stories these writers tell, and sometimes it is research that leads them to their subjects in the first place. Truman Capote's *In Cold Blood* was inspired, for example, by a newspaper article (see page 126) the author happened to read about the murder of the Clutter family in a small town in Kansas. Similarly, Orlean's work on orchids was triggered by a piece in a Florida newspaper.

The craft of using research in creative nonfiction is deciding, like any other source of information, whether the information is relevant to the story. Does it provide essential background? Might it help in constructing a scene? Can it be used as a springboard for thought? Integrating research into a memoir, essay, or work of literary journalism presents another dilemma: What effect will it have on the forward motion of the narrative? Exposition in a story is like a sea anchor to a sailboat in a stiff wind—it doesn't stop movement completely, but it can slow things down considerably. Nonfiction writers solve this problem in a number of ways. They may deeply embed fact within the narrative, perhaps in a scene. They may, as John McPhee often does, use characters as a vehicle for exposition, allowing them to explain things through dialogue. Skilled writers also colonize what easily could be dry information with their own voices, finding their own way of saying things. Or they might use surprising comparisons. For instance, Richard Conniff tells us that the movement of a housefly's wings is twice as fast as a hummingbird's, and the insect's eyesight is so acute that the moving frames of a movie would need to be ten times faster for a housefly for it to see anything but jerky images. Finally, facts are simply another kind of detail, and some of the qualities that make sensory detail shimmer in a story are the qualities that make facts memorable, too. One of these is surprise. Who would have guessed, for example, that a housefly spends 29.7 percent of its time throwing up its meal and blowing bubbles in its puke?

Writing With (and Against) Tradition

Definitions of literature have for so long focused exclusively on poetry, fiction, and drama that it's easy to forget that nonfiction preceded the novel and that the essay may have given birth to the short story. Of the many early published works of nonfiction—the treatise, the tract, the letter—it is the personal essay that may be said to have parented modern forms of creative nonfiction. In 1571, the French nobleman Michel de Montaigne retired to his chateau in Bordeaux following a legal career and spent his days in a book-filled tower writing what he called "essais." Carved in a wooden beam above his head was his motto, of sorts—*Que sais-je?* or "What do I know?" It was Montaigne's mission to explore not only this question but a related one: What kind of knowing matters most to a person—worldly knowledge or self-knowledge, received knowledge from the ancients or the knowledge that comes with paying close attention to the present? "...I hold that truth is none the wiser for being old," Montaigne wrote. "I often say it is pure foolishness that makes us run after foreign and bookish examples. The present is just as fertile in them as the time of Homer and Plato."

Montaigne's *essais*, which has its origins in the French verb *essayer*—to try, to attempt—upended the literary conventions of the time. Montaigne's essays were written in vernacular French rather than Latin (the language of the noble class); they refused to simply parrot what others, particularly ancient authorities, believed to be true; and they placed the author at the center of the work. "I want to appear in my simple, natural, everyday dress, without strain or artifice; for it is myself that I portray," Montaigne wrote to introduce *The Essays of Montaigne*, which was first published in 1580. Self-discovery was his motive, as was the belief that it is in the stuff of ordinary life that we can find the truth about ourselves, and in turn, about humankind. These are, of course, exactly the motives of contemporary essayists, and it is the Montaignian tradition that helps explain what drives Annie Dillard, Joan Didion, or Scott Sanders to the writing desk with its blank page or blank screen. "What do I know?" they ask themselves, as Montaigne did 400 years earlier.

Literary journalism also inherits much from the early essay. Some of the earliest forms of journalism were essays that coincided with the eighteenth-century rise of periodicals in England, published to entertain a growing middle-class readership. But more recent events in the United States, particularly the pioneering work of *New Yorker* writers like Joseph Mitchell and the publication of Capote's spellbinding *In Cold Blood*, inspired what Tom Wolfe in the 1960s called "The New Journalism," a movement that led directly to a revolution in conventions. The New Journalism or, alternatively, literary journalism, borrowed directly from the fiction writer's toolbox and attempted to tell stories in much the same way, exploiting character, scene, dialogue, and point of view. To a greater or lesser extent, these works focus on a subject other than the author. A famous exception would be Norman Mailer's account of the antiwar protests in 1967 at the Pentagon, *Armies of the Night* (see page 132), a story that gives us Mailer—in the guise of the Novelist, the Participant, the Historian, the Existentialist—as a central character.

The tradition of literary journalism, then, is rooted much more in the practices of reporting than are memoir and essay. Therefore, literary journalists, like Kidder, Wolfe, or McPhee, are much more likely to be dogmatic on issues of truth-telling, insisting on accuracy whenever possible. "The nonfiction writer is communicating with the reader about real people in real places," said McPhee. "So if those people talk, you say what those people said. You don't say what the writer decides they said." This kind of accuracy is only possible through immersion—what McPhee once called the "stone-kicking school" of journalism—in which writers spend enough time with their subjects to be able to confidently construct scenes, dialogue, and, in some cases, third-person point of view. Tracy Kidder, for example, spent eight months hanging out with engineers at a computer company to write *The Soul of a New Machine*. Capote spent a year in Holcomb, Kansas, collecting material for *In Cold Blood*. Imagine what kind of reporting was involved, for example, when Kidder crafted this scene with computer engineer Tom West for the book *The Soul of a New Machine*:

> One Holiday morning in 1978, Tom West traveled to a city that was situated, he would later say guardedly, "somewhere in America." He entered a building as though he belonged there, strolled down a hallway, and let himself quietly into a windowless room. Just inside the door, he stopped.
>
> The floor was torn up; a shallow trench filled with fat power cables traversed it. Along the far wall, at the end of the trench, enclosed in three large, cream-colored steel cabinets, stood a VAX 11/780, the most important of a new class of computers called "32-bit superminis." To West's surprise, one of the cabinets was open and a man with tools was standing in front of it. A technician, still installing the machine, West figured.

Here Kidder achieves what many thought was possible only in fiction—third-person point of view—and it is the kind of innovation that wooed novelists like Wolfe and Capote to nonfiction. Literary journalism was not, Capote concluded, a form that he might resort to when his imagination failed but rather a form that might have the same narrative power as a novel, except the story is true. What the "nonfiction novel" demanded, however, were things Capote thought most writers, and especially journalists, were unwilling or unable to do—transcribe pages and pages of verbatim interview, risk offending people who appear in the book, and especially "empathize with characters outside [a writer's] usual imaginative range." He was convinced that only skilled novelists were capable of pulling it off. However, "narrative reportage," as Capote called it, is now ubiquitous. *The New Yorker* and similar magazines routinely publish it, and *In Cold Blood* has plenty of company.

Using Crafting Truth

How to Read for Craft

Literature courses prepare us for a particular kind of reading that is certainly useful to creative writers. The critical essay, a typical assignment in a literature class, is a piece that argues for a particular take on the meaning of a work, or perhaps how it might be understood as seen through the eyes of other critics or theorists. Writing a critical essay demands close and thoughtful reading, and it's especially important because literary criticism focuses on *ideas*—what notions about the world a story or poem might be trying to communicate. It's too easy to forget that what makes stories compelling is not just that they are entertaining but that their authors have an intellectual interest in what it means to be human.

However, reading for craft is more concerned with *how* a text communicates its meanings than *what* those meanings might be. It is the kind of reading that an engineer, encountering the Brooklyn Bridge or a Roman aqueduct for the first time, might give: "The thing is beautiful, but how does it work?" Aesthetics do matter—we have to recognize and name what is moving in a piece of writing—but when we read for craft this is the starting point that leads to questions about the design of the story, the use of language, research methods, and narrative techniques. Following is a list of the kinds of questions creative nonfiction writers might ask if they wished to explore how an essay, memoir, or article works.

Analyzing the Story
- How is the narrative crafted to introduce tension?
- Why might the author have chosen a particular beginning or end?
- What is the relationship between narrative and exposition, showing and telling?
- What are the elements of a well-conceived scene?
- How is effective dialogue made?
- How is character constructed? Is this different in fiction?
- What literary devices—symbolism, metaphor, allusion, and so on—are used and to what effect?
- In what ways is the story in the service of ideas?
- What is the work's narrative point of view, and how does this influence the story?

Speculating About the Method
- What interview or research techniques might have this required?
- What can we infer about the writer's ethical stances toward truth-telling?
- How was the subject matter chosen and why?
- What does the author say about his or her methods for interviews, and how is this reflected in the work?

Analyzing the Style
- What are the patterns of sentences in a paragraph, and how do they work together?

- How are words or phrases placed to give them emphasis?
- What are the effects of certain word choices?
- What is the tone and how is this established?
- How are line spaces, italics, and other visual elements used?
- What is the ethos of the writer, and how does it influence readers' experience of the work?
- How is the prose style distinguished from that of similar works or other writers?

Theorizing About Genre

- How might the work reflect—or resist—certain traditions of the memoir, the essay, or literary journalism?
- What are the rhetorical qualities of the work? In what ways is it influenced by purpose, audience, or situation?
- Can the work be situated in a particular time or in response to a cultural or historical event, and how might these affect writers' approaches to telling their stories?
- How might writers in other genres, like fiction and poetry, approach the same material differently?
- How are the questions that writers ask about their subjects related to genre?

Reading excerpts rather than entire works has limitations for analysis of craft. For one thing, if you're not familiar with the rest of the piece, it's difficult to say much about how a passage might contribute to it thematically. You might also be tempted to generalize about a writer's approach based on the reading of three paragraphs. To say, for instance, that Truman Capote's work has a cinematic quality after reading a single scene of *In Cold Blood* would be a stretch. The best you could say is that *this scene* has a cinematic quality. Finally, in the absence of the text that surrounds the excerpt, you are forced to work with what I've provided. While I've labored over choosing the richest material, it's impossible to know whether I've always chosen the best. Despite these drawbacks, *Crafting Truth* is dedicated to the idea that working closely with short passages from a wide range of writers and nonfiction genres will be enormously useful for inexperienced and experienced writers alike. It is the kind of study that is most likely to provide insights into a variety of nonfiction techniques in the shortest possible time. A brief anthology in the back of the book introduces longer, often complete works by additional writers. These provide great opportunities to apply what you're learning to more than fragments.

While there is pleasure in simply reading these exquisite excerpts, serious students of creative nonfiction can learn a great deal more by *writing* about what moves them and how that might arise from the architecture of the passage. The brevity of the excerpts makes multiple readings easy. Consider following up each reading with five to seven minutes of fastwriting in your journal or notebook (see "A Method for Exploring Your Ideas in a Notebook" at right). Simply follow your thoughts in writing, no matter how meandering and awkward and even unintelligent they might be. You have to give yourself permission to write badly if this is to be useful.

The time you spend working things out in your journal or notebook will pay off. Fifteen minutes of "bad" writing about an excerpt will often lead to surprising discoveries you probably wouldn't have found if the writing hadn't led you to them. This is also material you can use to shape a more composed and coherent response to the excerpts if you're in a writing course that requires them. In addition, every excerpt in *Crafting Truth* is accompanied by questions that should help prompt some of this journal work or help focus your responses to the reading. And, finally, this is a book devoted

> A METHOD FOR EXPLORING YOUR IDEAS IN A NOTEBOOK
>
> 1. Give each excerpt at least three readings, and write quickly and openly in your journal for five to seven minutes after every reading.
> 2. After the first reading, fastwrite a narrative of thought, beginning with the phrase "The first thing I noticed when I read this was....And then....And then...."
> 3. After the second reading, use this phrase as an opening prompt: "What I'm beginning to notice now that I didn't notice at first is....And also....And also...."
> 4. After the third reading, copy a line or passage from the excerpt, and then below focus your fastwrite on why you chose the line or passage, how it might help you understand the writer's techniques, or what you notice.

not just to writing about writing but getting the most important work started: crafting your own memoirs, essays, or articles. In the "Practicing the Craft" sections after each excerpt I suggest preliminary journal work, which, while inspired by a particular excerpt, is often focused on generating material that may develop into your own work of creative nonfiction. Even if it doesn't, remember that every minute you spend with your butt in the chair writing, following the words wherever they lead, is always far better than merely thinking about writing.

Some successful writers say that the act of creation is a mystery that cannot be analyzed. If this is so, then the study of craft is a waste of time. It is true that the best thing you can do to improve your work is the simplest—to simply write—but what happens when you do is really not very mysterious, though it is often rich with surprise. When they work, writers constantly make choices, choosing this word rather than that one, shifting to dialogue rather than continuing exposition, doing research rather than staring off into space. The more aware you are of the multiple choices you might make, the more control you will have over the possibilities of your story. *Crafting Truth*, I hope, will help with this. Creative writing has as much to do with the heart as the head, and knowing what might be the right choice for a piece is something only you can know in your lonely encounters with the page. In those moments it will not be these voices you hear, but your own.

Part 1
The Essayists

∾∾∾

Introduction to the
Personal Essay

A Brief History of the Essay

More than 400 years ago, a French nobleman named Montaigne invented the essay, and somehow it got hijacked by the College Board, English teachers, college admissions officers, and textbook authors. We've all written "essays" in school, of course, but those won't be much help in understanding the essay tradition represented here. The school essay is deductive, the Montaignian essay is inductive; one is organized by logic and the other by experience; one cultivates certainty, the other confusion. Even the name "essay," which is now applied to anything from the five-paragraph theme to timed writing on the SAT, is far adrift from its original meaning.

In French, the term *essay* means "to attempt" or "to try," and Montaigne's "essais" were intended to portray himself "without strain or artifice." He added, "From these articles of my confession you can imagine others to my discredit. But whatever I make myself out to be, provided that I show myself as I am, I am fulfilling my purpose." The essays, which were collected in three books that were written consecutively over about ten years, represented Montaigne's attempts to understand himself in a Renaissance world that was awash with wars, plagues, and religious conflict. But instead of musing on the great events of the day, Montaigne wrote about friendship, education, vanity, experience, sex, doctors, smells, and numerous other commonplace subjects in an often digressive personal style. Although this first essayist could speak and write Latin, and referred often to the ancients, Montaigne chose to write in vernacular French and didn't hesitate to range freely in any essay, no matter what the subject. An essay on vanity could easily veer into a complaint about the weight of Italian umbrellas, or an essay on the poems of Virgil might turn suddenly to a meditation on penis size.

Others may have appropriated the form, but the essay tradition Montaigne inspired never died. On the contrary, it has been a vibrant literary form. From France, Montaigne's version of the essay emigrated to

21

England, where seventeenth- and eighteenth-century English writers like Goldsmith, Addison, Steele, and later Lamb, Hazlitt, Stevenson, Woolf, and Orwell all established reputations as first-rate writers of the personal or "familiar" essay. In the United States, Thoreau and Emerson were essayists, and so was Twain. In both countries, the rise in popularity of the personal essay coincided with the growth of periodicals and the growth of a middle class with the leisure to read them.

While early essayists were mostly men, women were often enthusiastic readers of essays. In England, magazines that featured essays by and for women thrived. Today, in fact, some of the best personal essayists are women; in the United States these include writers like Annie Dillard, Adrienne Rich, Joan Didion, Cynthia Ozick, Susan Sontag, and Nancy Mairs. All of these writers inherited from Montaigne a faith in "essaying," or the belief that dramatizing the process of coming to know, rather than simply presenting conclusions, is another kind of story that might be told. To "essay" something is to think about it, to try to figure it out. And in the figuring, essayists come to know themselves.

Essays as Narratives of Thought

Writers who are drawn to the essay see confusion as a field to cultivate. Rather than making arguments, they prefer to wonder: "What might be the truth about this experience? What do I understand now that I didn't understand then?" This impulse to reflect—to look back on things with fresh insight—isn't unique to the essay. It's a quality in much autobiography, especially memoir. But the personal essay is often a more intellectual form. It tells two stories and gives roughly equal weight to each: the story of what happened then, and the story of what the writer is making of it now. Put another way, essays have conventional narratives like other forms of storytelling, but they also have a narrative of thought. As Edward Hoagland said, essays follow "the mind's flow."

One way to distinguish essays is their relative emphasis on showing and telling. Unlike fiction, all essays show *and* tell; but some could easily be mistaken for short stories because the narrator's reflection is subtle. On the other extreme are essays like Montaigne's that are more exposition than narrative. In the selection of essayists that follow, you will find excerpts from essays all over this continuum. The key point is that the movement of the essay is not just in the story of writers' experiences but also in the story of how they are starting to understand those experiences.

This invitation to sort through the messy muddle of experience and to discover—at least tentatively—what you think, is why many writers turn to the essay. Some fiction writers, in particular, find the essay's explicitness about meaning—this is what I think at the moment—a welcome alternative to conventional storytelling for certain kinds of subjects. Andre Dubus, whose essay "Broken Vessels" is excerpted in this section of *Crafting Truth*, was until his death one of the great masters of the short story. But when Dubus lost the use of both legs after a devastating automobile accident, he turned to essay writing as a way of figuring out how his injuries had changed his life.

Essays are driven by questions—not answers. I often tell my students that the best material for essay writing comes from experiences that they can't quite sort out yet. For example, why is it that I am still drawn to the Midwest town in which I grew up, and yet when I go there to visit all I ever feel is sadness and melancholy? What's that about? Essay subjects can be less serious too. What is it about thumbs, for instance? (Montaigne had an essay about that.) Those of us who have never written a paper without an outline might find the essay crazy-making. Unlike a thesis-example paper, for instance, which is built logically from an assertion the writer corralled already, an essay can involve chasing after any number of wild horses, each running in different directions. The risk is that the writer ends with just a few runaway thoughts that don't seem to go anywhere.

To some extent, the personal essay allows for confusion. While the school essay typically offers a thesis and then assembles the evidence to support it, the personal essay is in hot pursuit of a point, something that may happen late in the piece. And what if it doesn't arrive at a definitive conclusion? Unlike academic essays, the authority of the personal essay doesn't depend on its certainty. Instead, readers believe essayists who are honest. To confess that things are not that simple, that a single thesis doesn't quite capture the truth of things, or even that what one ends up with is simply more questions are all acceptable results when writing or reading essays—just as long as readers feel that the essayist's insights are earned.

Yet the insights also have to be relevant to others. Though they may begin as an essayist's personal desire to understand himself or herself, the best essays ultimately transcend the small, self-interested world of the author and have something to say to someone else. Because essays, like most memoirs, are written and read by looking through the narrow keyhole of the letter "I," essayists must always answer the "So what?" question. Why should anyone else care that he had a rotten childhood, a love affair with turtles, or a glass eye? The wonder of the personal essay is how often readers *do* care. Most of us read essays for the same reason we read any story: to spend a little time in someone else's world. Even if this world is in a different time or place, or diverges from the particulars of readers' lives, the best essays ultimately arrive at someplace we all recognize—our struggles to love or feel at home with ourselves or find joy in what is extraordinary in otherwise ordinary things.

New Forms of the Essay

Since Montaigne, the essay continues to evolve. The "lyric" essay (see the Ander Monson selection in this section or Lia Purpura's piece in the anthology), for instance, which has emerged in the last 10 to 15 years, "remains loyal to that original sense of an essay as a test or a quest, an attempt at making sense"[1] but may take on the ambiguity—if not the form—of a poem. Lyric essays can be fragmented, inconclusive, and have an ambivalent relationship to fact and story. Some don't try to tell a story at all but traffic, like poems, mostly in images. Actually, it's hard to read most lyric essays and not wonder why they simply aren't called poems. Yet this hybrid form seems a natural child of another distinguishing feature of the modern personal essay: segments. Many contemporary essays use white space to create a collage (for instance, see the Momaday excerpt on page 85), breaking up narratives into shorter fragments or even getting several stories going at once. Segmented essays can present experience and thought as fractured and discontinuous, implicitly arguing that this is the way life today can be.

Lyric essays may be exciting experiments in the literary margins, but the personal essay has been revived for a popular audience as well on the radio and the Web. Programs like *This American Life* on National Public Radio have made the radio essay one of the hottest new forms of creative nonfiction (one of the program's regular contributors, David Sedaris, is featured in this section). These radio pieces might include not just the essayist's voice but music, ambient sound, and interview clips. Podcasts now do the same thing on the Web. Blogs are essays too. They are inspired by some of the same things that prompted Montaigne to climb his tower to pen his "essais": a sense that we are always selves in the making and that each moment of writing is a snapshot of that drama.

[1] In 2007, the literary journal *Seneca Review* devoted an entire issue to the lyric essay. Also, see David Shield's *Reality Hunger: A Manifesto.*

1.1

ORDER OUT OF WILD DISORDER

Excerpt from E. B. White's
The Ring of Time

∽

The Excerpt in Context

E. B. White, a frequent contributor to *The New Yorker* magazine
until his death in 1985, once said that the "essayist is a self-liberated
man, sustained in the childish belief that everything he thinks about,
everything that happens to him, is of general interest.... Only a person
who is congenitally self-centered has the effrontery and the stamina to
write essays." White's own essays—pieces about geese, raccoons, summer lakes, and circuses—celebrate the idea that an essayist can find
something transcendent in the quiet familiarity of ordinary things.

In this essay, "The Ring of Time," White watches a young girl, a circus rider, as she rehearses her performance, standing on the back of a
horse as it circles the ring. He admires her skill, and especially the ease in
which she accommodates the "wallowing" horse as it trots under her bare
feet. White writes that "a man has to catch the circus unawares to experience its full impact and share its gaudy dream." But this is more than an
essay about the circus. White also sees that the young rider is caught in a
"ring of time," an illusion easily sustained by youth and beauty; that time
can move in circles, ending and beginning again and again. "The enchantment grew not out of anything that happened or was performed,"
writes White, "but out of something that seemed to go round and
around and around with the girl, attending her, a steady gleam in the
shape of a circle—a ring of ambition, of happiness, of youth."

The "Ring of Time," ultimately, is an essay about the circus and
the immortality of youth, and also the persistence of racism in Florida,
beliefs that seem trapped by the same illusion that held White in a
trance watching the young girl. Time *does* move forward, and inevitably
Florida will change and the rider will become a middle-aged woman,
"wearing a conical hat and high-heeled shoes."

Apprentice fiction writers are often told "show, don't tell." Both
essayists and fiction writers are enchanted by stories that seem to carry

meaning, like a gray cloud carrying rain. But essayists are apt to "show *and* tell," to explain what happens when the rain falls—the rivulets, ridges, and gullies it carves in a landscape of ideas about the way things are. Novice essayists, particularly if they have a background in fiction, often resist this move to reflect and comment on the meaning of things. They want the story to do that work. They may be content with ambiguity about the story's meaning. Let the reader figure it out! Yet most essayists are very particular about what meanings readers take, partly because those insights were—through the writing—both eagerly sought and hard earned.

Yet explicit reflection is risky. Exposition can bog down the forward motion of a narrative, and if the reflection seems to state the obvious, readers are understandably impatient: *I already know that! Just get on with the story!* The key is to remember that the narrator of an essay is not a fictional character who could just as easily be a 5-year-old boy as an 80-year-old man. The narrator is the living writer, a person who can pretend to be 5 or 80 only with the reader's permission, and only for a short time. As readers of personal essays, we expect that writers share their knowledge and understanding of the events they relate. They may do this implicitly or explicitly, but they must do it. Writers who withhold their wisdom, however small and tentative it might be, indulge "in deceit or in concealment," and their fate, E. B. White warns, is "that they will be found out in no time."

"Ring of Time," published in 1956, is one of a number of essays White wrote about his time wintering in Florida. The excerpt that follows begins the second paragraph of the piece. White has paid a dollar admission to get access to the circus grounds on a hot March afternoon as the performers prepare for a later show. The essay begins as White watches an "older woman" in heels and a "conical hat" working out a horse in a ring.

♋ *The Excerpt* ♋

Behind me I heard someone say, "Excuse me, please," in a low voice. She was halfway into the building when I saw her—a girl of sixteen or seventeen, politely threading her way through us onlookers who blocked the entrance. As she emerged in front of us, I saw that she was barefoot, her dirty little feet fighting the uneven ground. In most respects she was like any of two or three dozen showgirls you encounter if you wander about the winter quarters of Mr. John Ringling North's circus, in Sarasota—cleverly proportioned, deeply browned by the sun, dusty, eager, and almost naked. But her grave face and the naturalness of her manner gave her a sort of quick distinction and brought a new note into the gloomy octagonal building where

From: E. B. White, *The Essays of E.B. White* (New York: First Perennial Classics, 1999), 179–180.

we had all cast our lot for a few moments. As soon as she had squeezed through the crowd, she spoke a word or two to the older woman, whom I took to be her mother, stepped to the ring, and waited while the horse coasted to a stop in front of her. She gave the animal a couple of affectionate swipes on his enormous neck and then swung herself aboard. The horse immediately resumed his rocking canter, the woman goading him on, chanting something that sounded like "Hop! Hop!"

In attempting to recapture this mild spectacle, I am merely acting as recording secretary for one of the oldest of societies—the society of those who, at one time or another, have surrendered, without even a show of resistance, to the bedazzlement of a circus rider. As a writing man, or secretary, I have always felt charged with the safekeeping of all unexpected items of worldly and unworldly enchantment, as though I might be held personally responsible if even a small one were to be lost. But it is not easy to communicate anything of this nature. The circus comes as close to being the world in microcosm as anything I know; in a way, it puts all the rest of show business in the shade. Its magic is universal and complex. Out of its wild disorder comes order; from its rank smell rises the good aroma of courage and daring; out of its preliminary shabbiness comes the final splendor. And buried in the familiar boasts of its advance agents lies the modesty of most of its people. For me the circus is at its best before it has been put together. It is at its best at certain moments when it comes to a point, as through a burning glass, in the activity and destiny of a single performer out of so many. One ring is always bigger than three. One rider, one aerialist, is always greater than six. In short, a man has to catch the circus unawares to experience its full impact and share its gaudy dream. ❧

Analyzing the Craft

1. The excerpt beautifully illustrates how well-written essays move from narrative to exposition, scene to reflection. The first paragraph describes a young rider, gracefully moving with her horse around a circus ring. The second paragraph immediately shifts in register. The tone is thoughtful, almost meditative: "In attempting to recapture this mild spectacle, I am merely acting as recording secretary for one of the oldest of societies—the society of those who, at one time or another, have surrendered, without even a show of resistance, to the bedazzlement of a circus rider." The seam between these two paragraphs doesn't show. Navigating from showing to telling is often a problem in the essay because the transition from story to exposition seems abrupt or awkward. How does White tackle this problem? What does he do to cement the two paragraphs together? How does he keep the second paragraph from drifting abstractly from the scene that precedes it?

2. E. B. White was a master of the paragraph. It's a skill he honed over many years writing very brief Notes and Comments pieces for *The New Yorker*. In *The Elements of Style*, the "little" book that he coauthored with his former professor William Strunk, the authors wrote that a paragraph "in narration and description" might begin with a "concise, comprehensive statement serving to hold together the details that follow." This may not, Strunk and White added, look anything like a topic sentence. Analyze the first sentences of each paragraph of the excerpts with this advice in mind. Do you see an organizing statement, and does it look like a topic sentence?

3. Obviously, to fully appreciate the themes in "Ring of Time" you need to read the whole essay. As the introduction to the excerpt mentions, the piece goes on to talk about "the race problem" in Florida and White's sense that people, like the young horseback rider, try to live as if change is escapable, and it is not. With that theme in mind, do you read the excerpt any differently?

Practicing the Craft

E. B. White's principle that humankind can best be understood by looking into the heart of one man or woman[2] is clearly at work here. White directs our gaze on a single young woman in a circus ring on a hot March afternoon in Florida, and through her we see a distant horizon, the idea that the circus is a microcosm of a larger world. The principle at work is something creative writers instinctively know: Abstract things can be understood best by seeing them revealed in concrete things. Essay writing is inductive like that; essayists are trying to look closely at the things in front of them to see how they might be hitched to larger ideas about the way things are. But you can also generate material for essays by working the other way around, beginning with an abstraction and then looking for a way to anchor it to the concrete world you live in.

- Begin with an abstraction (an idea or feeling) of your own, or choose one from the following list: Death, Fear, Youth, Friendship, Racism, Religion, Success, Failure, Happiness, Love, Loneliness, Food, Home, Family, Marriage, Hope, Education.

- Put the word you choose in the center of a blank journal page and circle it. Focusing on that word, build a quick branch of specific associations (names, places, facts, things, images, conversations, words, etc.) that come to mind without thinking. Follow these branches until they die, and then return to your abstract word and build a new

---

[2]This advice appears in White's essay "Some Remarks on Humor," perhaps one of the best pieces ever written on the genre, even though White admits in the opening of the essay that "humor can be dissected, as a frog can, but the thing dies in the process and the innards are discouraging to any but the pure scientific mind."

Figure 2 *A free-association cluster for the word "water"*

branch (see Figure 2).[3] Don't worry about repetition or logic. This generating phase should be playful and open ended. Do this for as long as it seems useful. Choose an alternative focusing word if you're disappointed with the results.

• Analyze your finished web for branches that you find particularly intriguing. Maybe they surprised you, or they suggest a story or scene. Choose a branch and use some of the information you generated (it might be merely one item) to craft a lead paragraph for a possible essay. Write one or two more leads in the same way, using different branches.

---

[3]This method of building a fast web of associations is called "clustering" or "mapping" and is particularly useful for first thoughts about a subject. The technique is described most fully in Gabriele Lusser Rico's 1983 book *Writing the Natural Way.*

This exercise is useful if it guides you toward scenes, stories, details, pro-files, or descriptions that in some way illuminate the abstraction you started with. Or, as White advised, find a way to start thinking about humankind by writing about a person. Your leads are just a start. Try following one of them to generate a longer draft, using relevant material from your web.

Recommended Nonfiction by
E. B. White

- *Essays of E. B. White* (1977). This selection of essays, containing White's handpicked favorites, is the best introduction to the essayist's finest work. It includes "The Ring of Time," as well as White's most-anthologized essay "Once More to the Lake." But there are many more less well-known pieces that will knock your socks off (a colloquialism of which White would not approve).

- *One Man's Meat* (1944). The nonfiction pieces that have, over the years, most enchanted E. B. White fans are his essays about living on a saltwa-ter farm in Maine, some of which he published in *Harper's Magazine*. These rural essays are the focus of this collection. It is a classic.

1.2

A FATHER'S FLAWS

Excerpt from James Baldwin's
Notes of a Native Son

༭

A scene from Harlem during the 1943 "race riots," the event that forms the backdrop for James Baldwin's essay "Notes of a Native Son." Triggered by the shooting of a black man by police, the riots resulted in four deaths and over three hundred arrests.

The Excerpt in Context

"Artists are the only people in a society," wrote James Baldwin, "who will tell that society the truth about itself." Baldwin sought to do this in novels, plays, and essays, including perhaps his most famous essay, "Notes of a Native Son," which is excerpted here. As an essayist,

Baldwin sought to tell the truth about the African American experience in this country, but he was also unsparing in his assessment of his own failings as a black man. In "Notes of a Native Son," Baldwin wrote about the bitterness he felt toward his father, a preacher, when he died. Baldwin found in the writing a way of understanding that his father's flaws were lodged dangerously close to Baldwin's own heart. They threatened to ruin the son just as they ruined the father.

The essay is set in Harlem in 1943 and opens with Baldwin's return there to attend his father's funeral on the same day that Harlem exploded in violence in "one of the bloodiest race riots of the century." Against the image of ruined neighborhoods and a "wilderness of smashed plate glass," Baldwin realized that it is the "weight of the white world" that led to the destruction of Harlem that summer, a weight that his father also carried and that burdens every black man in America: "I saw that this had been for my ancestors and now would be for me an awful thing to live with and that the bitterness which had helped to kill my father would also kill me." However, before Baldwin was ready to deal with that awful truth he had to confront his alienation from his father, a former preacher and a man with whom the writer had broken years before. There was a funeral to attend against the background of Harlem's "ruined streets," while James Baldwin's personal history converged with the history of race hatred in America.

The following excerpt from "Notes of a Native Son" ends the essay, and it's one of the finest endings in creative nonfiction. Crafting those final paragraphs of an essay—or any creative work—is often difficult, and it's not hard to figure out why. Readers have high expectations. The ending must somehow be tied, however tenuously, to what came before it; yet it must not be redundant. Often a strong ending is like dry wood added to a campfire on a black night—the surging flames suddenly cast light on everything in the story, bringing shadowy characters or moments or even ideas into sudden relief. In this moment of illumination, the reader can see everything that came before more clearly. The ending of a personal essay like "Notes of a Native Son," a piece in which the writer brings understanding to an experience that he didn't possess when it occurred, is particularly difficult to write. One must, at all costs, avoid moralizing, summing up, or inventorying life's lessons. None of these problems plague the following two paragraphs that end Baldwin's essay, despite his resort to abstractions that in the hands of a less capable writer would seem either obvious or pedantic. Even without reading the entire essay, there is in this ending a sense of earned insight, a feeling that the writer's understandings are not arrived at easily; nor are they expressed to conveniently "tie things together" or to deliver emotional punch. The ending, simply put, seems honest.

◦◦ *The Excerpt* ◦◦

"But as for me and my house," my father said, "we will serve the Lord."
I wondered, as we drove him to his resting place, what this line had meant
for him. I had heard him preach it many times. I had preached it once myself, proudly giving it an interpretation different from my father's. Now the
whole thing came back to me, as though my father and I were on our way to
Sunday school and I were memorizing the golden text: *And if it seem evil
unto you to serve the Lord, choose you this day whom you will serve; whether
the gods which your fathers served that were on the other side of the flood, or the
gods of the Amorites, in whose land ye dwell: but as for me and my house, we
will serve the Lord.* I suspected in these familiar lines a meaning which had
never been there for me before. All of my father's texts and songs, which I
had decided were meaningless, were arranged before me at his death like
empty bottles, waiting to hold the meaning which life would give them for
me. This was his legacy: nothing is ever escaped. That bleakly memorable
morning I hated the unbelievable streets and the Negroes and whites who
had, equally, made them that way. But I knew that it was folly, as my father
would have said, this bitterness was folly. It was necessary to hold on to the
things that mattered. The dead man mattered, the new life mattered; blackness and whiteness did not matter; to believe that they did was to acquiesce
in one's own destruction. Hatred, which could destroy so much, never failed
to destroy the man who hated and this was an immutable law.

It began to seem that one would have to hold in the mind forever two
ideas which seemed to be in opposition. The first idea was acceptance, the
acceptance, totally without rancor, of life as it is, and men as they are: in
the light of this idea, it goes without saying that injustice is a commonplace. But this did not mean that one could be complacent, for the second
idea was of equal power: that one must never, in one's own life, accept
these injustices as commonplace but must fight them with all one's
strength. This fight begins, however, in the heart and it now had been laid
to my charge to keep my own heart free of hatred and despair. This intima-
tion made my heart heavy and, now that my father was irrecoverable,
I wished that he had been beside me so that I could have searched his face
for the answers which only the future would give me now. ◦◦

Analyzing the Craft

1. The two most important sentences in an essay are, arguably, the first
   and the last. The first sentence not only attempts to capture the
   reader but also establishes the writer's emotional relationship with

From: James Baldwin, *Notes of a Native Son* (Boston: Beacon, 1984), 112–114.

the material. The last sentence is the last voice we hear, the final words we remember, and the thought that resonates when we, as readers, shift our gaze from the page. Look closely at the final sentence of Baldwin's ending. In particular, consider the idea that the words (or phrases) that directly precede punctuation in any sentence—a comma, period, semicolon, and so on—have particular emphasis.

> This fight *begins*, however, in the heart and it now had been laid to my charge to keep my own heart free of *hatred and despair*. This intimation made my *heart heavy* and, now that my father was *irrecoverable,* I wished that he had been beside me so that I could have searched his face for the answers which only the future *would give me now.*

Stylistically speaking, then, what is the effect of Baldwin's sentence structure here? What ideas or feelings does he seem to emphasize most? Can you imagine why the final sentence might be written with different words emphasized and why that might not be as effective?

2. We've all written "bad" endings, and we've all read them, too. One of the most common bad endings in school writing is the kicking-the-dead-horse ending—a conclusion (which often begins "in conclusion") that essentially reminds readers of what they should already know if they've read the piece. Obviously, Baldwin's ending is not one of those. But what kind of ending is it? What do the final two paragraphs of "Notes of a Native Son" do that "good" endings should do?

3. If essays both "show" and "tell"—dramatize through scene, dialogue, description, and so on as well as *explain* what these narrative moments might mean—then Baldwin's ending seems an excellent example of how these two elements can be woven together. Using two different colored markers, highlight the passages that "show" and the passages that "tell." What does the pattern reveal about how Baldwin does the weaving? In particular, what would you say about the balance between narration and reflection and where they occur in these two paragraphs?

Practicing the Craft

Once, many years ago, I wrote an essay about my own father that was later published in a Boston newspaper. My father was an alcoholic, and a former journalist, who died when I was in my early twenties. If anyone asked, I always said I was relieved when he died, and ten years later I wrote the essay to try to figure out if I was being honest with myself. Was I really relieved? The essay led me in a different direction, however, and became a piece about the fear that must haunt the children of alcoholics that they, too, will turn to the bottle to fill an empty heart. This was the ending of the essay:

> It is good, I think, that we live the rest of our lives a little afraid.
>
> Maybe it is that fear that has brought me back to this old typewriter, to peck away at painful memories and to try—through the writing—to understand the loss of a man who could give me a rose bush on my 21st birthday and drink himself to death before it had the chance to bloom.

Donald Murray, a Pulitzer Prize–winning journalist and a fine personal essayist, once handed out laminated cards to his writer friends, printed with the acronym S.O.F.T.—"Say One F—ing Thing"—which he believed was one of the best pieces of advice he could pass along about essay writing. Endings are usually where this one thing gets said in an essay. In my ending above, it was the bit about being "a little afraid" that was most important. Select one or more of your own personal essays, reread them, and when you're done turn over the manuscripts and finish this sentence: *What I understand now about this that I didn't understand then is...* Follow that sentence for three to five minutes in your journal. Then compose new endings to your essays that say—directly or indirectly—the one thing that is most important to say.

Make a study of essay endings. Select a quiver full of published essays that you admire and retype the endings—the last paragraph or two—on a separate sheet of paper. Copying them will give you more intimacy with what it is that's powerful about how the endings were written. Collaborating with other members of your class or writing group, use this collection of endings to develop a taxonomy of endings; in other words, can you see patterns in strong essay endings, and might you invent categories that describe them?

Recommended Nonfiction by James Baldwin

- *Notes of a Native Son* (1955). This essay collection, of course, takes its title from Baldwin's famous essay, which is excerpted in this chapter. The book, which was republished in 1984 with a new introduction, includes several extraordinary personal essays, including a remarkable piece titled "Stranger in the Village." Some of these essays focus on criticism (there's a controversial piece on Richard Wright), on race in America, and on Baldwin's life as an expatriate in France.

PRICKLY DREAD ON BANYAN STREET

Excerpt from Joan Didion's
Some Dreamers of the Golden Dream

Lucille Miller (seen here) and her attorney discuss her case, the subject of Joan Didion's classic essay, "Some Dreamers of the Golden Dream." Miller was accused—and convicted—of burning her husband alive in the family Volkswagen. The tire from that car, key to Miller's defense, frames the shot.

The Excerpt in Context

In "Why I Write," Joan Didion confesses that no matter how hard she tried to enjoy the "world of ideas," her "attention veered inexorably back to the specific, the tangible, to what was generally considered, by everyone I knew, then and for that matter have known since, the peripheral." This passion for the particular is a sensibility that many good writers share. It is, in one sense, the practice of inductive reasoning, but logic does not seem at the heart of it. Perhaps it comes down to faith—the belief that everyday things can carry a charge of meaning, and it's the job of the writer to see what that might be.

The excerpt that follows is the three paragraphs that open Joan Didion's 1966 essay about the trial and conviction of Lucille Miller, accused of burning her husband alive in the family Volkswagen. Banyan Street is where the couple lived in the San Bernardino Valley, then much more sparsely settled. It's obvious that Didion brings to this material that passion for the particular, but it would be a mistake to say that this isn't an essay about ideas, too. The piece is a work of cultural criticism, not just a murder story. Didion writes about a time in California when it was a place to reinvent oneself, a place to live the "golden dream," living as if "time past has no bearing on time present." The problem, writes Didion, is that when the "dream teaches the dreamers how to live" it cultivates dangerous illusions. In creative nonfiction it's simply not enough to inventory the "telling" details; they must be put to work in the service of something larger, reflections that arise from those details without seeming to bully them to conform to some preconceived ideas about what is true. Tom Newkirk calls this "earned insight."

Much is said about what makes beginnings—or "leads," to use the journalist's term—succeed in getting a piece out of idle and into gear. Strong openings obviously should capture the reader's interest, but they must do more. John McPhee once said that "leads are like flashlights that shine into the story." They illuminate the writer's purpose and subject, give a piece of writing at least a hint about where it's headed. A good lead, like the stem of an old watch, puts tension on the spring that drives the work forward and keeps readers engaged because they wonder what will happen next. That a paragraph, in a short essay, and perhaps several pages in a longer one, can do so much work is quite stunning. The potency of a strong lead to make a compelling promise about what is to follow without giving away the store may be why they are often so hard to write. Another reason, according to McPhee, is that when you begin, all the material is unused, and the possibilities about *where* to begin are many. "What will you choose?" he asks. A careful study of good leads offers some clues, and Didion's beginning to "Some Dreamers of the Golden Dream" is among the most memorable in creative nonfiction.

∾ *The Excerpt* ∾

This is a story about love and death in the golden land, and begins with the country. The San Bernardino Valley lies only an hour east of Los Angeles by the San Bernardino Freeway but is in certain ways an alien place: not the coastal California of the subtropical twilights and the soft westerlies off the Pacific but a harsher California, haunted by the Mojave just beyond the mountains, devastated by the hot dry Santa Ana wind that comes down through the passes at 100 miles an hour and whines through the eucalyptus windbreaks and works on the nerves. October is the bad month for the wind, the month when breathing is difficult and the hills blaze up spontaneously. There has been no rain since April. Every voice seems a scream. It is the season of suicide and divorce and prickly dread, wherever the wind blows.

The Mormons settled this ominous country, and then they abandoned it, but by the time they left the first orange tree had been planted and for the next hundred years the San Bernardino Valley would draw a kind of people who imagined they might live among the talismanic fruit and prosper in the dry air, people who brought with them Midwestern ways of building and cooking and praying and who tried to graft those ways upon the land. The graft took in curious ways. This is the California where it is possible to live and die without ever eating an artichoke, without ever meeting a Catholic or a Jew. This is the California where it is easy to Dial-A-Devotion, but hard to buy a book. This is the country in which a belief in the literal interpretation of Genesis has slipped imperceptibly into a belief in the literal interpretation of *Double Indemnity,* the country of the teased hair and the Capris and the girls for whom all life's promise comes down to a waltz-length white wedding dress and the birth of a Kimberly or a Sherry or Debbie and a Tijuana divorce and a return to hairdressers' school. "We were just crazy kids," they say without regret, and look to the future. The future always looks good in the golden land, because no one remembers the past. Here is where the hot wind blows and the old ways do not seem relevant, where the divorce rate is double the national average and where one person in every thirty-eight lives in a trailer. Here is the last stop for all those who come from somewhere else, for all those who drifted away from the cold and the past and the old ways. Here is where they are trying to find a new life style, trying to find it in the only places they know to look: movies and the newspapers. The case of Lucille Marie Maxwell Miller is a tabloid monument to that new life style.

Imagine Banyan Street first, because Banyan is where it happened. The way to Banyan is to drive west from San Bernardino out Foothill Boulevard, Route 66: past the Santa Fe switching yards, the Forty Winks Motel. Past the motel that is nineteen stucco tepees: "SLEEP IN A WIGWAM—GET MORE FOR YOUR WAMPUM." Past Fontana Drag City and the Fontana Church of the Nazarene and the Pit Stop A Go-Go; past Kaiser Steel, through Cucamonga, out to the Kapu Kai Restaurant-Bar and Coffee Shop, at the corner of Route 66 and Carnelian Avenue. Up Carnelian Avenue from the

From: Joan Didion, *Slouching Towards Bethlehem* (New York: Noonday, 1992), 3–5.

Kapu Kai, which means "Forbidden Seas," the subdivision flags whip in the harsh wind. "HALF-ACRE RANCHES! SNACK BARS! TRAVERTINE ENTRIES! $95 DOWN." It is the trail of an intention gone haywire, the flotsam of the New California. But after awhile the signs thin out on Carnelian Avenue, and the houses are no longer the bright pastels of the Springtime Home owners but the faded bungalows of the people who grow a few grapes and keep a few chickens out here, and then the hill gets steeper and the road climbs and even the bungalows are few, and here—desolate, roughly surfaced, lined with eucalyptus and lemon groves—is Banyan Street. ❧

Analyzing the Craft

1. In "Some Dreamers of the Golden Dream" place is not merely a backdrop for the story of Lucille Miller; it *is* the story. One of the extraordinary qualities of the essay's opening is how evocative it is of the San Bernardino Valley in the mid-sixties. To evoke a place in prose is no small task. It demands both texture and mood—what we sometimes call "ambience"—and, of course, visual description that is less a snapshot than a realistic painting, one that bears the painter's brushstrokes and color. To evoke a place is to provide a deeply subjective view of it. Explain how Didion manages to craft such a view of the Valley. What exactly gives her lead texture and mood, and in what sense does it implicitly reflect her own strong feelings and ideas about the place?

2. There are few essayists who are more attuned to irony than Joan Didion, and "Dreamers" is a profoundly ironic piece. There is a kind of innocence to California's "Golden Dream" and the people like Lucille Miller who believe in it, and this is a view that Didion clearly doesn't share. Though it might appear that her treatment here is "objective"— after all, Didion doesn't explicitly intrude on the narrative—this essay is highly critical of the culture it describes. Where in the excerpt does this criticism seem most devastating?

3. As John McPhee suggests, one of the challenges of beginning a piece is deciding where to start, an especially difficult problem when you have so much material to choose from. What does Didion's lead suggest about some of the things that might guide that choice?

Practicing the Craft

In news journalism the "lead" (or "lede") of an article is usually the first paragraph of the piece, but in an essay—depending on its length—the lead can be much longer. Still, the first paragraph of an essay, and especially the first and last lines of the first paragraph, are particularly important. These sentences should be carefully crafted. For example, here is Didion's first line: *This is a story about love and death in the golden land, and begins with the country.* And this is the line that ends that lead paragraph: *It is the season of suicide and divorce and prickly dread, wherever the wind blows.* Both sentences do necessary work, setting the tone of the essay, giving it a sense of direction, and immediately raising questions. But how we choose to begin affects writers as well as readers. The first line, especially, signals to writers their emotional relationship to the material, and, to use McPhee's metaphor, that first sentence is a "light that shines down into the story," illuminating a particular part of the material. It stands to reason that trying out several first lines is a useful revision strategy, helping writers see alternative trajectories for the work.

Practice crafting three different first lines to a draft you've written or might write. Each of these should be written in ways that might make a reader anxious to read the sentence that follows. If you're working with a draft, you might find one or more of these first sentences buried somewhere in the material. Here are three first lines to a piece on landscapes that I'm currently working on:

1. The first caller is Charlie, who reports that Kuba, his German shepherd, has a strange behavior—one that isn't necessarily a problem except that it's so odd.

2. In the American West it is still possible for a landscape to bust free of visual borders, inviting us to slowly pivot on our heels to take it all in.

3. Who you are is where you were, and it is in the Midwest where my stories of myself are set.

Which of the three lines you wrote seem most promising? When you share them with others, what do they say?

After you've written three possible openings to your piece, consider which might be most interesting to follow. Jot that sentence down in your journal, and for seven minutes follow it to see where the line leads you. Try not to push the material around to conform to some preconceived notions about how you should tell the story. Let the language lead by writing fast. Do this at least one more time with another of your first lines. Can you see how each different opening line redirects the beam of light, illuminating different parts of the story?

Recommended Nonfiction by
Joan Didion

- *Slouching Towards Bethlehem* (1969). This is, perhaps, Didion's most successful essay collection, providing a penetrating, often disturbing look at California in the 1960s. The title essay in the collection is a wonderful example of the "segmented" or collage essay and a magnificent piece of reporting.

- *The White Album* (1979). Didion widens her critical gaze in this essay collection from California to the women's movement in the late sixties and early seventies. This collection also includes some of her most personal essays, including the widely anthologized piece on her migraine headaches, "In Bed."

- *The Year of Magical Thinking* (2005). This account of surviving the sudden death of her husband, the novelist John Gregory Dunne, is an extraordinary work of insight into grief and a compelling example of the essayistic spirit—one begins with questions and follows them where they seem to lead. This is Didion's best work in decades.

1.4

YOU DID NOT CHANGE

Excerpt from Alice Walker's
Beauty: When the Other Dancer Is the Self

∽

The Excerpt in Context

Alice Walker's personal essays rarely get the attention her novels and even her criticism receive, but they shine with intelligence, honesty, and political conviction. All of her work focuses on relationships between people, particularly women, and while her personal essays may *seem* less political than her criticism, they are often stories that turn on the cruelty of sexism or racism. Yet they are also optimistic, celebrating the tenacity of the human spirit.

Walker's first and best collection of essays, *In Search of Our Mother's Gardens*, from which "Beauty: When the Other Dancer Is the Self" is drawn, is an eclectic bounty of autobiographical pieces, criticism, reviews, and "statements" on civil rights, all written between 1966 and 1982. In the book, she coins a term for her work—"womanist prose"—which she borrows from an expression some African-American women use to describe girls who are "outrageous, audacious, or willful." Walker adds that "womanist prose" is "committed to the survival and wholeness of entire people, male *and* female."

In "Beauty," Walker tells the story of losing her eye in an accident when she was eight. Her brothers receive BB guns ("Because I am a girl, I do not get one," she writes) and as they play cowboys and Indians, Walker is accidentally shot in the right eye. When a white mass forms in the eye, a cataract that blinds her for good, Walker writes, "It was great fun being cute. And then one day it ended." The afflicted eye becomes a source of torment, even when the cataract is removed, and she struggles for much of her life with the "anguish of not looking up." The essay is organized in a series of scenes, each separated by line breaks or sometimes an italicized sentence. The excerpt that follows is from the middle of the piece.

It is hard to imagine writing about 36 years in 4,000 words, but Walker manages it here, sometimes disrupting the chronology if it serves her purpose. Nonfiction writing may be about "real life," but it often defies its rules, including the necessity of telling a story "exactly the way it happened." Indeed, essay time and real time may be very different things. In essay time, the story of what happened is the warehouse from which writers initially shop for meaning, and once they discover it, they select only the relevant events. Segmented essays,[4] like Walker's "Beauty: When the Other Dancer Is the Self," are structures that can help manage time in an essay, not only allowing the narrative to shift abruptly from time and place but representing experience as fractured; the story is a puzzle of pieces that somehow fit together in a meaningful way, which is something like the way we experience life. No matter what the structure, though, essay time also involves the shift between present and past. There are two narrators, essentially—the one to whom things happened and the one who is beginning to understand what it all means. What is interesting about this excerpt is Walker's use of the present tense, a move that would seem to surrender one narrator for the other. Present tense has emotional impact, but does it sacrifice the reflective quality that we come to expect from a personal essayist?

∾ *The Excerpt* ∾

My mother is lying in bed in the middle of the day, something I have never seen. She is in too much pain to speak. She has an abscess in her ear. I stand looking down on her, knowing that if she dies, I cannot live. She is being treated with warm oils and hot bricks held against her cheek. Finally a doctor comes. But I must go back to my grandparents' house. The weeks pass but I am hardly aware of it. All I know is that my mother might die, my father is not so jolly, my brothers still have their guns, and I am the one sent away from home.

"You did not change," they say.

Did I imagine the anguish of never looking up?

I am twelve. When relatives come to visit I hide in my room. My cousin Brenda, just my age, whose father works in the post office and whose mother is a nurse, comes to find me. "Hello," she says. And then she asks, looking at my recent school picture, which I did not want taken, and on which the "glob," as I think of it, is clearly visible, "You still can't see out of that eye?"

From: Alice Walker, *In Search of Our Mother's Gardens* (San Diego, CA: Harcourt, 1983), 366–368.

[4] To learn more about the segmented essay form, see Robert Root's piece "Beyond Linearity: Writing the Segmented Essay," in Michael Steinberg and Robert Root, eds., *The Fourth Genre*, 5th ed. (New York: Longman, 2009).

"No," I say, and flop back on the bed over my book.

That night, as I do almost every night, I abuse my eye. I rant and rave at it, in front of the mirror. I plead with it to clear up before morning. I tell it I hate and despise it. I do not pray for sight. I pray for beauty.

"You did not change," they say.

I am fourteen and baby-sitting for my brother Bill, who lives in Boston. He is my favorite brother and there is a strong bond between us. Understanding my feelings of shame and ugliness he and his wife take me to a local hospital, where the "glob" is removed by a doctor named O. Henry. There is still a small bluish crater where the scar tissue was, but the ugly white stuff is gone. Almost immediately I become a different person from the girl who does not raise her head. Or so I think. Now that I've raised my head I win the boyfriend of my dreams. Now that I've raised my head I have plenty of friends. Now that I've raised my head classwork comes from my lips as faultlessly as Easter speeches did, and I leave high school as valedictorian, most popular student, and queen, hardly believing my luck. Ironically, the girl who was voted most beautiful in our class (and was) was later shot twice through the chest by a male companion, using a "real" gun, while she was pregnant. But that's another story in itself. Or is it?

"You did not change," they say.

It is now thirty years since the "accident." A beautiful journalist comes to visit and to interview me. She is going to write a cover story for her magazine that focuses on my latest book. "Decide how you want to look on the cover," she says. "Glamorous, or whatever."

Never mind "glamorous," it is the "whatever" that I hear. Suddenly all I can think of is whether I will get enough sleep the night before the photography session: if I don't, my eye will be tired and wander, as blind eyes will.

At night in bed with my lover I think up reasons why I should not appear on the cover of a magazine. "My meanest critics will say I've sold out," I say. "My family will now realize I write scandalous books."

"But what's the real reason you don't want to do this?" he asks.

"Because in all probability," I say in a rush, "my eye won't be straight."

"It will be straight enough," he says. Then, "Besides, I thought you'd made your peace with that."

And I suddenly remember that I have.... ॐ

Analyzing the Craft

1. Many years ago, when I was visiting a friend in Vermont, he told me about his neighbor's toolshed. The neighbor, a dairy farmer, had an old, ramshackle place that was, nonetheless, meticulously

organized, and of the toolshed the farmer was especially proud. All of the tools he used most often were near the door, neatly hung on the wall within easy reach. He put the important things in places where he knew he could find them. Writers do, too. We know intuitively that first lines and last lines are incredibly important. But there are other locations in an essay that matter as well, places where writers are likely to put important information and strong language. Interestingly, the segmented essay creates some new points of emphasis, places that will occupy readers' attention. Where are these in the Walker excerpt? In other words, which are the most important lines, and where are they? Does this reveal a pattern of emphasis?

2. "In writing memoir," writes Phillip Lopate, "the trick, it seems to me, is to establish a double perspective, that will allow the reader to participate vicariously in the experience as it was lived (the confusions and misapprehensions of the child one was, say), while conveying the sophisticated wisdom of one's current self."[5] As I noted earlier, Walker's decision to write in present tense, as if she were still that child that would not look up, would seem to limit her access to the narrator that has the "sophisticated wisdom of one's current self." Is that true?

3. The distinguishing feature of the segmented essay is the white space that separates the blocks of text. How does that white space affect readers' experience of an essay?

Practicing the Craft

A lot of personal essays these days use a segmented structure, or at least try to make artful use of line breaks. But I find that segments are far more useful as a way of generating material than organizing the finished product. Just as visual collages can trigger unexpected ways of seeing, writing a series of segments in your journal, one after another, can lead to surprises. This can be a particularly rich exercise if you start with a thematic idea and then quickly generate three or four segments on scenes or stories that you associate with that theme. When it works, the segments collide in ways you don't expect, revealing things you didn't know you knew.

One reason that the segmented essay—a work that is structured in sections divided by line breaks—is such a popular form for the personal essay is

[5]Phillip Lopate, "Reflection and Retrospection: A Pedagogic Mystery," *The Fourth Genre* 7.1 (2005): 143–156.

that it seems to mimic the nature of modern experience, which often feels fragmented, disjointed, and hard to assemble into a linear narrative that makes much sense. But the segmented essay is also powerfully generative for writers as well. By freeing them from the constraints of trying to make experience a single coherent story, writers can experiment with juxtaposing a range of scenes, pieces of information, and observations. The collision of these fragments can sometimes encourage accidental meanings. To explore these possibilities, try this journal exercise:

1. Begin with an abstract idea or feeling: fear, death, friendship, community, curiosity, guilt, intelligence, and so on.

2. Generate a list of possible scenes, moments, and situations from your own experience that you associate with the idea you chose. To help with this, finish the following "seed sentence" as many times as you can in your journal:

   _____ makes me think of the time that I . . .

3. Title the journal exercise "_____: Four Examples," focusing on the abstraction you chose.

4. Begin with a single scene and, drawing on all your senses, fastwrite the scene. Write for seven minutes.

5. Skip a line. Fastwrite for another seven minutes and generate another scene on the same word.

6. Do this one more time.

7. Look critically at the material you have generated and consider the following questions:

   a. Aside from the broad focus on the abstract idea or feeling you chose, how are the fragments related?

   b. Do any of them seem to speak to each other about similar things?

   c. What surprised you? What do you understand about _____ that you didn't understand before?

   d. If you reorder the fragments, does the pattern of the sequence unleash unexpected meaning?

   e. What scenes that you haven't written yet (but should) suddenly seem relevant?

   f. What outside information might help you understand the idea you're exploring or the question you seem to be asking?

8. Write a draft with the same title—"_____: Four Examples"— that includes three scenes and at least one segment based on relevant research.

Recommended Nonfiction by
Alice Walker

- *Anything We Love Can Be Saved* (1997). This eclectic collection of essays largely focuses on Walker's political activism, with pieces on topics ranging from the unfortunate iconography of Aunt Jemima to the author's cat. The book also includes interesting backstories on the writing of some of her work, including the Pulitzer Prize–winning novel, *The Color Purple*, and the essay collection excerpted here, *In Search of Our Mother's Gardens.*

- *Living by the Word* (1988). Composed of selected essays and journal entries Walker wrote between 1973 and 1987, this collection illuminates her evolution as a writer and includes a lovely essay about her father.

1.5

CUTTING IT STRAIGHT

Excerpt from Scott Russell Sanders's
The Inheritance of Tools

∾

Scott Sanders's childhood living on or near Ohio's Ravenna Arsenal—pictured here producing bombs during WWII—provides the setting for his essay collection, The Paradise of Bombs.

The Excerpt in Context

Scott Sanders's widely anthologized essay, "The Inheritance of Tools," from which the following excerpt comes, describes growing up with a father who taught him the virtues of right angles, how to appreciate the bite of a saw in raw wood, and the proper swing of a framing hammer. The piece opens with the news that Sanders's father has died, a passing that coincides with Sanders banging his thumb with his father's hammer, one tool among others he inherited from him. The joining of the abstract and the particular—in this case a father's death and a sudden blow to a thumbnail—is a commonplace movement in Sanders's essays, and in most other personal essays as well. That movement is certainly apparent in the following passage as Sanders describes his father's tools and at the same time meditates on the "unspoken morality in seeking the level and plumb."

In the personal essay, the conventional movement of narrative—this happened and then this and then this—often dances with a "narrative of thought," the often explicit "movements of the mind" that follow a story's lead. Sanders says as much in his introduction to the essay collection from which this excerpt comes, *The Paradise of Bombs*: "For me the writing of a personal essay is like finding my way through a forest without being quite sure what game I am chasing.... The pleasure in writing an essay—and when the writing is any good, the pleasure of reading it—comes from this dodging and leaping, this movement of the mind."

One scholar of the essay called the arc of this narrative the "reflective turn." In less capable hands, this reflection may be a distraction or perhaps a statement of the obvious. It might feel forced. But when done well, the "narrative of thought" is as interesting as any other kind of story. We want to know not just what happened but what the writer understands about what *happens*. The work of Scott Russell Sanders is exemplary in this regard. His is a mind we want to follow, wondering along with him what "game" he's following through the woods, reassured that whatever it is, Sanders will find it.

⟪ *The Excerpt* ⟫

The saw I use belonged to him, as did my level and both of my squares, and all four tools had belonged to his father. The blade of the saw is the bluish color of gun barrels, and the maple handle, dark from the sweat of hands, is inscribed with curving leaf designs. The level is a shaft of walnut two feet long, edged with brass and pierced by three round windows in which air bubbles float in oil-filled tubes of glass. The middle window serves for testing whether a surface is horizontal, the others for testing whether it is plumb or vertical. My grandfather used to carry this level on the gun rack behind the seat in his pickup, and when I rode with him I would turn around to watch the bubbles dance. The larger of the two squares is called a framing square, a flat steel elbow so beat up and tarnished you can barely make out the rows of numbers that show how

From: Scott Russell Sanders, *The Paradise of Bombs* (Boston: Beacon, 1987), 106–107.

to figure the cuts on rafters. The smaller one is called a try square, for marking right angles, with a blued steel blade for the shank and a brass-faced block of cherry for the head.

I was taught early on that a saw is not to be used apart from a square: "If you're going to cut a piece of wood," my father insisted, "you owe it to the tree to cut it straight."

Long before studying geometry, I learned that there is a mystical virtue in right angles. There is an unspoken morality in seeking the level and the plumb. A house will stand, a table will bear weight, the sides of a box will hold together only if the joints are square and the members upright. When the bubble is lined up between two marks etched in the glass tube of a level, you have aligned yourself with the forces that hold the universe together. When you miter the corners of a picture frame, each angle must be exactly forty-five degrees, as they are in the perfect triangles of Pythagoras, not a degree more or less. Otherwise the frame will hang crookedly, as if ashamed of itself and of its maker. No matter if the joints you are cutting do not show. Even if you are butting two pieces of wood together inside a cabinet, where no one except a wrecking crew will ever see them, you must take pains to insure that the ends are square and the studs are plumb.

I took pains over the wall I was building on the day my father died. Not long after that wall was finished—paneled with tongue-and-groove boards of yellow pine, the nail holes filled with putty and the wood all stained and sealed—I came close to wrecking it one afternoon when my daughter ran howling up the stairs to announce that her gerbils had escaped from their cage and were hiding in my brand-new wall. She could hear them scratching and squeaking behind her bed. Impossible! I said. How on earth could they get inside my drum-tight wall? Through the heating vent, she answered. I went downstairs, pressed my ear to the honey-colored wood, and heard the scritchscritch of tiny feet.

"What can we do?" my daughter wailed. "They'll starve to death, they'll die of thirst, they'll suffocate."

"Hold on," I soothed. "I'll think of something." ◌

Analyzing the Craft

1. Consider this sentence from the excerpt:

> The level is a shaft of walnut two feet long, edged with brass and pierced by three round windows in which air bubbles float in oil-filled tubes of glass.

Now consider this revision of that sentence:

> The level is a narrow piece of wood about two feet long, edged with metal and containing three holes in which there are bubbles in tubes of glass.

Which of the two sentences do you prefer? Why? Your answer to these questions speaks, of course, to the importance of being concrete in writing. This advice applies to all kinds of prose, but especially to creative writing, where novice writers learn two things: first, that concrete language helps readers see and, second, that particulars can say more than they say. These "revealing details" can imply things about character and status, among other things. But then there is the danger of overwriting, of excessive detail or adjectives that can turn prose purple. With these things in mind, what would you say about Sanders's sentence and its revision?

2. In the second long paragraph of the excerpt, the one that begins "Long before studying geometry," Sanders subtly shifts from the story narrator to the reflective narrator, or the one who sees meaning in the situation. This often involves a move to abstract and a subtle shift in the register of the voice. How would you describe what distinguishes that paragraph from the rest of the narrative?

3. Map the movement of each sentence in that second paragraph on a grid that uses a simple scale like this:

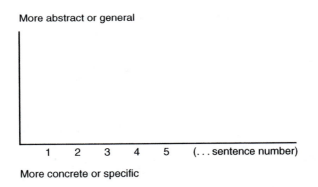

What do you notice about the pattern?

Practicing the Craft

In an essay published many years ago, the scholar Richard Ohmann confessed his uneasiness over the advice in Strunk and White's classic *The Elements of Style* that writers should always use "definite, specific, concrete language."[6] Their point was a good one: Specifics are more interesting to read than abstractions. Yet Ohmann wondered whether this

[6] Richard Ohmann, "Use Definite, Specific, Concrete Language," in Gary Tate and E. J. Corbett, eds., *The Writing Teacher's Sourcebook* (New York: Oxford, 1981), 379–389.

advice didn't sometimes rob writers of a kind of thinking that moves them away from "immediate experience" and toward language that might help them analyze, understand, and even "transform" it. Fiction writers won't lose much sleep over this. Stories are built from attention to the particular—what it looked like, how it smelled, and so on—and meanings are usually the providence of the reader. But nonfiction both shows *and* tells. The personal essay, especially, is often explicit. "The essay is distinguished from the short story," wrote Scott Sanders, "not by the presence or absence of literary devices, not by tone or theme or subject, but by the writer's stance towards the material. In composing an essay about what it was like to grow up on that military base, I *meant* something quite different from what I mean when concocting a story. . . . I wanted to speak directly out of my own life into the lives of others."[7] This "direct" speech is not the "specific and concrete" language that Strunk and White encouraged but the more general, analytical language that they discouraged.

Essayists must write with both languages; they build stories from particulars and then reflect on their significance with analysis (though never too much). Try the following journal exercise to see the power of each kind of writing.

1. Imagine a room you spent a lot of time in as a child. Put yourself back there and look around. For three minutes, brainstorm a list of everything you see, drawing on all of your senses. Write "the green, down-stuffed chair with the coffee stain" rather than simply "the chair."

2. Choose one of these details as a starting point for a story or anecdote, and follow it, fastwriting for six full minutes. Don't worry if you leave the room or stay; just let the writing lead. Try writing in present tense, however, and keep the prose as detailed as your list was in the previous step.

3. Skip a line in your journal. Now analyze the material you just generated by *crafting* (thinking about what you're going to say before you say it) a fat paragraph that begins this way: "What I understand now that I didn't understand then was . . ."

How would you compare the writing in steps two and three of this exercise in terms of levels of specificity or abstraction, register, voice, and especially the cognitive demands each made on you? Did you find that each demanded a different kind of thought? Is there a personal essay lurking here?

[7]From Scott Russell Sanders, "The Singular First Person," *Secrets of the Universe* (Boston: Beacon, 1991), 203.

Recommended Nonfiction by
Scott Russell Sanders

- *Secrets of the Universe* (1991). Choosing a few from Sanders's many collections of essays is nearly impossible, but this volume, along with *The Paradise of Bombs*, is my favorite. *Secrets of the Universe* includes another remarkable essay on his father that presents a different angle on the man than the one in "Inheritance of Tools." The collection also includes Sanders's essay on the genre of the essay, "The Singular First Person," one of the best contemporary pieces on the subject.

- *A Private History of Awe* (2006). This is Sanders's memoir of his early childhood in Tennessee and move to the Ravenna Arsenal in Ohio, where his father took a job in a munitions plant. The work is beautifully structured. Sanders frames his own memories of the past with two present-day narratives—one about his granddaughter Elizabeth and the other about his mother, who suffers from Alzheimer's. This device reinforces the idea that the narrowness of childhood soon opens up to wonder, only to return to a another kind of narrowness.

1.6

THE BEGINNING AND END
OF A MAN'S LIFE

Excerpt from Andre Dubus's
Broken Vessels

$\curlyvee$

The Excerpt in Context

On July 23, 1986, Andre Dubus stopped to help Luis and Luz
Santiago, whose car was stalled on the side of a Massachusetts highway.
The impulse to stop, Dubus later wrote, arose from his Marine Corps
training years before—an impulse to act even if it seemed counter to
one's instinct for survival. The decision was a tragic one. An oncoming
car swerved, killing Luis and crushing Dubus's legs; his left leg was later
amputated and his right one permanently disabled. He spent the remain-
der of his life, which ended with a heart attack 13 years later, in a wheel-
chair, though he continued to write fiction and nonfiction, building on a
literary career that was well established before the accident. Dubus is well
known for his short fiction, but his essays—a genre he turned to especially after his injuries—are lyrical and deeply felt works, brutally honest
yet tempered with insight that seems earned at great cost.

One of the great accomplishments of Dubus's essays is that they
often risk sentimentality but never give into it. Phillip Lopate once observed that the essay is a form especially suited for authors who are
middle-aged and older and, if true, it may be because older writers
quickly recognize that their experiences are not singular and that this is
exactly what makes them powerful. *How it felt* is most moving when
said with restraint, even understatement, because writers never imagine that they are the first to feel such things. And yet Andre Dubus's
tragic accident and the difficulties that followed would seem to invite
exclamations of some kind. The excerpt that follows is from the title essay of a collection of work, much of which was written in the few years
after the accident. In "Broken Vessels" Dubus writes not only about
toiling to recover from his injuries but learning to live "the life of an
amputee when he realizes that everything takes three times as long,"

including cooking pork chops and reading stories to his two daughters, Madeline and Cadence. In this key passage, Dubus seems to understand that this means much more than mere logistics.

✎ *The Excerpt* ✎

The best person for a crippled man to cry with is a good female physical therapist, and the best place to do that crying is in the area where she works. One morning in August of 1987, shuffling with my right leg and the walker, with Mrs. T in front of me and her kind younger assistants, Kathy and Betty, beside me, I began to cry. Moving across the long therapy room with beds, machines, parallel bars, and exercise bicycles, I said through my weeping: *I'm not a man among men anymore and I'm not a man among women either.* Kathy and Betty gently told me I was fine. Mrs. T said nothing, backing ahead of me, watching my leg, my face, my body. We kept working. I cried and talked all the way into the small room with two beds that are actually leather-cushioned tables with a sheet and pillow on each, and the women helped me onto my table, and Mrs. T went to the end of it, to my foot, and began working on my ankle and toes and calf with her gentle strong hands. Then she looked up at me. Her voice has much peace whose resonance is her own pain she has moved through and beyond. *It's in Jeremiah*, she said. *The potter is making a pot and it cracks. So he smashes it, and makes a new vessel. You can't make a new vessel out of a broken one. It's time to find the real you.*

Her words and their images rose through my chest like a warm vapor, and in it was the man shattering clay, and me at Platoon Leaders' Class at Quantico, a boy who had never made love, not when I turned nineteen there, not when I went back for the second six weeks just before becoming twenty-one; and memories of myself after my training at Quantico, those times in my life when I had instinctively moved toward action, to stop fights, to help the injured or stricken, and I saw myself on the highway that night, and I said: *Yes. It makes sense. It started as a Marine, when I was eighteen; and it ended on a highway when I was almost fifty years old.* ✎

Analyzing the Excerpt

1. Dubus, primarily a fiction writer, is a master at crafting scene. Much can be learned by studying his method in the excerpt. Scenes typically have the following elements: vantage point, characters, setting, and action. Something happens to someone somewhere as seen from a particular

From: Andre Dubus, *Broken Vessels* (Boston: David R. Godine, 1991), 171–172.

point of view. The action may or may not be dramatic. In this excerpt, for instance, the moment is utterly ordinary—a man undergoes a physical therapy session, and in frustration he weeps. But "Mrs. T" says something unexpectedly poignant, and suddenly the scene takes on an emotional charge that moves us. Obviously, we don't render scenes in exact detail, describing everything we can remember about what happened where. We select details sparingly, things that do necessary work in the scene. Talk about the details that Dubus chooses here, and also what he chooses to leave out. What does that tell you about a method for crafting a scene?

2. There are many ways for a writer to give certain material—a line, a passage, or even a word—emphasis. Here Dubus uses italics, a method that is more common with the advent of word processing programs. Aside from drawing readers' attention to these sentences, the italics here affect how we read them, how the lines resonate in our heads. How would you describe this effect?

3. Stylistically, Dubus, like Joan Didion, is a lover of the embedded clause. Consider, for example, this sentence from the excerpt: "I cried and talked all the way into the small room with two beds that are actually leather-cushioned tables with a sheet and pillow on each, and the women helped me onto my table, and Mrs. T went to the end of it, to my foot, and began working on my ankle and toes and calf with her gentle strong hands." This sentence could easily be broken into several by dropping an "and" and converting a comma to a period. What would be lost and what would be gained from such a move?

Practicing the Craft

Scene is the foundation of literary journalism, memoir, and often essay. You can't practice it enough. Material for scenes in nonfiction comes from primarily three sources: memory, observation, or interview. The Dubus excerpt is an inspiring example of scene writing that draws on his own recollections of a day in 1987. More-journalistic approaches would be to observe and take notes that can later be crafted into a scene or to interview people who were there, especially if the writer was not, and create a scene based on what the interviewees say. Using Dubus's excerpt as an example of a scene drawn from memory, write a scene about a conflict with a family member or a friend. Remember to deploy some of the key elements of scene by anchoring it to a particular time and place and perhaps vantage point.

You might begin in your journal by simply listing sensory details that you recall from the moment, material that you can later select from as you give the scene shape. When I was in high school, I ran cross-country and track, and though I was a mediocre runner, I developed thick thighs and good endurance. My father was a drunk. One evening after dinner, he challenged me to a foot race, a proposal that enraged me and, later, made me profoundly sad. Here are some details I recall from that scene:

Thick black plastic glasses slipping to end of nose

Adidas running shoes, white with green stripes

Linden Ave.

Summer evening, fading light

The jingle of change

Heavy-lidded eyes

"You think you can still beat me? Let's find out."

Labored breath

Salem cigarettes

Blur of wooden fence

Sallow complexion

> One summer night when I was 16, my father challenged me to a footrace. As a young man my age, my father was a sprinter and a football player, but now, at 52, he spent his days racing to the basement where he stashed a bottle of vodka on the shelf that held cigar boxes full of nuts and bolts. "You think you can still beat me?" Dad said. "You think you can outrun your old man? Let's find out, okay? Let's just see who is the best runner in this family." I don't recall what exactly inspired the challenge, though my obvious contempt for him was reason enough. "I don't think so, Dad," I said. But he persisted, and the chance to humiliate my father was irresistible. So we stood there in the fading light, both toeing some imaginary line on the street in front of our old stucco house—a young man in shorts and white Adidas, and his father with clenched fists and a forehead wet with sweat—both listening to the beating of their empty hearts. I took off in a burst, and I heard behind me the jingling of loose change in my father's pockets, a sound that still reminds me of him, and of that night. A few years later, when my Dad died of a cerebral hemorrhage, my brother found him in his filthy kitchen, lying in a pool of blood, and though I wasn't there, I imagine that a few silver coins had fallen from his pocket.

Because our memories are already embedded in stories we tell about ourselves, it isn't difficult to craft a scene from them that is organized around a feeling or idea. It's much more difficult to write a scene that we observe rather than one we remember. For one thing, we have no idea what story we want to tell. What will all our observations add up to? Try to craft a scene from your notes of an event or place that you observe for 30 minutes or more. Try to choose a situation or location that is potentially interesting, where there might be a little story to tell—a sporting event, last call at a cowboy bar, seniors playing a video game at a nursing home. What demands does this kind of scene make on you as a writer that crafting a scene from memory doesn't make?

Recommended Nonfiction by Andre Dubus

- *Meditations from a Moveable Chair* (1998). This is Dubus's second collection of essays and, sadly, the last essays he published before his death in 1999. The writer was 62. Much of the work in this volume focuses on writing, and one essay, "Letter to a Writer's Workshop," should be required reading for anyone involved in a writer's group or workshop class.

1.7

A GREAT MOMENT OF NEED

Excerpt from Nancy Mairs's
On Touching by Accident

∽

The Excerpt in Context

"Socrates' maxim about the unexamined life not being worth living has undergone a noteworthy mutation in late twentieth-century America," writes Nancy Franklin in a recent *New Yorker*. "In the last few years, as the best-seller lists have seen a steady march of memoirs and biographies that tell all—or purport to tell all—an observer of our culture could reasonably conclude that we believe that a life isn't worth living unless *everyone* examines it." Perhaps no American nonfiction writer is more identified with "the literature of personal disaster" than Nancy Mairs, an essayist whose collections have among other things recounted her adulteries, her sexual interests, and her psychiatric and physical problems. For years, Mairs has bravely endured multiple sclerosis, an experience she explores in her best-known essay, "On Being a Cripple."

Critics of "confessional" writing complain that this genre is too often meant to merely shock, fails to enlighten, or is simply excessive. Writing about a memoir that included a series of sexual disclosures, one critic asked, "How does a reader respond when the writer creates a hapless, damaged character, barely afloat and apparently without a clue, and confirms, 'Yes this is me, my life has been hell, please give me a hug'? It's disarming, but is it literature?" All essayists ultimately confront the question of how much they will disclose about themselves. Because the writer is the subject of the personal essay, this dilemma is nearly unavoidable. But how do you make this decision? It's certainly a personal question—How safe do you feel sharing the details of your life, how willing are you to expose the personal lives of others?—but it's also a question of craft: Does personal confession serve a particular purpose in the piece, and how does this affect how you are read by others?

The excerpt that follows is from *Plaintext*, one of Mairs's earliest essay collections and arguably her best. It's typical in some ways of much of her work: frank and deeply personal, and at times even quietly distressing. In the piece titled "On Touching by Accident," Mairs narrates one of her suicide attempts. The excerpt is drawn from the last third of the essay, and it describes a Friday night in October when she decided to take too many pills.

❧ *The Excerpt* ❧

When I got home, the back yard of my little apartment building, where I parked my car, was dark; but there was a moon, and I'd left my porch light on, so I could find my door. As I stuck the key into the lock, a figure danced out of the darkness—a clown, I think, in a pink ruffled suit—and pleaded, "Oh, can I use your bathroom? I'm at this party over there"—vague gesture—"and the line to the bathroom is *miles* long and I've been drinking all this *beer* and I'm about to *burst* and..." "Sure," I said, swinging the door in. "It's in there." While she peed torrentially, I turned on the radio, opened a beer, and put down fresh food for Bête Noire, who was twisting around my ankles like a dervish. The clown flushed and came out, yanking at her ruffles. "This is so *hard* to get in and out of," she moaned. "Oh, thank you. You saved my *life*. I just couldn't have waited any longer." She was pink and plump. I didn't think she was old enough for the beer. "Oh, *there* you are," she called to a shadow that loomed on the doorstep, and off she bounded, recounting my heroic rescue of her in her moment of greatest need.

I closed the door behind her. I went into the bathroom and started taking Elavil while I washed my face and undressed. I went back into the tidy white bedroom/living room/kitchen/study and sat down at my desk. Still taking the Elavil, three by three, I finished my letter to George and tried to write in my journal, but my vision was too badly blurred. I dropped the bottle of Elavil and couldn't see to pick up the small yellow tablets. That clumsiness probably saved my life. That, and Bête Noire. I had at first thought I would turn on my stove and heater, which had no pilot lights, and thus hasten the work of the drug. But Bête was so tiny that I knew that the gas would kill her long before me, and I couldn't bear the thought of her black body still and lifeless. By this time I had no sense of myself or anyone else as a living creature; and when, later, a psychiatrist asked if I hadn't tried to call for help after taking all those pills, I had to say that I didn't know there was anyone to call; yet I couldn't kill the kitten.

George[8] found me eighteen hours later and took me to the emergency room, where, after a few hours on a heart monitor and the obligatory psychiatric interview, I was pronounced a survivor and sent home. I had at

From: Nancy Mairs, "On Touching by Accident," *Plaintext* (Tucson, AZ: University of Arizona, 1992), 23–24.
[8]George is Mairs's husband.

some point roused having to go to the bathroom and, unable to get even to my hands and knees, had dragged myself around my apartment, battering my body and smearing the floor with blood and urine; but I heal quickly. Before long the bruises faded and the scabs fell off. I was still shaky, but no longer suicidal. I had let a lot of my responsibilities slide, so I threw myself into activity and forgot the whole mess as much and as quickly as possible.

Then one day, six weeks or so later, when I was having lunch with a friend and we were swapping stories of failed love and suicide, I saw suddenly the round pink ruffled form of the little clown dancing through my door and into my bathroom. I had wholly forgotten her and the young man waiting for her in the shadows under my cedar trees. I was startled by the memory—so quick, so complete—startled and amused, and I began to describe it to my friend. Just then, though, the man who had thrown me over, with whom I was still in love, asked if he might join us, and naturally we had to speak of other things. I never finished my story about the clown. ◌

Analyzing the Craft

1. There is a difference between self-help books and literature, though literature may be helpful and self-help books well written. But in her essay on "The Literature of Personal Disaster,"[9] Nancy Mairs writes that the "true value of victim art" is that it "make[s] one's pain not pitiable but exquisite, exemplifying the human spirit's tenacity and triumph." Humor, she adds, is often an essential ingredient as well. The excerpt isn't funny, but it is certainly devoid of self-pity. Some might even read it as lacking much feeling at all. What do you think?

2. Elsewhere in *Crafting Truth* we've explored the ethics of nonfiction, particularly writers' responsibility to the people they write about. In this excerpt, for example, Mairs's husband George enters the story briefly as her rescuer. Mentioned once, he exits the narrative for good after Mairs notes that George took her to the ER, where she was subsequently released after the "obligatory psychiatric interview." It isn't hard to imagine that for George the experience of finding his wife nearly dead on a floor covered with "blood and urine" was traumatic. Does Mairs err in not acknowledging this? What are her responsibilities, if any, to her husband in how she tells this story?

3. In the last line of this excerpt from "On Touching by Accident," Mairs writes simply: "I never finished my story about the clown." In some ways, this is an apt ending because it returns to the odd image in the scene of a stranger in a clown suit with the mundane problem of a full bladder just

[9]Nancy Mairs, *Voice Lessons* (Boston: Beacon), 1994.

minutes before Mairs starts taking Elavil, three pills at a time. And yet, it seems so understated, almost bland. What do you think?

Practicing the Craft

When dramatic things happen to us—whether they're good or bad—they trigger dramatic emotional responses: fear, joy, rage, grief, self-pity, pride, and so on. Undoubtedly Nancy Mairs felt things very deeply when she planned, attempted, and recovered from the suicide she described in the excerpt, though we can only guess what those feelings were. In writing workshops I often hear the complaint that writers in their drafts don't say enough about what they were feeling. "You must have been devastated when this happened," someone might say. "But you don't tell us that." The advice seems simple. Add a sentence that says "I was devastated." Most of the time this falls flat because it states the obvious. The Mairs excerpt suggests another solution: understatement. Paradoxically, perhaps writers should trust that a situation that calls for sentiment can express it most strongly by withholding feeling.

No subject is more vulnerable to sentiment than essays about pets. The beloved dog dies or the cute kittens get caught in a raccoon trap or the parrot mourns the loss of his life partner. It's almost impossible to tell these stories without oversentimentalizing. And yet, some of the most powerful pet stories rely on understatement, on trusting that the reader will "get it" even if the feeling is not named. Try composing a paragraph in your journal about a death—of a pet or even a person—that had a strong impact on you. If possible, choose a death that you witnessed or were close to in some way. For this exercise, focus on the scene, perhaps the moment when you saw the death occur or learned about it; this should be some moment that was charged with feeling for you, but don't talk about those feelings. Instead, let the details and your observations do that work.

Here's what I did with the exercise:

Years before I would weep at the movie "Old Yeller—a film that my teenage daughter refuses to watch because she is quite certain she would "fall apart"—I watched a milk truck run over my poodle. I was three or four and had no experience watching things die. The dog, Buster, was wooly white and six hands high, his head even with mine. We lived at the time in a Chicago suburb, and in the mid-fifties milk was still delivered twice weekly in glass bottles with cardboard tops. I was alone with Buster in the front yard when the dog trotted to the middle of Glencoe Avenue, and lay down. I called him, but at that age I had no authority over a standard poodle. The Wanzer milk truck hit him broadside and never stopped. The dog wasn't killed instantly because I remember that for a few moments after the truck disappeared down the street, his tail was still wagging. I've often wondered what kind of greeting that was, and for whom.

Recommended Nonfiction by Nancy Mairs

- *Voice Lessons* (1994). The subtitle of this book is "On Becoming a (Woman) Writer" and includes several powerful essays on how she found her voice as an essayist, stories that many writers will recognize. One of the most important pieces here is her essay "Literature of Personal Disaster," an inquiry into the motives behind confession in autobiographical writing.
- *Remembering the Bone House* (1989). Fans of Mairs's essays will find that this memoir fills in many of the narrative spaces that the shorter pieces must leave out. Mairs calls *Remembering the Bone House* her "memoir of my life as a female body." She writes in her preface to the 1995 edition of the book that it is her favorite work because it is "raw-boned" and "gawky," much "like the girl I once was."

1.8

VAMOOSE TO THE VOMIT CORNER

Excerpt from David Sedaris's
The SantaLand Diaries

This "Entrance Elf" could have been David Sedaris (it is not) when he found seasonal employment at Macy's department store in its "SantaLand" display, though it appears that they've toned down the elf outfit since Sedaris wrote about his experience in "The SantaLand Diaries."

The Excerpt in Context

Humor, says E. B. White, "plays close to the hot fire which is Truth, and sometimes readers feel the heat." It seems like an oddly serious thing to say about writing that is meant to amuse. But White's point is that humorists are writers with serious things to say who have chosen to say them humorously. Humorists who are just after the laughs,

White might say, aren't serious writers. An interest in getting at the truth of things is something that humorists share with other essayists. But the comic essay, with its mix of fact and exaggeration (fiction?), doesn't always seem to belong in nonfiction's otherwise big tent. It's a hybrid form—a blend of essay and short story—but most readers seem to give it a pass on the usual expectation that nonfiction must be true, though we expect it to generate the heat of truth.

There is a long tradition of American humor writing, which Mark Twain distinguished from European forms this way: "The humorous story is American, the comic story is English, the witty story is French. The humorous story depends for its effect upon the manner of the telling; the comic story and the witty story upon the matter."[10] Twain, like many American humorists, told funny stories to an audience; the humor essay was really based on a speaking engagement. The oral delivery of humorous stories has been revived by a new generation of humorists, and none is better known than David Sedaris, whose audio essays have been featured for the last 15 years on National Public Radio's *This American Life*.

The following excerpt is from "SantaLand Diaries," the essay that first established Sedaris's fame when he read it on the radio in 1994. The piece tells the story of his temporary job as a Christmas elf in Macy's department store. (He took the name "Crumpet," though later entertained the idea of changing it to "Blisters.") The commercialization and excess of Christmas is fair game for humor but often falls flat; perhaps the narrator comes across as sanctimonious, or we've heard the same complaints about the holiday again and again. "SantaLand Diaries" has none of these problems. It's simply flat-out funny. It's also a scathing critique of the lengths people will go to to demand their piece of the Christmas "spirit." Keep in mind, too, that this essay was originally written to be read aloud, a fact that influences Sedaris's prose style in interesting ways.

❧ The Excerpt ❧

This morning we were lectured by the SantaLand managers and presented with a Xeroxed booklet of regulations titled "The Elfin Guide." Most of the managers are former elves who have worked their way up the candy-cane ladder but retain vivid memories of their days in uniform. They closed

From: David Sedaris, "SantaLand Diaries," *Holidays on Ice* (New York: Back Bay, 1997), 10–12.
[10]Mark Twain, "How to Tell a Story," *How to Tell a Story and Other Essays* (1897) (New York: Oxford, 1996).

the meeting saying, "I want you to remember that even if you are assigned Photo Elf on a busy weekend, YOU ARE NOT SANTA'S SLAVE."

In the afternoon we were given a tour of SantaLand, which really is something. It's beautiful, a real wonderland, with ten thousand sparkling lights, false snow, train sets, bridges, decorated trees, mechanical penguins and bears, and really tall candy canes. One enters and travels through a maze, a path which takes you from one festive environment to another. The path ends at the Magic Tree. The Tree is supposed to resemble a complex system of roots, but looks instead like a scale model of the human intestinal tract. Once you pass the Magic Tree, the light dims and an elf guides you to Santa's house. The houses are cozy and intimate, laden with toys. You exit Santa's house and are met with a line of cash registers.

We traveled the path a second time and were given the code names for various posts, such as "The Vomit Corner," a mirrored wall near the Magic Tree, where nauseous children tend to surrender the contents of their stomachs. When someone vomits, the nearest elf is supposed to yell "VAMOOSE," which is the name of the janitorial product used by the store. We were taken to the "Oh, My God, Corner," a position near the escalator. People arriving see the long line and say "Oh, my God!" and it is an elf's job to calm them down and explain that it will take no longer than an hour to see Santa.

On any given day you can be an Entrance Elf, a Water Cooler Elf, a Bridge Elf, Train Elf, Maze Elf, Island Elf, Magic Window Elf, Emergency Exit Elf, Counter Elf, Magic Tree Elf, Pointer Elf, Santa Elf, Photo Elf, Usher Elf, Cash Register Elf, Runner Elf, or Exit Elf. We were given a demonstration of the various positions in action, performed by returning elves who were so animated and relentlessly cheerful that it embarrassed me to walk past them. I don't know that I could look someone in the eye and exclaim, "Oh, my goodness, I think I see Santa!" or "Can you close your eyes and make a very special Christmas wish!" Everything these elves said had an exclamation point at the end of it!!! It makes one's mouth hurt to speak with such forced merriment. I feel cornered when someone talks to me this way. Doesn't everyone? I prefer being frank with children. I'm more likely to say, "You must be exhausted," or "I know a lot of people who would kill for that little waistline of yours."

I am afraid I won't be able to provide the grinding enthusiasm Santa is asking for. I think I'll be a low-key sort of an elf. ✧

Analyzing the Craft

1. The radio essay—or the podcast—is likely the most popular form of the essay genre these days. *This American Life* writers like David Sedaris, Ira Glass, and Sarah Vowell are the closest thing we have to creative nonfiction rock stars. Telling humorous stories to an audience isn't new, as noted earlier, but technology now makes it possible to edit

and add not only voices but also music and ambient sounds. But essayists like Sedaris who write for radio or podcast operate under a condition that print authors don't: An audio essay is likely to be heard only once. Imagine, for example, tuning into public radio while driving and hearing a Sedaris essay. You listen but you can't reread. And most of us will stop listening pretty quickly if the speaker isn't engaging. With this in mind, what do you notice in the excerpt that seems fashioned to appeal especially to a listener rather than a reader?

2. In memoir and essay the narrator is always a character (an "I-Character," Phillip Lopate put it), and this seems especially important in the humor essay. The success of Sedaris's work is due in large part to our eagerness to see things as he does and to spend time not only in his world but also in his head. Crafting an "I-Character" with whom readers want to spend time is difficult, especially in humor essays, because the narrator can come across as a wise-ass—superior, sarcastic, cynical, or unsympathetic. How would you describe the Sedaris-narrator? And where, exactly, is there evidence of this persona, even in this relatively short excerpt?

3. Okay, the holidays invite excess, and certainly Sedaris is commenting on that here, but is he making any more-nuanced or subtle arguments in the excerpt? In other words, what might be some of the serious truths behind the humor?

Practicing the Craft

The audio essay is a new frontier for personal essayists. Montaigne's 500-year-old form has found new and enthusiastic audiences online and on the radio. Yet what is more interesting is how different it is to write essays that are meant to be *heard* rather than read. When I work with advanced nonfiction students on writing and producing radio essays, one of the first things they say is how much more it matters that they believe what they are saying. There's something about speaking your words, rather than leaving them on a printed page, that seems to inspire the honesty and commitment that was always the hallmark of the personal essay. "You can't be a bullshitter," one student said to me. "You just can't stand to hear yourself saying anything you don't believe." Speaking essays influences prose in other ways, too. Radio essayists report that they are more vigilant about making every word count and about making their meanings clear even through repetition. They are also particularly sensitive about the balance between narrative and exposition. People who listen to essays especially need the backbone of story to stay engaged with the telling.

Even if you don't want to podcast or broadcast essays, the practice of crafting prose that will be heard only once is excellent training for all writers. Hearing is one of the senses that must be a part of all writing—printed or spoken—though it is one of the most difficult to cultivate. Work on this by producing a four-minute podcast—about three double-spaced pages of manuscript. Consider revising an existing draft for this exercise if you don't want to generate new material. Imagine that your audience is a distracted driver who is listening to you on the radio.

1. As you prepare the manuscript, keep the following in mind:
   - Edit for simplicity.
   - Try to say one thing in the piece, and don't hesitate to repeat it.
   - Emphasize story over exposition, showing over telling.
   - Keep paragraphs short—three or four sentences at most.
2. Before you record, read your piece out loud to help you with editing it further.
3. To record your piece, you will need the following:
   - A computer with a microphone (external or internal).
   - Recording software. This may already be bundled into your computer (e.g., Mac computers usually have "Garage Band"), but you can download free software that is more than adequate from Audacity (http://audacity.sourceforge.net/). The tutorials on the site will guide you on how to use the program. It's quite simple to use, especially if you are recording just a voice track.
4. Record your essay. You may edit the track, including rerecording and then inserting segments you want to do over, or simply work to produce one clean-sounding version of your essay. If you wish, you may decide to add music to your piece later.
5. Share the result with your writing group or others. Discuss whether the piece was engaging, and how it can be more so. Try to determine what one idea your listeners thought seemed most important after listening to the essay only once.
6. Revise and rerecord.

Other Recommended Nonfiction
by David Sedaris

- *Me Talk Pretty One Day* (2000). Most of these laugh-out-loud essays were first heard on National Public Radio's *This American Life,* and it's particularly amusing to not only read the pieces but also listen to them as they were originally written for broadcast. You can find some of them in the program's audio archives online. Fans of bathroom humor (that would include me) will particularly enjoy the essay "Big Boy" in this collection.
- *Dress Your Family in Corduroy and Denim* (2004). This is an extraordinary essay collection that followed the success of *Me Talk Pretty One Day.*

A SCAFFOLD FOR LANGUAGE

Excerpt from Ander Monson's
Outline Toward a Theory of the Mine Versus
the Mind and the Harvard Outline

The 2000 film Memento, *a low budget thriller, defied the usual conventions of film by narrating one story in reverse chronology and the other chronologically, with both narratives converging at the end. By defying expectations,* Memento *raised questions about film genres much like the lyric essay challenges nonfiction genres.*

The Excerpt in Context

No one in a creative writing class wants to talk about genre. "What difference does it make what we call it?" Then we encounter an "essay" like Ander Monson's, excerpted here, or the work of Lia Purpura (see "Autopsy Report" in the anthology) and other "lyric essayists," and suddenly genre is all we want to talk about. The personal essay, like any literary form, balances precariously between tradition and experiment. The tradition is often tacit; writers at least know intuitively what it means to write an essay or a short story because they've been exposed to the genres for a long time. On the other hand, a poet who takes up nonfiction will import what she knows about writing poems into a personal essay, and before long a hybrid form arises. This gets our attention. As readers, we work from our own tradition, too, and we have certain tacit expectations about what an essay "should" look like and may conclude that "this ain't it," or we learn from Oprah that James Frey faked parts of his memoir and share her sense of betrayal.

Clearly, genre does matter. But maybe it shouldn't? "I suspect that genre, like gender, with which it shares a root," wrote essayist Eula Biss "is mostly a collection of lies we have agreed to believe."[11]

Ander Monson's essay "Outline Toward a Theory of the Mine Versus the Mind and the Harvard Outline," from his award-winning nonfiction work *Neck Deep and Other Predicaments,* is likely to get you thinking about form, even if it doesn't make you wonder about genre. The excerpt, drawn from the beginning of his essay, starts with a meditation on the Harvard outline by using it to structure his thoughts. Eileen Pollack uses the term "found form" to describe this kind of appropriation of worldly things to organize material in literary nonfiction.[12] Examples abound. The literary journalist John McPhee uses the board game Monopoly to structure his essay about Atlantic City, "In Search of Marvin Gardens," and Terry Tempest Williams (see page 106) uses the changing levels of the Great Salt Lake to structure her memoir. It's not hard to imagine promise in "found forms" of all kinds, depending on your subject: An essay on music could be organized in tracks, or a piece on eating might read like a menu.

However, what makes Monson's essay poignant isn't the form it takes but how he ultimately finds in the form a way of understanding things that seem to have nothing to do with the outline: his family's legacy of hard-rock mining in northern Michigan, and how the Harvard outline might provide the right "architecture" for boring into his own past. The excerpt only hints at the larger dimensions of the essay, but the

---

[11]Eula Biss, "It Is What It Is," *Seneca Review* 37.2 (2007): 56. This issue of the journal is devoted to answering the question "What is the lyric essay?"

[12]Eileen Pollack, "The Interplay of Form and Content in Creative Nonfiction," *The Writer's Chronicle* 39.5 (March/April 2007): 56.

opening to "Outline Toward a Theory of the Mine Versus the Mind and the Harvard Outline" provides a good sense of how Monson exploits the form—not just for verbal play but as a method of thought.

∾ *The Excerpt* ∾

I. Start with the Roman numeral I with an authoritative period trailing just after it. This is the Harvard Outline, which comes in Caps and is a method of organizing information
  a. remembered from high school as a major step toward creating an essay
      i. though there was a decimal method, too
  b. but I've never been comfortable with the thing—its seeming rigor, its scaffolding so white against the language
      i. never felt the top-down structuralist method of constructing writing to be useful or effective; the mind, so idiosyncratic, unusual
        1. its strangeness and its often-incoherence
            a. the lovely anomaly
  c. and the Harvard Outline is the reason that I get 55 5-paragraph essays every month
  d. it is, I think, suspect, (its
  e. headings
      i. subheadings
        1. sub-subheadings
            a. etc.
            b. though there is a pleasure to this iteration, this recursion—like mathematics and the algorithms I played with and admired in computer-science classes, writing functions that called themselves
                i. which called themselves
                  1. which called themselves
                      a. until they were satisfied
                  2. and exited
              ii. right back
        c. out
            i. like those Russian nesting [Matryoshka] dolls; a lovely symmetry; such satisfaction comes in nesting
          ii. such starkness
              1. elegance)

From: Ander Monson, "Outline Toward a Theory of the Mine Versus the Mind and the Harvard Outline," *Neck Deep and Other Predicaments* (Saint Paul, MN: Graywolf, 2007), 3–4.

    f. all those steps out and down across the page—like the writing task
is that of going downhill, like a waterfall in its rush
       i. or the incremental, slow plod down the slope, skis buried be-
hind in some drift ⁕

Analyzing the Craft

1. A critic once expressed his reservations about the "lyric essay"
because, he wrote, it often seems like a "license for vagueness." He
wondered whether the form, "a wedding of contemporary poetry and
nonfiction," might be, in the end, just another kind of poetry. What
seems obvious from the excerpt is that alternate forms of the essay do
at least free writers from the usual kinds of storytelling. Martha Ronk
observed that the lyric essay may be seeded with anecdote but is likely
to "spin out from it not toward narrative or fact, not toward information separate from words, but toward constructed and artificial shape
dependent on analogy." How do these departures from the conventional essay change the reader's experience of the work? What was
your experience reading the excerpt, and did it matter that it defied
your expectations? To what extent do you think genre matters to you
as a writer?

2. In an appendix to Monson's collection, he writes that what attracts him
to unconventional essay forms, ironically, is that it shields him somewhat
from the reader: "I employ methods of obfuscation, of complication, of
precipitation that stand between the word and world, between you and
me." Did you think that the excerpt's imitation of the Harvard outline
shifted your gaze away from Monson the narrator in some ways? More
generally, is the narrator in a personal essay always vulnerable to some
extent, no matter what devices he invokes to find cover?

3. What argument is Monson making in the excerpt?

Practicing the Craft

For a long time, I was on the side of those who believed that the material *finds* its appropriate form. Maybe you begin writing an essay and it
becomes a short story, or you begin writing fiction and it becomes memoir. Perhaps it was my experience with writing instruction that works
from the mistaken premise that form is a container into which you pour
information, but I've always believed that you discover your purpose
through writing *and then* find an appropriate form for that purpose. But
my friends who are poets have convinced me otherwise. They find that

forms like sonnet are often *generative* and a source of discovery about the subjects and themselves.

Ander Monson provides a wonderful model for these kinds of experiments with form. The Harvard outline is familiar to most of us, and it's particularly intriguing because it's a method of structuring thought as well as information. The possibilities for these "found forms" are endless. Consider the promise of borrowing some of the following forms to organize material for an essay on turning points in your own life:

- Google search page results
- Entries from a field guide to birds
- A menu
- An instruction manual
- A series of Tweets or Facebook posts
- Tracks from a record album
- A passage with multiple-choice questions modeled on the SAT
- A job application

In this exercise, choose one of these forms or another that is more appropriate to organize a two- or three-page sketch on what you consider turning points in your own life. Try beginning this exercise in your journal with the following fastwrite:

- Spend at least seven minutes generating material in your journal in response to the following prompt:

  When you think about moments in your life that you consider "turning points," what do you think of? And then what? And then? What stories do these turning points inspire? Tell some.

Generate as much material as you can on the subject of turning points before you attempt to craft anything. Most important is to enjoy the verbal play and possibility that this experiment inspires.

Recommended Nonfiction by Ander Monson

- http://otherelectricities.com. A memoir is forthcoming from Ander Monson, but in the meantime the author's website is a showcase of his talents as an essayist, poet, and technophile. The site includes a link for *Neck Deep and Other Predicaments*, the essay collection from which the excerpt is drawn. It is a visually arresting and fascinating addendum to the book.

Part 2
The Memoirists

❧❧❧

Introduction to Memoir

Frank McCourt, the author of the Pulitzer Prize–winning memoir *Angela's Ashes*, once recalled that getting started on the book was hell. He knew he wanted to be a writer and yet he couldn't figure out what he wanted to write. At first it never occurred to him that he might write about himself, so he dabbled in fiction, including crime and spy stories. An Irish Catholic, McCourt was taught in parochial school that the "lives of the saints" might be an appropriate topic for writing about but certainly not his own life. "I simply didn't know that my own experiences were of any value," he said. When he published *Angela's Ashes* at age 65, McCourt learned otherwise, in spectacular fashion. McCourt had to believe that *his* was the story he needed to tell, and *that* faith doesn't come easily. It's risky to believe your story will matter to anyone but you.

Both memoirs and personal essays depend on writers' faith that their experiences have value. But how does one find this faith? To some extent, you can't know before you've at least tried to tell your story—the writing might help you discover what you didn't know you knew. However, some critics of the memoir argue that the real problem is not that too few writers have this faith but that too many do. For every *Angela's Ashes* there are scores of memoirs published every year that, as one editor put it, suffer from "gimmickry, trendiness, and self-promotion."[1] All forms of autobiography are vulnerable to the charge that their authors are egotistical or that what they disclose about themselves is in bad taste. These are not new complaints. Jean-Jacques Rousseau was so mortified by the potential public reaction to portions of his memoir, *The Confessions*, that he chose to publish it posthumously in 1782. And yet, despite all of this, the public hunger for memoirs has not abated, beginning with what was arguably the first: *The Confessions of St. Augustine*, published in the fourth century. Today, memoirs still dominate best-seller lists. During the week of this writing, for example, number one on *The New York Times* best-seller list is tennis great Andre Agassi's memoir *Open*, a book that opens up about a lot of personal things, including Agassi's drug use.

[1]Gerald Howard, "Room for Debate: The Golden Age Has Passed," *New York Times*, July 24, 2009, http://roomfordebate.blogs.nytimes.com/2009/07/24/memoirs-and-mccourt/.

Ethics in the Age of Memoir

How much do readers really need to know about someone else's private life, including that of a celebrity like Agassi? *Need* is probably the wrong word. In the "age of memoir," which some say began in the last 20 or 30 years, there seems to be no limit to our interest in the private lives of others, whether it's stories about incest or about living with a really bad dog. That's not to say, however, that our interest in personal disclosure necessarily reflects our opinion about the quality of the work. These can be really bad books. "Confessional literature can be wearing because it is so often based on the fallacy that the unvarnished truth is the whole truth and the only truth,..." wrote Nancy Franklin in *The New Yorker*. "The virtues of craft, of approaching and finishing the job with restraint and care, should not be overlooked as communicative tools in their own right: see how putting on a coat of varnish brings out the grain of the wood."

While the celebrity memoir is an easy target for the complaint that it's missing varnish, literary memoirs aren't spared criticism either. The controversy over Joyce Maynard's 1990 memoir *At Home in the World*, which includes explicit material about her affair with the late writer J. D. Salinger when he was 52 and she was 18, not only raised eyebrows about the ethics of violating the privacy of the reclusive author but raised complaints about how Maynard allowed that part of her story to hijack the memoir. (And yet, how could it not?)

More often, literary memoirs get a bad rap when they lie. James Frey's best-selling memoir *A Million Little Pieces* (2003) raised Oprah's ire when she discovered, after recommending the book, that Frey fictionalized some scenes and falsified key events in his life history. There was controversy, too, over Augusten Burroughs's *Running with Scissors*, a memoir of the author's boyhood living with an extraordinarily strange family following his parents' divorce. The memoir, a best seller, prompted a lawsuit from the people he portrayed in the book—all members of the Northhampton, Massachusetts, family Burroughs lived with. They strongly disputed the accuracy of his story. The libel suit was settled in 2007 when the publisher agreed to call *Running with Scissors* a "book" and not a memoir.

Life history is inescapably subjective. After all, a memoir isn't a documentary: The author's motive isn't merely to write what happened but to reflect on what he or she makes of what happened. Memory isn't photographic, either (at least not for most mortals), so it's impossible to achieve complete accuracy. What, then, is the memoirist's obligation to get things right?

Although the ethics of truth-telling pose issues in the essay genre, they are particularly troublesome in memoir because memoirists so often write about people other than themselves. This fact prompted one critic to coin the term "the genre of appropriation" to describe books like *Running with Scissors* or *At Home in the World*, stories with characters that sometimes elbow the author into the background. Nonfiction characters "live both inside and outside the story," noted journalist David Lehman. Should creative nonfiction writers worry about both kinds of characters—the literary and the literal? Annie Dillard, who wrote *An American Childhood*, an acclaimed memoir about growing up in Pittsburgh, offered this answer: "Literature is an art, it's not a martial art...and no place from which to launch an attack." And yet, don't writers of autobiography also have an obligation to tell the truth about their experiences, even if it might inflict hurt on others?

Is There a Story Worth Telling?

Given all these ethical complexities, why might anyone write a memoir in the first place? The motives vary, of course, but rarely do memoirists turn to the genre because they think they have lived extraordinary lives that they just *know* other people will find fascinating. On the contrary, many successful memoirists believe their lives are absolutely ordinary. They come to the work for the same reason essayists write personal essays: self-discovery. Sometimes this means beginning with the parts of writers' lives that they find puzzling, dark, or transformative. "Write about the biggest, scariest darn elephant in the living room of your soul," suggested one published memoirist.[2] Other writers *do* something that becomes the basis of their memoir: read the encyclopedia from the beginning to the end, make every recipe in Julia Child's cookbook for a year, or sail around the world as a teenager. But what makes any memoir successful is almost always the way a writer elevates the ordinary into something much more than that. The memoirist does this through extraordinary writing, a good story, and, perhaps most important, the insight necessary to make that story move people.

Because memoirs, unlike personal essays, are *extended* narratives, they do present writers with particular problems. Generally speaking, when you have a lot of material the structure becomes especially important. Chronology is the default approach to organizing autobiography: Start at the beginning and go from there. This tactic can create narrative problems by robbing the story of the insight that might come from what Laurie Uttich called the "present moment" narrator. One of the things that memoirs share with personal essays is "the double vantage point"—the time shift between then and now. Sometimes this shift is very subtle—detectable by a change in tense or voice—but there can also be pretty obvious signage: "I now know..." Subtle or obvious, this shift is an essential part of the memoir. Without it, the story is merely about what happened and not about what *happens*.

[2]Gus Lee, "How You Can Find Your Story," Jennifer Traig, ed., *The Autobiographer's Handbook* (New York: Holt, 2008), 29.

But even more vexing than point of view is a more basic question: Is there a story to tell, and if so, how do you tell it? In other words, said Annie Dillard, it always comes down to this: "what to put in and what to leave out." But how do you make this decision? That, of course, is the art of the memoir. Tobias Wolff, author of *This Boy's Life*, believed that he saw the "narrative shape" of his memoir at the beginning of the project but also accepted that this was always subject to change as he wrote. Frank McCourt gravitated to the "hot" moments—life stories that tend to be significant: "a child dying, or your first communion, ... or your first day of school." More frequently, the decision about what to put in and what to leave out of a memoir is determined by the thematic heart of the book. What is it about? Loss? Friendship? Identity? Anything that doesn't belong under the thematic umbrella is cut. Alternatively, memoirist Janice Erlbaum offers this advice: "You find the 'story of your life' by asking yourself this question: What did you want more than anything?"[3]

The memoir excerpts that follow show some of the happy results when writers choose well. While you can't fully appreciate this decision without reading the whole work, you *can* see significant pieces of the stories these masters of the memoir choose to tell. For example, Gretel Ehrlich pauses to describe Wyoming's winter landscape in the excerpt from *The Solace of Open Spaces*, Mary Clearman Blew remembers looking through the blurry windshield of a pickup truck at a Montana river threatening to sweep some pigs away in the opening to *All But the Waltz*, and Maxine Hong Kingston imagines herself into the legend of Fa Mu Lan in a moment from *The Woman Warrior*. Each of these are moments that give the memoirs not only their "narrative shape" but their meaning as well. While they are small parts of larger stories, the excerpts in this section all demonstrate how craft elevates something ordinary into something much bigger than itself.

---

[3]Many of these comments by authors about the craft of memoir are included in *The Autobiographer's Handbook*, edited by Jennifer Traig, an excellent resource.

2.1

I MADE HIM OUT OF DREAMS

Excerpt from Tobias Wolff's
This Boy's Life

∽

The Excerpt in Context

Chronology can be a straitjacket for writers. Though at first we may need to lean on chronology to help us remember, chronology may not be the best way to structure a memoir. Typically, a writer's departure from chronological telling is motivated by a desire to introduce dramatic tension. The thinking goes something like this: If I begin at the ending, then readers will want to discover how it happened. This kind of manipulation of time is mostly about exploiting the tension in causality. Yet there is a subtler, and possibly equally significant, danger in organizing a nonfiction story chronologically: Writers may become constrained by a too-limited point of view. In most creative nonfiction, there are really two narrators: the "time-now" narrator and the "time-then" narrator, and both combine to tell a story. Chronology can favor the "time-then" narrator, thrusting memoirists back into their pasts but depriving the story of the wisdom that comes through reflection. That's the knowledge that the writer has *now* about the significance of what happened back then. If the time-then narrator were missing, we wouldn't have much of a story; if the time-now narrator were missing, the story wouldn't have much poignancy or meaning.

While it's quite possible to write a strictly chronological memoir that incorporates both narrators, it's more difficult. This is one reason why writers choose to disrupt the timeline, interrupting the narrative with scenes or reflective moments that show little respect for how things really happened. In the excerpt that follows, drawn from Tobias Wolff's best-selling memoir *This Boy's Life* (1989), Wolff reflects on his biological father, a figure who was absent through all of the writer's boyhood growing up with his mother and abusive step-father, Dwight, in the Pacific Northwest. What is striking about this passage is how Wolff suddenly breaks with the chronological narrative and sets off on another story that occurs years later—one that illuminates an understanding about his father that could only come with time. This break

79

with the main story, which otherwise proceeds chronologically, is unexpected and yet gives this moment in the narrative an emotional reality that could not be achieved as easily any other way. Wolff manages the shift gracefully, reminding us that we need not be bound by time and place or point of view.

∽ *The Excerpt* ∽

I also missed my father. My mother never complained to me about him, but sometimes Dwight would make sarcastic comments about Daddy Warbucks and Lord High-and-Mighty. He meant to impugn my father for being rich and living far away and having nothing to do with me, but all these qualities, even the last, perhaps especially the last, made my father fascinating. He had the advantage always enjoyed by the inconstant parent, of not being there to be found imperfect. I could see him as I wanted to see him. I could give him sterling qualities and imagine good reasons, even romantic reasons, why he had taken no interest, why he had never written to me, why he seemed to have forgotten I existed. I made excuses for him long after I should have known better. Then, when I did know better, I resolved to put the fact of his desertion from my mind. I visited him on my way to Vietnam, and then again when I got back, and we became friends. He was no monster—he'd had troubles of his own. Anyway, only crybabies groused about their parents.

This way of thinking worked pretty well until my first child was born. He came three weeks early, when I was away from home. The first time I saw him, in the hospital nursery, a nurse was trying to take a blood sample from him. She couldn't find a vein. She kept jabbing him, and every time the needle went in I felt it myself. My impatience made her so clumsy that another nurse had to take over. When I finally got my hands on him I felt as if I had snatched him from a pack of wolves, and as I held him something hard broke in me, and I knew that I was more alive than I had been before. But at the same time I felt a shadow, a coldness at the edges. It made me uneasy, so I ignored it. I didn't understand what it was until it came upon me again that night, so sharply I wanted to cry out. It was about my father, ten years dead by then. It was grief and rage, mostly rage, and for days I shook with it when I wasn't shaking with joy for my son, and for the new life I had been given.

But that was still to come. As a boy, I found no fault in my father. I made him out of dreams and memories. One of these memories was of sitting in the kitchen of my stepmother's beautiful old house in Connecticut, where I had come for a visit, and watching him unload a box

From: Tobias Wolff, *This Boy's Life* (New York: Harper & Row, 1989), 121–122.

full of fireworks onto the table. It was all heavy ordnance, seriously life threatening and illegal. My stepmother was scolding him. She wanted to know what he planned to do with them. He pushed a bunch of cherry bombs over to me and said, "Blow 'em up, dear, blow 'em up."

Analyzing the Craft

1. The movement in this excerpt between the time-then narrator and the time-now narrator isn't obvious until you start looking for it. The passage begins with the time-then narrator: "I also missed my father. My mother never complained to me about him, but sometimes Dwight would make sarcastic comments about Daddy Warbucks and Lord High-and-Mighty. He meant to impugn my father for being rich and living far away and having nothing to do with me, but all these qualities, even the last, perhaps especially the last, made my father fascinating." However, in the very next sentence, that narrative point of view changes with this reflection: "He had the advantage always enjoyed by the inconstant parent, of not being there to be found imperfect." This is something that the boy clearly did not, and perhaps could not know. Follow this narrative movement, sentence by sentence, for one or two paragraphs. You might even graph it.

2. When we tell stories to friends, we naturally tell the stories chronologically. We begin at the beginning and take off from there. Is there a parallel in oral storytelling to the time and point-of-view shift that takes place in the second paragraph of the excerpt? Is this a move that only writers can make?

3. What do you notice about the pattern of short and long sentences in Wolff's prose?

Practicing the Craft

When my father died I was relieved. We sat at a restaurant, my mother, brother, and I, just a few blocks from the hospital where his breathing stopped, and we all agreed that we expected him to live much longer. "Drunks can live forever," I said, "and I was sure he would. I'm glad he didn't." Everyone at the table nodded. I understand this moment differently now than I did back in 1975. The relief was real, but as years passed it camouflaged grief, something that I never allowed myself to see. Taken together—the scene at the restaurant 35 years ago and my understanding of it now—is what Vivian Gornick calls the "situation and the story." Something happened and now I can see what *happens*. This is possible because two narrators—the young man who just lost his father and the writer who sits here now—collaborate in the making of meaning.

In an earlier exercise, you may have experimented with summoning up these two narrators when you were prompted to write about a room you remember from childhood (see page 52). The trick, in part, was related to a shift in tenses. When we write in the present tense about the past, we naturally move to the voice of the time-then narrator. Past tense widens the distance between what happened then and what we feel or think now. Yet shifting tenses is a device that doesn't always work, nor is it always necessary. In the excerpt, Wolff does something even simpler than manipulating tenses: He explicitly says that the rage he felt at his father, triggered years later when a nurse clumsily searched for a vein in Wolff's new baby boy, was an understanding that was "still to come."

More-experienced memoirists and essayists don't need to rely on devices like these; they naturally weave back and forth from remembering what happened and considering its meaning. Both narrators cooperate to find meaning (if there is any), and both are present at the same time as the writing unfolds. This involves a reasoning process that isn't unique to writers: inductive thinking, or the back and forth between one's observations of things and ideas about them, between the concrete and the general, and between showing and telling. In this exercise, try to bring both narrators to your work at one time but without forcing it. Just see if they are there naturally.

At the top of a fresh journal page, write this heading: "My Face." Is there anything with which we are more familiar than our own faces? And yet, there are stories there that we haven't told ourselves, perhaps about resemblances, insecurities, old scars, or aging. Think about your own face, and perhaps begin a seven-minute fastwrite with a description. Let the writing lead, and if a door opens to a story go through it, returning to your face when the story dies off. If it helps you get started, go to a mirror and look. Here's my attempt:

> There is a scar on my forehead, high up near my scalp. It is a faint discoloring of the skin, and a tiny depression—a groove, really—that I suspect no one else notices. I don't remember the details of the injury; it is a scar, unlike many others on my body, including my face, that is orphaned by an imperfect memory. And yet whenever I see the scar, there is a scene. I am with my friends in the densely wooded ravine behind our houses in a Chicago suburb. Ruth Cook is there—a dark-haired beauty two years older than me—and Chris Field. Possibly the Cape brothers. There is a grassy clearing, a sagging wire fence, and we are holding sticks, I think. There is also a weathered wooden garage from which, on some other day, we would drop a board riddled with rusty nails on a neighbor boy's head. Whenever I see my own scar, it is that incident I remember—Mark Rose's bloody head, his screams of

outrage, and my own fear—even though I wasn't the one hurt that day. I don't really know what to make of a scar on my own face that seems to belong to someone else.

This is quite possibly the beginning of something, but what interests me most here is the shadow dancing of the two narrators: one who remembers Ruth Cook and a weathered wooden garage—and the other who, especially in the last sentence, is beginning to meditate on the oddities of memory. Look for these kinds of narrative shifts in your own fastwrite. Are they there? Where exactly do you see each narrator—the "time-then" narrator and the "time-now" narrator—make an appearance? Then, if you'd like to develop the piece further, skip a line and write three or four more segments triggered by the title "My Face."

Recommended Nonfiction by Tobias Wolff

* *In Pharaoh's Army* (1994). Though *This Boy's Life* is his most famous work of nonfiction, *In Pharaoh's Army*, Wolff's memoir about his service as an Army lieutenant in Vietnam, is among the best accounts of that war, joining books like Michael Herr's *Dispatches* and Tim O'Brien's stories. Wolff's 1994 memoir essentially picks up where *This Boy's Life* leaves off.

2.2

LONG AGO WHEN DOGS COULD TALK

Excerpt from N. Scott Momaday's
The Way to Rainy Mountain

Sa'tank, the Kiowa chief pictured here, was one of the tribe's last leaders before confinement to an Oklahoma reservation. He was killed 10 or so years before Momaday's grandmother was born, a time the writer describes as the "last great moment" in Kiowa history.

The Excerpt in Context

Huck Finn, like many characters in American literature, must leave home and "strike out for the territories" to find himself. In his journey away, Huck can define himself *against* where he came from and who he was there. This idea that hitting the road is the path to individualism is so ingrained in our cultural mythology that it's easy to ignore how often it is the *return home* that characterizes the search for self-understanding in much Native American literature. The challenge is not to define oneself against the tribe but to find oneself within it. Momaday's memoir, *The Way to Rainy Mountain*, describes just such a journey, when he returns one July to Rainy Mountain, a landmark of the Kiowa people in Oklahoma, to see the grave of his grandmother, who died that spring. Momaday's grandmother, Aho, was a tribal elder, and when she was born, "the Kiowas were living the last great moment of their history." For Momaday, this return to his ancestral home in Oklahoma is less an effort to understand his personal heritage than it is the glorification of the idea that a people— through story—can imagine themselves into being, and that these stories with each telling extend their tendrils into generations, transcending time and place. It is a "whole journey," writes Momaday, "…made with the whole memory, that experience of the mind which is legendary as well as historical, personal as well as cultural."

The structure of Momaday's memoir reflects this belief. Nearly every chapter is structured like the following excerpt—with three chunks of text , each in a different font—all floating near each other surrounded by white space. The first fragment typically narrates a Kiowa legend, the second a bit of historical information about the tribe, and the third a personal reminiscence. The form of Momaday's memoir isn't the only thing that makes it unique. The oral tradition, while threatened in Native American cultures, remains a vital part of storytelling, and even in print some of these oral qualities remain. The work of Momaday comes from a distinctly different narrative tradition than that of many of the writers in this book, and you can detect this in the role he assumes as narrator, his relationship to what is narrated, the language he chooses, and his motives for the telling, among other things. This excerpt comes early in *The Way to Rainy Mountain*.

◈ *The Excerpt* ◈

III

Before there were horses the Kiowas had need of dogs. That was a long time ago, when dogs could talk. There was a man who lived alone; he had been thrown away, and he made his camp here and there on the high

From: N. Scott Momaday, *The Way to Rainy Mountain* (Albuquerque, NM: University of New Mexico Press, 1969), 20–21.

ground. Now it was dangerous to be alone, for there were enemies all around. The man spent his arrows hunting food. He had one arrow left, and he shot a bear; but the bear was only wounded and it ran away. The man wondered what to do. Then a dog came up to him and said that many enemies were coming; they were close by and all around. The man could think of no way to save himself. But the dog said: "You know, I have puppies. They are young and weak and they have nothing to eat. If you will take care of my puppies, I will show you how to get away." The dog led the man here and there, around and around, and they came to safety.

A hundred years ago the Comanche Ten Bears remarked upon the great number of horses which the Kiowas owned. "When we first knew you," he said, "you had nothing but dogs and sleds." It was so; the dog is primordial. Perhaps it was dreamed into being.

The principal warrior society of the Kiowas was the Ka-itsenko, "Real Dogs," and it was made up of ten men only, the ten most brave. Each of these men wore a long ceremonial sash and carried a sacred arrow. In time of battle he must by means of this arrow impale the end of his sash to the earth and stand his ground to the death. Tradition has it that the founder of the Ka-itsenko had a dream in which he saw a band of warriors, outfitted after the fashion of the society, being led by a dog. The dog sang the song of the Ka-itsenko, then said to the dreamer: "You are a dog; make a noise like a dog and sing a dog song."

There were always dogs about my grandmother's house. Some of them were nameless and lived a life of their own. They belonged there in a sense that the word "ownership" does not include. The old people paid them scarcely any attention, but they should have been sad, I think, to see them go. ꙮ

Analyzing the Craft

1. The structure of this excerpt—three fragments of text, each in a different font and separated by white space—is repeated throughout *The Way to Rainy Mountain*. We often think that structure, particularly in memoir, should be more or less invisible. Why distract the reader by drawing attention to the seams holding the story together? There must be a very good reason whenever writers draw attention to the design of their texts. What might be the logic behind Momaday's decision to structure his memoir this way? What does this excerpt suggest about that?

2. We're so used to certain kinds of storytelling that it's easy to ignore other narrative traditions. The oldest, of course, is oral—someone telling a story to others who are present to hear it. The shift to writing things down rather than telling them fundamentally changed the way stories were told.[4] Tribal cultures like the Kiowa had a strong oral tradition, one that Momaday and other Native American writers experienced growing up. *The Way to Rainy Mountain,* like much contemporary Indian literature, reflects Momaday's sensitivity to two storytelling traditions—the oral tradition and the more familiar narrative typical of the American memoir. What does the excerpt suggest about how Momaday preserves elements of oral storytelling?

3. Another selection in the memoir section, the excerpt from Maxine Hong Kingston's *The Woman Warrior* (see page 90), is an interesting one to pair with Momaday's. Both seem to shift from fact to fantasy and realism to allegory, moves that we don't normally consider typical of nonfiction. Taken together, what do the passages from Momaday and Kingston suggest about how creative nonfiction writers can imagine their lives in a memoir?

Practicing the Craft

In *The Way to Rainy Mountain,* Momaday enlarges our idea of memory in two ways. He suggests that who we are is what we remember and that memory is not confined to what we've actually experienced. His grandmother, Aho, for example, can "tell of the Crows, who she had never seen, and of the Black Hills, where she had never been." This is the kind of memory that runs in the blood, a kind of genetic inheritance. Memoirists, who are in the business of remembering, don't have to be Kiowa to expand the reach of memory beyond what they have seen. Nonfiction writers do this all the time, in fact, when they do historical and genealogical research.

Imagine this challenge: You would like to describe the neighborhood your family lived in the day you were born. You may remember the neighborhood from your early childhood, and this will help with the description some, but you can't possibly know what it was like on that first birthday. There are at least two ways to take possession of that memory: Interview people who lived in the neighborhood before you were born, and research the history of the neighborhood (or perhaps neighborhoods like it at that time). Was the old school still there? Who lived next door? How did people spend their time? What did people wear?

---

[4]For more on the shift from oral storytelling to writing, see Walter Ong's masterwork on the subject, *Orality and Literacy.*

Try this exercise: Write a two- or three-paragraph description of a Sunday morning in your neighborhood at about the time you were born. Old family photographs and online research—images, historical documents, census data, old newspapers, and so on—can be a useful sources of information for this. Interview your older family members as well. What do they remember about a Sunday morning in the neighborhood? Who would walk by arm in arm? What were the street sounds? What kinds of cars did people drive then? You will also, undoubtedly, draw on your own memories of the place, particularly the things that did not change in the years after you were born. In a few paragraphs, try to evoke a sense of place, drawing on all of the senses.

To develop this further, use this scene (at least initially) as a launching place for writing about your parents at that time. You've described a place at a time you couldn't have known it, so now put people in it and see where that leads.

Recommended Nonfiction by
N. Scott Momaday

- *The Names: A Memoir* (1987). While *The Way to Rainy Mountain* is considered Momaday's finest autobiographical work, *The Names* is his most personal. The memoir focuses on his memories of growing up in Oklahoma and the Southwest, and like much of Momaday's work, *The Names* departs from the conventional approaches to memoir by combining essays, poems, photographs, and stories.

- *The Man Made of Words: Essays, Stories, and Passages* (1997). This appealing collection of work includes essays about Native American literature as well as a wonderful personal essay about a subsequent return to Rainy Mountain.

TELLING THE TRUTH ABOUT DREAMS, VISIONS, AND PRAYERS

Excerpt from Maxine Hong Kingston's
The Woman Warrior

ॐ

San Francisco's Chinatown, the setting for Kingston's memoir Woman Warrior, *as it appeared in the 1940s when the author grew up there.*

The Excerpt in Context

Maxine Hong Kingston's 1976 memoir about growing up as a first-generation Chinese-American in Stockton, California, redefined the possibilities of nonfiction by expanding its imaginative reach into a writer's

89

inner life—her dreams, fantasies, and visions. In *The Woman Warrior,* Kingston appropriates the Chinese fables told to her by her mother, a native Chinese, and weaves them tightly into the fabric of Kingston's own remembrances. These "talk stories" of ghosts, emperors, and fabulous beasts are not merely anecdotal, nor are they documentary—an attempt to record and preserve village tales. Instead, Kingston sees these stories as a way of sorting through her conflicting identities. Is she American, is she Chinese, or is she some odd hybrid? In one extended narrative, for example, Kingston assumes the identity of Fa Mu Lan, the legendary girl who became a warrior so her father would not be conscripted by the emperor.

The excerpt that follows, which is drawn from the book's second chapter, "White Tigers," begins the Fa Mu Lan story, and it captures the dramatic transition from Kingston's memory of hearing her mother tell the tale (a quite conventional autobiographical moment) to Kingston's own participation in the story as Fa Mu Lan herself (a shift into fantasy we rarely see in nonfiction). Moves like this in *The Woman Warrior* drew fire from some critics who complained that the author crossed over into fiction. Kingston later said that it was her "mission," in fact, "to invent a new autobiographical form." "I think that some of our truths are things that are not dealt with in standard autobiography," she once told an interviewer. "I think that dreams are very important to women—and important to everybody's psyche—and to have access to those dreams is a great power. Also visions that we have about what we might do, also prayer— that's another 'silent, secret' kind of thing. I think part of what we have to do is figure out a new kind of autobiography that can tell the truth about dreams and visions and prayers."

⚘ *The Excerpt* ⚘

At last I saw that I too had been in the presence of great power, my mother talking-story. After I grew up, I heard the chant of Fa Mu Lan, the girl who took her father's place in battle. Instantly I remembered that as a child I had followed my mother about the house, the two of us singing about how Fa Mu Lan fought gloriously and returned alive from war to settle in the village. I had forgotten this chant that was once mine, given me by my mother, who may not have known its power to remind. She said I would grow up a wife and a slave, but she taught me the song of the warrior woman, Fa Mu Lan. I would have to grow up a warrior woman.

The call would come from a bird that flew over our roof. In the brush drawings it looks like the ideograph for "human," two black wings. The

From: Maxine Hong Kingston, *The Woman Warrior* (New York: Vintage, 1976), 24–25.

bird would cross the sun and lift into the mountains (which look like the ideograph "mountain"), there parting the mist briefly that swirled opaque again. I would be a little girl of seven the day I followed the bird away into the mountains. The brambles would tear off my shoes and the rocks cut my feet and fingers, but I would keep climbing, eyes upward to follow the bird. We would go around and around the tallest mountain, climbing ever upward. I would drink from the river, which I would meet again and again. We would go so high the plants would change, and the river that flows past the village would become a waterfall. At the height where the bird used to disappear, the clouds would gray the world like an ink wash.

Even when I got used to that gray, I would only see peaks as if shaded in pencil, rocks like charcoal rubbings, everything so murky. There would be just two black strokes—the bird. Inside the clouds—inside the dragon's breath—I would not know how many hours or days passed. Suddenly, without noise, I would break clear into a yellow, warm world. New trees would lean toward me at mountain angles, but when I looked for the village, it would have vanished under the clouds.

The bird, now gold so close to the sun, would come to rest on the thatch of a hut, which, until the bird's two feet touched it, was camouflaged as part of the mountainside. ⌒

Analyzing the Craft

1. There was no bird except in a dream. And yet, when we read this excerpt, the movement from Kingston's memory of her mother telling her the Fa Mu Lan story to the author's entry into fantasy seems nearly seamless. Do you agree? Are there particular lines in which fact and fantasy merge? Can you imagine a reader failing to notice this shift from nonfiction to fiction, and if so, does this raise questions for you about the nature of nonfiction writing or, more specifically, of memoir? Does Kingston take enough care to signal to the reader that she is moving from memory into fantasy, her lived experience into a dream? Does it even matter?

2. You may have noticed that Kingston refers a number of times in the excerpt to drawings, particularly pen-and-ink representations of certain things in her dream. What do you make of that?

3. If you read N. Scott Momaday's excerpt from *The Way to Rainy Mountain* (see page 85), it might have occurred to you that it has some similarities to Kingston's passage here. What are they? One that strikes me has to do with language and a certain intonation that I associate with the telling of fables or allegories. The Fa Mu Lan story is one that Kingston first heard spoken. Is it simply that this excerpt has qualities of an oral tradition, or is there more going on here with style and language?

Practicing the Craft

When I was a boy, I repeatedly dreamed about gorillas. Typically these dreams involved being chased by a large gorilla that bore a strong resemblance to Bushman, a huge mountain gorilla who was once a popular attraction at Chicago's Lincoln Park Zoo. When in a defiant mood, Bushman would throw dung at visitors. He is now stuffed and on permanent exhibit at the city's Field Museum. In these dreams, Bushman would chase me and always corner me, and on many occasions, terrified, I would fight back with the only weapon at my disposal—disbelief. "You're only a dream," I would say. "Go away." And he did, dissolving into black vapor. Maxine Hong Kingston believes that dreams have "great power," as did Jung, Freud, and a host of others, but can they be useful to the nonfiction writer?

I found interesting thematic material when writing about my dreams of the great Bushman, and the one that struck me most was the power I sometimes summoned to make him go away. This does not square with my memory of myself as a helpless child. This is a contradiction that I might explore.

Write about your dreams, focusing, if you can, on the dreams that you often have (or often had). This is journal work. Write fast without thinking too much about what you want to say before you say it. What images recur? Do they illuminate some idea or feeling about yourself or about your situation? Does your dream tell the same story, over and over? What is its theme? After you've done some "bad" writing about this, revise the best material into a lead paragraph for a possible essay that (at least tentatively) is the doorway into an exploration of what those dreams say about you, about your life, or about the things you've always wanted.

Recommended Nonfiction by
Maxine Hong Kingston

- *China Men* (1980). While *The Woman Warrior* focused on Kingston's experiences growing up with the women in her family, especially her mother, *China Men* focuses on her father. Like the earlier work, this memoir combines autobiography, fable, and history of the Chinese-American experience. It won the American Book Award for nonfiction.

2.4

THE ACHE MADE PHYSICAL

Excerpt from Gretel Ehrlich's
The Solace of Open Spaces

ೲ

The Excerpt in Context

In 1976, Gretel Ehrlich moved to Wyoming to begin a film on sheep ranching. Her collaborator on the project, David, who was also Ehrlich's lover, remained in New York, dying of cancer. His death at age 30 triggered a grief in Ehrlich that Wyoming's great empty spaces seemed to heal. Ehrlich wrote her memoir of that time, *The Solace of Open Spaces*, "in fits and starts" over five years while she lived in Wyoming, living alone, working on sheep ranches, and finally marrying a man with whom she honeymooned at the National Finals Rodeo. Ehrlich's memoir, a work of remarkable beauty, is a personal narrative, but it is also an examination of what she understood was the real West, stripped of its mythology. She finds ruggedness and individualism and also finds a place where tenderness is a brand of courage.

The Solace of Open Spaces belongs to a long literary tradition in which writers try to come to terms with the richness, diversity, and often-terrifying loneliness of the American landscape. The largely treeless and dry terrain of the American West was a particular challenge to nineteenth-century writers, many from New England, who lacked the palette to adequately describe a place whose dominant color was brown, not green. Arguably, it took another generation of prose writers like Wallace Stegner, N. Scott Momaday, Ivan Doig, Richard Rodriguez, and Joan Didion—all of whom were born and raised in the West—to find an adequate language for expressing the power of its landscape in nonfiction. *The Solace of Open Spaces* is one of the best of these works. It is composed of 12 chapters in roughly chronological order. In the excerpt that follows, drawn from the chapter titled "The Smooth Skull of Winter," Ehrlich describes Wyoming's winter—a long, drawn-out affair that both "strips away" what is "ornamental" in people and at the same time brings them together. The passage is typical of Ehrlich, poetic in its use of language, often metaphoric, and remarkably perceptive. Descriptions of place, and particularly of changing seasons, are so prone to cliché that it's especially instructive to look closely at how a fine writer handles them. It will not do to simply pile on the descriptive details, and because most of us have seen plenty of winters, writers must help us to see what we may not have noticed.

∾ *The Excerpt* ∾

A Wyoming winter laminates the earth with white, then hardens the lacquer work with wind. Storms come announced by what old-timers call "mare's tails"—long wisps that lash out from a snow cloud's body. Jack Davis, a packer who used to trail his mules all the way from Wyoming to southern Arizona when the first snows came, said, "The first snowball that hits you is God's fault; the second one is yours."

Every three days or so white pastures glide overhead and drop themselves like skeins of hair to earth. The Chinese call snow that has drifted "white jade mountains," but winter looks oceanic to me. Snow swells, drops back, and hits the hulls of our lives with a course-bending sound. Tides of white are overtaken by tides of blue, and the logs in the woodstove, like sister ships, tick toward oblivion.

On the winter solstice it is thirty-four degrees below zero and there is very little in the way of daylight. The deep ache of this audacious Arctic air is also the ache in our lives made physical. Patches of frostbite show up on our noses, toes, and ears. Skin blisters as if cold were a kind of radiation to which we've been exposed. It strips what is ornamental in us. Part of the ache we feel is also a softness growing. Our connections with neighbors—whether strong or tenuous, as lovers or friends—become too urgent to disregard. We rub the frozen toes of a stranger whose pickup has veered off the road; we open water gaps with a tamping bar and an ax; we splice a friend's frozen water pipe; we take mittens and blankets to the men who herd sheep. Twenty or thirty below makes the breath we exchange visible: all of mine for all of yours. It is the tacit way we express the intimacy no one talks about. ∾

Analyzing the Excerpt

1. A common mistake of novice writers is to discover a lovely metaphor and then beat it to death, returning to it again and again, teasing out every possible meaning. A metaphor's magic—that it can explain something in a fresh and original way through an unexpected comparison— is also its poison. We like it too much. In the second paragraph of the

From: Gretel Ehrlich, *The Solace of Open Spaces* (New York: Penguin Books, 1986) 72–73.

excerpt, Ehrlich uses the word "oceanic" to describe Wyoming winters, and she plays with that metaphor for several sentences without overdoing it. Clearly, the relative brevity of the treatment is a strength. But what else does Ehrlich do when handling the metaphor that makes it so powerful? How does she deploy simile effectively in other passages?

2. The excerpt is, among other things, a work of description, but it is quite different from the descriptive prose featured in the excerpt by James Agee (see page 122). In this passage by Agee, he uses 600 words to describe the smell of the homes of tenant farmers. Explore both Agee's and Ehrlich's techniques for description. What does the comparison reveal about method?

3. Obviously, verbs make things happen in prose. But just any verbs won't do. Time and again in this collection, you might notice how carefully writers choose the verbs to pump life and movement into the work. In this excerpt, we see this technique from the very beginning with the word "laminates," an oddly appropriate choice to describe what the snow does to the Wyoming landscape in deep winter. Examine the rest of the excerpt—and perhaps other excerpts in the book as well—with a focus on verbs and what kind of work they do in a sentence.

Practicing the Craft

Changing seasons are events with which we are so familiar—and so sentimentally attached—that our prose descriptions often suffer from the same things: familiarity and sentimentality. This is not the case with Ehrlich's description of the Wyoming winter. For one thing, she uses novel comparisons that surprise us—like the "oceanic" quality of winter—and uses strong verbs that make things happen rather than passively tick off visual details. Perhaps most striking, though, is how she puts her description of winter to work as part of her larger project to explore the character of not just the land but also the people who live on it. The winter, she writes, produces an "ache in our lives made physical . . . a softness growing."

In much nonfiction, place is a character like a person can be a character. Place has moods, it can be complicated, and yet it still creates a dominant impression. The relationships people have with important places in their lives also illuminate human character, as Ehrlich shows us. All of this suggests that place is not merely setting, a backdrop against which stories are told, but is often a crucial *part* of those stories. For practice, choose a place to write about.[5] This may be where you

---

[5]For inspiration, I strongly recommend that you read Patricia Hampl's "The Dark Art of Description," which appears in the *Best American Essays 2009*.

now live or where you once lived. You will craft a description of this place—perhaps a season there—in one or two paragraphs built around a particular *characterization* of it.

First, brainstorm a list of places that have left an impression on you. Then choose one and spend five minutes making a long and fast list of details about the place, drawing on all of your senses. (You may also go and observe the place if it's convenient.) Look at your list, and answer these questions: *What is my dominant impression of this place? What one word (or two words) sums up the feeling I get from this place or the personality it seems to embody?* Craft a description in which the particulars contribute to showing that feeling or personality to someone unfamiliar with the place.

Here's what I wrote in my journal:

> In midsummer, the high deserts of southern Idaho shimmer with heat, and a truck on any rural road creates an angry brown cloud that covers everything with fine dust. In contrast, this is the season of unsullied skies, at least away from the city—a resonant blue is punctuated by a few clouds—and the hot sun has clear sailing until late in the evening, sometimes setting as late as ten. This is an optimistic sky, reliably sunny day after day, that is at odds with the heat on the ground, which can easily hover at 100 degrees and cooks desert grasses to a uniform brown.

While I'm not wild about what I wrote, I can see how the description of the Idaho landscape here is starting to do the work I wanted it to: to create the sense that the high desert in the summer is a place of contrasts in clarity, in temperature, and in mood. This is something I can build on.

Other Recommended Nonfiction by Gretel Ehrlich

- *A Match to the Heart* (1994). If Wyoming's landscape gave Ehrlich solace it also gave her a jolt that becomes the starting point of this memoir, in which she describes her recovery from a lightning strike.
- *This Cold Heaven* (2003). After she recovered from the lightening strike, Ehrlich visited Greenland, and this collection of essays about her travels in that desolate land includes some of her finest writing since *The Solace of Open Spaces*.

2.5

POWERFUL PRAYERS

Excerpt from Frank McCourt's
Angela's Ashes

∾

The Excerpt in Context

Among the many extraordinary qualities of Frank McCourt's Pulitzer Prize–winning memoir, *Angela's Ashes* (1996), is the richness of his memory. Memoirs demand that their authors' recall is sufficiently detailed to craft scenes, of course, but McCourt's account of growing up poor in Limerick, Ireland, reads like a novel. We are treated to many long and lively stretches of dialogue as well as closely observed scenes; the excerpt that follows is typical. It's a common experience that the writing itself helps to bring it all back, and while McCourt likely found this true when he sat down to write *Angela's Ashes* in his 60s, he also reported that it was his decision early in the book to shift to present tense that seemed to unleash the story. After the first 20 pages of background on his family—his birth in Brooklyn, New York, his parents' marriage, and a portrait of their troubles with poverty and drink—McCourt suddenly shifts point of view. "I'm in a playground on Classon Avenue in Brooklyn with my brother Malachy," he writes. "He's two, I'm three. We're on the seesaw."

From this point on, *Angela's Ashes* is narrated by the boy McCourt as he grows up in Limerick's slums, ending with his return to America at age 18. In fiction we accept the illusion that a child narrator thinks and feels like a child and may not know any better, but in nonfiction this illusion seems more difficult to sustain. After all, readers know that the narrator writing the book is no longer a child but the adult writer looking back with the knowledge the child lacked. McCourt's narrative, particularly when he was quite young, has an innocent, wide-eyed quality, and the excerpt that follows seems faithful to a young boy's point of view. But the storyteller is not a young boy anymore. He is a retired high school teacher in his 60s, writing his first book and remembering what it was like to live in Limerick's slums. Why is it, then, that we seem to accept the boy's point of view as

97

authentic? Are there hints of the adult writer lurking behind the narrator? How does McCourt seem to address the problem of writing from a child's point of view?

❧ *The Excerpt* ❧

I'm nine years old and I have a pal, Mickey Spellacy, whose relations are dropping one by one of the galloping consumption. I envy Mickey because every time someone dies in his family he gets a week off from school and his mother stitches a black diamond patch on his sleeve so that he can wander from lane to lane and street to street and people will know he has the grief and pat his head and give him money and sweets for his sorrow.

But this summer Mickey is worried. His sister, Brenda, is wasting away with the consumption and it's only August and if she dies before September he won't get his week off from school because you can't get a week off from school when there's no school. He comes to Billy Campbell and me to ask if we'll go around the corner to St. Joseph's Church and pray for Brenda to hang on till September.

What's in it for us, Mickey, if we go around the corner praying?

Well, if Brenda hangs on and I get me week off ye can come to the wake and have ham and cheese and cake and sherry and lemonade and everything and ye can listen to the songs and stories all night.

Who could say no to that? There's nothing like a wake for having a good time. We trot around to the church where they have statues of St. Joseph himself as well as the Sacred Heart of Jesus, the Virgin Mary and St. Therese of Lisieux, the Little Flower. I pray to the Little Flower because she died of the consumption herself and she'd understand.

One of our prayers must have been powerful because Brenda stays alive and doesn't die till the second day of school. We tell Mickey we're sorry for his troubles but he's delighted with his week off and he gets the black diamond patch which will bring the money and sweets.

My mouth is watering at the thought of the feast at Brenda's wake. Billy knocks on the door and there's Mickey's aunt. Well?

We came to say a prayer for Brenda and Mickey said we could come to the wake.

She yells, Mickey!

What?

Come here. Did you tell this gang they could come to your sister's wake? No.

But, Mickey, you promised...

She slams the door in our faces. We don't know what to do till Billy Campbell says, We'll go back to St. Joseph's and pray that from now on

From: Frank McCourt, *Angela's Ashes* (New York: Scribner, 1996), 171–172.

everyone in Mickey Spellacy's family will die in the middle of the summer and he'll never get a day off from school for the rest of his life.

One of our prayers is surely powerful because next summer Mickey himself is carried off by the galloping consumption and he doesn't get a day off from school and that will surely teach him a lesson. ❧

Analyzing the Craft

1. The art of the memoir (and the personal essay, for that matter) is what Sven Birkerts writes is "the collision of original perception and hind-sight realization: the revision of the *then* by the *now*."[6] Typically, creative nonfiction writers signal the shift between these two pers-pectives by changes in tense—from present to past—or a switch in pronouns—from *I* to *we*. But a memoir like *Angela's Ashes*, which is largely narrated from the point of view of McCourt as a boy growing up in Limerick, presents problems dramatizing this "collision" between then and now. The book, except for the first 20 pages, doesn't shift from the present tense. And yet, we *know* that it is the 60-year-old writer narrating his story, not the boy. How, then, does McCourt maintain the illusion of an unknowing narrator while at the same time bringing the hindsight that makes the story so poignant? How does he do this in the excerpt?

2. You may have noticed that McCourt doesn't punctuate dialogue in the usual way, omitting quotation marks. What might explain his reasoning behind this decision?

3. Creating dialect in prose is considerably harder than doing verbal imitations, because the writer must create not only the sound but also the language that will produce that sound. McCourt's advantage, of course, is that he speaks the Irish dialect that he recreates here. Mickey's voice, and his use of the word *ye*, is an obvious move to recreate the sounds of Limerick, but the rest of the passage does this just as effectively without resorting to local language forms. How does it do that?

Practicing the Craft

Before we lost him to an assassin's bullet, I would do John Kennedy imitations. I was eight or nine, and I was intrigued by our young presi-dent's Massachusetts dialect. It was widely parodied by comedians ("pahked my cah in havahd yahd") back then, reflecting the novelty in early 1960s America of having a president who spoke with a distinct

[6]Sven Birkerts, *The Art of Time in the Memoir* (Minneapolis, MN: Graywolf, 2008), 37.

regional dialect that wasn't from the South. I could not then, and I cannot now, do believable imitations. If I can't speak with a dialect (other than my faint Chicago accent), I'm wary of trying to reproduce it in prose. Often enough, fortunately, it's unnecessary. But you may find it useful to create dialogue with dialect in nonfiction if it contributes to character.

Are you thinking this is hard? You bet it is. The greatest danger is that instead of crafting a character you create a stereotype. It makes sense, then, to practice this skill. Go online to the International Dialects of English Archive: http://web.ku.edu/~idea/index.htm.

You will see a list of "dialects and accents" from speakers around the world. These have links to audio files you can play on your computer of these speakers reading a passage about rainbows. Listen to several of these, and then choose one you'd like to work with. Listen carefully to the recording, replaying as necessary, and craft one or two sentences that attempt to capture the sound of the speaker in prose. What is difficult about this? What does it help you to see about rendering nonfiction characters using dialect?

Recommended Nonfiction by
Frank McCourt

- 'Tis (1999). While it didn't receive the critical acclaim that made Angela's Ashes a Pulitzer Prize winner, 'Tis embodies McCourt's unique literary voice—honest, unsentimental, and humorous—a voice that will be sorely missed with the writer's death in 2009. This memoir picks up where Angela's Ashes left off, as McCourt tries to make a life in the United States after leaving Ireland.

- Teacher Man (2005). This final memoir in McCourt's trilogy describes his 30 years as a high school teacher in New York City. Readers will appreciate seeing how he brings his storytelling skills to his Stuyvesant classroom and coaxes inspired writing from his students. Angela's Ashes was written after McCourt retired from teaching, and it's compelling to see how his understanding of story as an instructor illuminates his later work.

2.6

SAFE IN THE CENTER

Excerpt from Mary Clearman Blew's
All But the Waltz

⁓

The Excerpt in Context

"Truth in a memoir," writes essayist Vivian Gornick, "is achieved not through a recital of actual events; it is achieved when the reader comes to believe that the writer is working hard to engage with the experience at hand. What happened to the writer is not what matters; what matters is the large sense that the writer is able to make of what happened." The extraordinary meaning a good writer can find in what are often ordinary events may be the best route to truth in memoir or essay, but often experience bends from the weight of significance that is *imposed* on the material. For instance, we don't quite believe that a scene in the supermarket made the writer reflect on his empty heart. We want to believe that it's true, but somehow the way the scene is drawn or the reflection is offered makes us suspect that the meaning is forced. We wonder, did the writer truly "engage with the experience at hand"?

When we come to write about an experience, we are usually quite far removed from it. From this distance, we are in a position to know things about what an experience meant that we were unlikely to know when it happened to us. This gap in knowing can easily be dramatized if the story is explicitly narrated by that older, wiser self—the writer who comes to the past from the present. But how is this handled when the work is written in present tense and the narrative point of view creates the illusion that what happened is happening *now*? In one of the scenes that follow, excerpted from Mary Clearman Blew's remarkable memoir, *All But the Waltz*, we are asked to believe it is the sight of pigs stranded in the raging current of a river that stuns Blew into the realization that her life is as precarious as theirs. Like Frank McCourt's excerpt from his memoir, *Angela's Ashes* (see page 98), Blew seems to write from the point of view of a child. This rendering does seem authentic, and yet we

101

know that the child would be unlikely to comprehend the significance of these scenes until much later. How does Blew manage to maintain the illusion that a child is telling this story while clearly giving readers the sense that she has wisdom about the significance of the event that a child could not possess?

All But the Waltz, published in 1991, tells the story of five generations of ranchers in the beautiful and isolated landscape of central Montana. It's really Blew's story, of course, as she seizes the strands of memory and fragments of family history and tries to come to terms with what they might mean to her. The book was winner of the 1992 Pacific Northwest Booksellers Association Award; Blew is widely recognized as one of the most important voices in contemporary writing about the American West. She currently teaches at the University of Idaho.

The excerpt that follows is part of the opening chapter of *All But the Waltz*, titled "The Sow in the River."

✑ *The Excerpt* ✑

Light flickers. A kerosene lamp in the middle of the table has driven the shadows back into the corners of the kitchen. Faces and hands emerge in a circle. Bill has brought apples from the box in the dark closet. The coil of peel follows his pocketknife. I bite into the piece of quartered apple he hands me. I hear its snap, taste the juice. The shadows hold threats: mice and the shape of nameless things. But in the circle around the lamp, in the certainty of apples, I am safe.

The last of the kerosene tilts and glitters around the wick. I cower behind Grammy on the stairs, but she boldly walks into the shadows, which reel and retreat from her and her lamp. In her bedroom the window reflects large pale her and timorous me. She undresses herself, undresses me; she piles my pants and stockings on the chair with her dress and corset. After she uses it, her pot is warm for me. Her bed is cold, then warm. I burrow against her back and smell the smoke from the wick she has pinched out. Bill blows his nose from his bedroom on the other side of the landing. Beyond the eaves the shapeless creatures of sound, owls and coyotes, have taken the night. But I am here, safe in the center.

I am in the center again on the day we look for Bill's pigs. I am sitting between him and Grammy in the cab of the old Ford truck while the rain sheets on the windshield. Bill found the pigpen gate open when he went to feed the pigs this morning, their pen empty, and now they are nowhere to be found. He has driven and driven through the sagebrush and around the

From: Mary Clearman Blew, *All But the Waltz* (New York: Penguin, 1991), 4–6.

MARY CLEARMAN BLEW *All But the Waltz*   103

gulches, peering out through the endless gray rain as the truck spins and growls on the gumbo in low gear. But no pigs. He and Grammy do not speak. The cab is cold, but I am bundled well between them with my feet on the clammy assortment of tools and nails and chains on the floorboards and my nose just dashboard level, and I am at home with the smell of wet wool and metal and the feel of a broken spring in the seat.

But now Bill tramps on the brakes, and he and Grammy and I gaze through the streaming windshield at the river. The Judith has risen up its cutbanks, and its angry gray current races the rain. I have never seen such a Judith, such a tumult of water. But what transfixes me and Grammy and Bill behind our teeming glass is not the ruthless condition of the river— no, for on a bare ait at midcurrent, completely surrounded and only inches above that muddy roiling water, huddle the pigs.

The flat top of the ait is so small that the old sow takes up most of it by herself. The river divides and rushes around her, rising, practically at her hooves. Surrounding her, trying to crawl under her, snorting in apprehension at the water, are her little pigs. Watching spellbound from the cab of the truck, I can feel their small terrified rumps burrowing against her sides, drawing warmth from her center even as more dirt crumbles under their hooves. My surge of understanding arcs across the current, and my flesh shrivels in the icy sheets of rain. Like the pigs I cringe at the roar of the river, although behind the insulated walls of the cab I can hear and feel nothing. I am in my center and they are in theirs. The current separates us irrevocably, and suddenly I understand that my center is a precarious as theirs, that the chill metal cab of the old truck is almost as fragile as their ring of crumbling sod.

And then the scene darkens and I see no more. ❧

Analyzing the Craft

1. Often scenes in nonfiction, or fiction for that matter, have a cinematic quality. We see the scene as we might through a camera that is either fixed or moving, and we know exactly where this camera is at any given moment. Blew's excerpt has this cinematic feel as we follow her descriptions from a table to the stairs and then up to Grammy's bedroom. In the next paragraph, we cut to the cab of a truck where Blew looks through a rain-blurred windshield. What are the advantages of this cinematic approach to the writer and to the reader? Can you imagine any other way the scene might be crafted?

2. When we remember, we naturally use the past tense: "The light flickered." A writer's decision to narrate a work in the present tense— "The light flickers"—is usually carefully considered. Why might a memoirist or essayist make that choice? What are the disadvantages of narrating in the present tense?

3. In the section that follows the excerpt, Blew describes a moment, years later, when she and her father drive past the spot where she remembered the sow and her piglets stranded in the rising Judith River. "That's where the pigs were," she said. "What pigs?" he said. Blew's father doesn't remember the scene described in the excerpt, and claimed it never happened: "The Judith never got that high, and there never was any pigs up there." This is a moment that could happen to any nonfiction writer who writes memoirs or personal essays. The landscape of memory is seen differently by the people who once shared its places. Yet don't writers who craft stories from reality have some obligation to what really happened? Should Blew feel any responsibility for finding out whether those pigs really were there on the Judith River that night?

Practicing the Craft

The memoir requires extraordinary skill in resurrecting the particulars of events that may have happened decades ago. No one expects, of course, that these memories be completely accurate, but they should be richly detailed, recreating a world that the people who shared it will at least recognize. Fortunately, a photographic memory isn't necessary because the writing itself opens doors you may have thought were closed. Imagine, for example, *a moment* in your past that you considered a "turning point." Perhaps it was the confrontation that night with your best friend that changed things between you forever; or that conversation with the teacher who made you feel, for the first time, that you weren't stupid; or that scene at the café in Paris when you first understood what it meant to be an American in Europe. When you have selected one of these moments to write about, draft the scene with as much detail as you can. Before you begin, consider writing fast in your journal for a full seven minutes without censoring yourself. Writing in the present tense, put yourself back into that moment and follow the words. Use this material to craft your scene. Here's a scene I remember when I stood next to my father, a few years before he died, watching a wooden sloop shattered by a storm:

When I was growing up, I lived a quarter mile from Lake Michigan, and on days when a Northeaster blew, I could hear the muffled roar of the waves through the woods behind my house. The wind smelled faintly of fish and wet sand. Once I watched a wooden sloop that had run aground in the shallow water near my house as it was battered to pieces by those waves. The lake was terribly beautiful as angry waves clawed at the sand in the shallows, tinting the water brown, and the scene was one of the saddest things I ever saw. The owner, who had restored the boat in Chicago and was sailing it on its maiden voyage when it ran aground, stood on the shore for hours and helplessly collected the pieces as they washed in—broken lengths of teak planking, fractured mahogany bright work, and sodden sails. "Poor bastard," my father said, shielding his pipe from the wind as he touched a match to tobacco. Some years later, I began to understand that I felt much like the man with his feet in the soft sand waiting for the fragments of a dream to wash in.

Tom Wolfe once wrote that "scene-by-scene construction" is a fundamental element of literary journalism. The same could be said of memoir and essay. Scenes are a fundamental unit of nonfiction storytelling. For this reason, a study of how writers like Mary Clearman Blew craft scenes is time well spent. Using excerpts from this book or other published creative nonfiction, examine how well-written scenes are made. What do you notice, for example, about the choice of details, the pattern of development, or the management of vantage point? How does the writer signal the significance of the scene, and what is the balance between showing and telling?

Recommended Nonfiction by Mary Clearman Blew

- *Balsamroot* (1994). Following the critical success of *All But the Waltz*, Blew published her second memoir, *Balsamroot,* which continues the narrative of the author's departure from her Montana ranch and her relationship with her Aunt Imogene.

- *Bone Deep in Landscape* (1999). This is a delightful collection of essays about living in Idaho, and about writing.

2.7

A CORRESPONDENCE WITH THE EARTH

Excerpt from Terry Tempest Williams's Refuge

ॐ

The Excerpt in Context

  Memoirs and essays are unruly offspring, setting off without the writer's permission in unexpected directions. Terry Tempest Williams's *Refuge* (1991) was at first, she says, a book about birds. Williams wrote the memoir in the late 1980s, when the Great Salt Lake experienced record flooding and one of Williams's favorite haunts, the Bear River Migratory Bird Refuge, was underwater. This dramatic public event, one that inspired Utah politicians to launch several massive engineering efforts to control lake levels, coincided with her mother's and grandmother's diagnoses of cancer. Both were victims, Williams believes, of decades of nuclear bomb testing on the Utah desert that caused generations of residents to suffer from a range of deadly cancers. The book about birds became a book about where a grieving heart might find refuge; it also emerged as an eloquent plea to break the silence on the impact of the nuclear fallout because "the price of obedience has become too high."

  Yet birds flutter through much of *Refuge*, and Williams observes them both as a naturalist and a poet. They often carry the symbolic weight of the narrative, and one of the great achievements of the book is that this never becomes tiresome or overly sentimental. The birds and the lake also become central to the design of the memoir. Each chapter except the last is titled after a particular bird, and internal chapter sections are often marked by the Great Salt Lake's flood level. This is a structure that Eileen Pollack called a "found form," or one that borrows its design from things in the world relevant to the work's subject.

  The very brief excerpt that follows, drawn from the first 100 pages of *Refuge*, follows the inclusion of a remarkable letter Williams's mother wrote to a friend, who also suffered from cancer. Terry's mother, Diane, asks her daughter whether it was "all right to send." The following

106

passage is Terry Tempest William's response to her mother's question. In many ways, it's typical of the reflective turns in the narrative—moments that combine intellect and heart, particulars and abstraction, and that are often moving.

∾ *The Excerpt* ∾

Our correspondences show us where our intimacies lie. There is something very sensual about a letter. The physical contact of pen to paper, the time set aside to focus thoughts, the folding of the paper into the envelope, licking it closed, addressing it, a chosen stamp, and then the release of the letter to the mailbox—are all acts of tenderness.

And it doesn't stop there. Our correspondences have wings—paper birds that fly from my house to yours—flocks of ideas crisscrossing the country. Once opened, a connection is made. We are not alone in the world.

But how do we correspond with the land when paper and ink won't do? How do we empathize with the Earth when so much is ravaging her?

The heartbeats I felt in the womb—two heartbeats, at once, my mother's and my own—are heartbeats of the land. All of life drums and beats, at once, sustaining a rhythm audible only to the spirit. I can drum my heartbeat back into the Earth, beating, hearts beating, my hands on the Earth—like a ruffed grouse on a log, beating, hearts beating—like a bittern in the marsh, beating, hearts beating. My hands on the Earth beating, hearts beating. I drum back my return. ∾

Analyzing the Craft

1. Memoirists are time travelers, moving back and forth between *then* and *now*; and they also zigzag between exposition and narrative. Read nearly any memoir or personal essay and you can often see this movement—in one section a writer explains or reflects, and in another we are guided back to a scene, a description, or a bit of dialogue. The balance between telling and showing is part of the art of nonfiction narratives. Stories can stall if the explaining goes on too long, or they can seem pointless if there is no explaining. One signal that a writer is shifting to telling is the use of collective pronouns like *we* or *our*, as Williams does in the excerpt. There is little showing here. Williams doesn't say she is mailing *a* letter but that

From: Terry Tempest Williams, *Refuge* (New York: Vintage, 1991), 84–85.

when we mail *letters* we show "where our intimacies lie." This raises an important question of craft: What does Williams risk when she includes her readers in her reflections by using a pronoun like *we*? In a way, she does this without our consent. We may not agree, for instance, that letter writing carries such significance. How can a writer get away with this?

2. One important principle of style is called *end focus*. When we read a sentence, we usually give the last word or phrase—the information right before the end punctuation—the most weight. We remember it and infer that it's important. For instance, Williams could have written the first sentence of the excerpt this way: "Our intimacies are revealed by our *correspondence*." Which version do you prefer and why?

3. Maybe the most striking sentences in this excerpt come at the end, as Williams repeats the word *beating*. These deliberate recurrences are meant, obviously, to make us pay attention to the word. This device is familiar in poetry. It is less common in nonfiction. Is it effective here?

Practicing the Craft

"Our correspondence has wings," writes Terry Tempest Williams, "paper birds that fly from my house to yours—flocks of ideas crisscrossing the country." Metaphors are both concrete and abstract. They must be anchored to the particular (wings, birds, houses, flocks), but they also imply a relationship between things that is an idea, an abstraction about how the world is. Usually writers discover metaphors by accident, and it surprises them as much as it might later surprise readers. When they are forced, metaphors often fail. But they can be terrifically useful ways of thinking about material if done playfully.

Use metaphor (or simile) as a journal exercise to generate "seed" sentences that may serve as prompts for more writing.

1. Draw a line down the middle of a journal page. Label the left column "Things" and the right column "Passages."

2. In the left column, spend a few minutes brainstorming a list of concrete things. Try looking around the room you're sitting in and listing what you see.

3. In the right column, brainstorm a list of significant moments in your life, things like fatherhood or marriage or first kiss that can be labeled in a word or two.

4. Look for a figurative connection between an item in each column, and craft a sentence that expresses that relationship as a metaphor. Don't hesitate to ignore either list if you come up with a better idea.

Here's what I did:

Things	Passages
Nautilus shell	Being 15
Bird	Fatherhood
Fountain pen	Birth of child
Cedar	Marriage
Icicle	Mary
Compass	Dad's death
Book	First apartment
Letter	Fiat
Chair	Graduation
Post-it	First book
Front porch	

> Like many men, I resisted marriage because it seems like a closing off of options, a Post-it on my forehead that said, simply, "Never Again."

5. Finish by following your sentence for as long as you can in a fastwrite to see where the writing takes you.

Recommended Nonfiction by Terry Tempest Williams

- *An Unspoken Hunger* (1995). Four years after the publication of *Refuge*, Terry Tempest Williams published this collection of essays. Some of the essays explore her responses to the landscapes of the American West, but others take her to places like the Serengeti. The collection also features one of Williams's finest essays, "Yellowstone: The Erotics of Place."

- *Finding Beauty in a Broken World* (2008). Mosaic is the metaphor that binds together this extraordinary meditation on how to "mend a broken world." Three separate narratives wind around each other in the work—a visit to Italy to learn the art of mosaic, an investigation of endangered prairie dogs, and a visit to Rawanda to build a memorial to victims of genocide. This is not only a work of great beauty but also one that experiments with genre, creating in prose a kind of mosaic as well.

2.8

I COULD BE GOING OUT, SURE

Excerpt from Dave Eggers's
A Heartbreaking Work of Staggering Genius

∾

Eggers cofounded Might *magazine and in its most infamous issue, left, featured a story about the death of child star Adam Rich. Rich, who was not dead, cooperated with the ruse, a story that is recounted in Eggers's memoir.*

The Excerpt in Context

"In 2000," writes Ben Yagoda in *Memoir: A History,*[7] "Dave Eggers made an impressive attempt to kill the memoir, or at least deconstruct it until it was unrecognizable." The memoir is, of course, alive and well, but Eggers's *A Heartbreaking Work of Staggering Genius* offered a fresh answer to a persistent question about autobiography: Is it true? Not entirely, Eggers concedes in his memoir's preface, which includes notes, sometimes keyed to particular pages in the memoir, that explain omissions ("some really great sex scenes"), character alterations, time

---

[7]Ben Yagoda, *Memoir: A History* (New York: Riverhead, 2009).

compression, and inaccuracies about certain locations. This is followed by a 25-page acknowledgments section that urges readers "who are bothered by the idea of this being real" to just go ahead and "PRETEND IT'S FICTION."

All of this metacommentary on what he is up to makes the beginning of Eggers's memoir unusual but not entirely unprecedented. Forty years earlier, Mary McCarthy's *Memories of a Catholic Childhood* made a similar move to take time in the narrative to talk about the making of the narrative when she included inter-chapters that questioned the accuracy of some of her memories. Yet Eggers does much more than that. By beginning *A Heartbreaking Work* with the admission that the memoir is an act of imagination that might, on occasion, stray from the truth, Eggers conspires with the reader to give him license to do just that—imagine what might have happened and make that integral to the narrative. It's a clever move, all the more so because Eggers is not, he would insist, trying to be ironic but honest: This is how I tell my true story, so take it or leave it.

It's a good story, by the way. When Eggers was 21, both of his parents died, leaving him and his sister Beth to care for their 10-year-old brother, Toph. They all decide to move to San Francisco from the family home in Lake Forest, north of Chicago, and the memoir explores Eggers's struggle to be both a parent and a single 20-something against the background of a grief that rumbles beneath the narrative's comic surface. The excerpt that follows opens a section of Eggers's memoir in which he tries to navigate his sense of responsibility to his brother, Toph, and his competing impulses to act his age. Thomas Larson[8] puts *A Heartbreaking Work* in the category of "sudden memoir," work that explores an author's more recent experiences, and he notes that one quality of such a memoir is the sense of immediacy in the writing. The story seems to be happening now. This can rob a memoir of insight, the kind that comes with finding some distance from the narrated events. But Eggers's memoir has a quality that is essayistic: We are presented with the drama of a self in the making.

As you will see from the excerpt, Eggers has an extravagant, eruptive prose style that is reminiscent of Tom Wolfe's when he burst on the scene with the publication of *The Kandy-Colored Tangerine-Flake Streamline Baby*, his 1965 essay collection. But more interesting, perhaps, is the narrative persona in Eggers's memoir. In *The Situation and the Story*,[9] Vivian Gornick writes that her attempts to write her memoir depended on her struggle to discover "just who was telling the story." This narrator, she notes, is both "me and at the same

[8]Thomas Larson, *The Memoir and the Memoirist* (Athens, OH: Swallow Press, 2007).
[9]Vivian Gornick, *The Situation and the Story* (New York: Farrar, Strauss, and Giroux, 2001).

time not me"—someone who is capable of finding the story in a situation, a narrator who can find a way to "organize" the writer's experience. In the absence of this persona, the work stalls. This narrator, or "I-character," as Phillip Lopate calls it, may vary from piece to piece, and therefore the autobiographical "I" might be chameleon-like. The narrator of *A Heartbreaking Work of Staggering Genius* is more iguana than chameleon. His is a commanding presence, and for that reason, Eggers's persona in the memoir seems to provoke strong reactions. Yet it may have been the persona that he needed to tell this story and to "serve its insights." See what you think.

∾ *The Excerpt* ∾

Oh I could be going out, sure. It's Friday night and I should be out, across the Bay, I should be out every night, with the rest of the young people, fixing my hair, spilling beer, trying to get someone to touch my penis, laughing with and at people. Kirsten and I are *taking a break,* which we have done twice already and will do ten or twelve times in the future, meaning that we (ostensibly) date other people. So yes, I could be out, enjoying this freedom specifically and that of youth generally, exulting in the richness of my time and place.

But no.

I will be here, at home. Toph and I will cook, as usual—"Can you get the milk?"

"It's right there."

"Oh. Thanks."

—and then we will play Ping-Pong, and then we'll probably drive to that place on Solano and rent a movie, and, on the way back, buy a few push-ups at 7-Eleven. Oh I could be out, rollicking in the ripeness of my flesh and others', could be drinking things and eating things and rubbing mine against theirs, speculating about this person or that, waving, indicating hello with a sudden upward jutting of my chin, sitting in the backseat of someone else's car, bumping up and down the San Francisco hills, south of Market, seeing people attack their instruments, afterward stopping at a bodega, parking, carrying the bottles in a paper bag, the glass clinking, all our faces bright, glowing under streetlamps, down the sidewalk to this or that apartment party, hi, hi, putting the bottles in the fridge, removing one for now, hating the apartment, checking the view, sitting on the arm of a couch and being told not to, and then waiting for the bathroom, staring

From: Dave Eggers, *A Heartbreaking Work of Staggering Genius* (New York: Vintage, 2001), 105–106.

idly at that ubiquitous Ansel Adams print, Yosemite, talking to a short-haired girl while waiting in the hallway, talking about teeth, no reason really, the train of thought unclear, asking to see her fillings, no, really, I'll show you mine first, ha ha, then no, you go ahead, I'll go after you, then, after using the bathroom she is still there, still in the hallway, she was waiting not just for the bathroom but for me, and so eventually we'll go home together, her apartment, where she lives alone, in a wide, immaculate railroad type place, newly painted, decorated with her mother, then sleeping in her oversized, oversoft white bed, eating breakfast in her light-filled nook, then maybe to the beach for a few hours with the Sunday paper, then wandering home whenever, never—

Fuck. We don't even have a baby-sitter. ❧

Analyzing the Craft

1. Bill writes an essay in my creative nonfiction workshop, and when we talk about it in class, how do we talk about the Bill on the page? Do we simply call him *Bill* (this is nonfiction, after all) or do we borrow a term from fiction: The Narrator? The question seems relatively minor, but it does highlight a significant issue: Is the "I" who narrates his autobiography equivalent to the "I" who holds the pen to write it? Consider the Eggers excerpt. If Vivian Gornick is right that we often need to find the persona who can tell the story before we know how to tell it, how might the narrator in the excerpt serve Eggers's purpose? How would you describe that persona, and what evidence would you offer from the passage that contributed most strongly to that impression?

2. Take a moment to reflect on how we create "I-characters" in nonfiction. Where do we begin? What are some of the elements that shape a narrative persona?

3. Much of the excerpt is one long sentence that switchbacks from one embedded clause to another until finally ending breathlessly before the simple sentence about the absence of a babysitter. What effect does that 270-word sentence have on you as a reader? Why might have Eggers crafted it that way?

Practicing the Craft

Most of us don't think of ourselves as characters, certainly not of the literary kind. Most of us think of ourselves as rather uninteresting. Fortunately, being ordinary doesn't disqualify anyone from writing good autobiography because much nonfiction literature focuses on ordinary things: a young man's struggle with grief, the difficulty of returning home, an unsettling response to ourselves in the mirror one morning, and so on. But stories need characters, and for first-person stories like memoir or essay, the main character is you. How do you make yourself into a character? Phillip Lopate suggests this: "Mine your quirks." Most of us are quite ordinary and yet we have mannerisms, habits, interests, or obsessions that make us, at times, slightly strange or at least somewhat interesting.

I revel in potty humor at the dinner table and make grocery lists that I always forget to bring with me to the supermarket. I feel compelled to pretend that I know what I'm talking about when someone asks me about, say, how ocean tides work, or any other subject about which I have just a little knowledge. I have never learned how to spit.

Now it's your turn. In your journal, generate a list of your quirks. List at least ten things.

Next, keeping your quirk list in mind, craft a character sketch about yourself, but do this in third person. For example,

> He had a strange taste in clothes, an often-unhappy marriage of preppy and cowboy, button-down oxfords and riding boots, Levi's and horn-rimmed glasses. He did not possess a Stetson but sometimes wore a beret. Had there been a brass belt buckle for sailboat racing like those worn by rodeo champions, he might have worn that, but instead preferred a large leather belt with a modest metal buckle, purchased at a discount at the Eddie Bauer factory outlet.

Even if you can't immediately use the material you generated in this exercise, learn from the experience of rendering yourself as a character. Seeing yourself that way will help you to better understand the often subtle—and essential—differences between the you who is sitting at the writing desk and the you who is telling a story on the page.

Recommended Nonfiction by Dave Eggers

- *Zeitoun* (2009). Eggers's most recent work of nonfiction is a dramatic departure from his memoir. The book focuses on Abdulrahman Zeitoun, a Syrian-born painting contractor in New Orleans who endured Hurricane Katrina only to be arrested on suspicion of terrorism. *Zeitoun* demonstrates Eggers's impressive range as a nonfiction writer. Here his narrative persona is appropriately subdued, compared to the memoir, and he masterfully builds a narrative from his research on others.

Part 3
The Literary Journalists

❧❧❧❧❧

Introduction to Literary Journalism

New and Not New

In 1963, a young reporter for *The New York Herald Tribune* pitched a story to the editors at *Esquire* about people who are into the custom car and hot rod scene. The journalist, Tom Wolfe, had done a story on a convention of car freaks for the newspaper but thought that he had missed the real story: Some of the people involved in customizing cars—adorning them with wild paint jobs, furry steering wheels, and curving chrome— were genuine artists, and some of these cars were works of art. *Esquire* sent Wolfe to California to cover a teen festival that featured a custom car show. Wolfe took notes and, on deadline, returned to New York to write the piece. But he couldn't. "I had a lot of trouble analyzing what I had on my hands," Wolfe later wrote.

In despair, Wolfe wrote a memorandum to his editor about his California trip, thinking that another writer might be able to finish the job. *Esquire* published the memo as a feature article in the magazine titled "The Kandy-Kolored Tangerine-Flake Streamline Baby." That was the beginning of Tom Wolfe's foray into what he called the "New Journalism," a fresh form of nonfiction that he realized could use not only techniques usually associated with the short story but also "any literary device," including third-person point of view. With good-enough notes, a nonfiction writer could get into someone's head enough to actually render him or her as a character with knowable thoughts. Wolfe went on to do this in a number of his nonfiction books, most notably *The Electric Kool-Aid Acid Test*, his examination of Ken Kesey's "acid tests" in the 1960s.

But Wolfe wasn't the only one pioneering literary journalism. At about the same time, Truman Capote was working on his epic "nonfiction novel" *In Cold Blood*, the story of the brutal murder of the Clutter family in rural Kansas in 1959. Capote, a fiction writer, had become enamored with the possibilities of applying "all the techniques of fictional art" to reportage that was "nevertheless immaculately factual." It was Capote's contention that a work like this could only be done by fiction writers, not journalists like Wolfe, because only first-rate fiction writers had "complete control" over literary craft. *In Cold Blood* was a huge success, and it ignited a debate over what exactly it means to write "literary journalism." Must it be factually accurate? Is that even possible?

Although Capote claimed that his was the first "nonfiction novel," and Wolfe described narrative journalism in the 1960s as "new," the seeds of American literary journalism were sown much earlier, in the work of writers like Stephen Crane, Richard Harding Davis, Lafcadio Hearn, and Jack London. Reporters had been telling stories for years, of course, and some, like Stephen Crane, who are now known primarily as novelists, began by writing nonfiction stories about street life in American cities. Inspired by Crane and others, Lincoln Steffens, a late-nineteenth-century editor of *The New York Evening Post*, argued that newspapers need more stories that are "personal, literary, and immediate." Stories like that take time. Steffens once told a reporter, "Here...is a report that a man murdered his wife, a rather bloody, hacked-up crime....There's a story in it. That man loved that woman well enough once to marry her, and now he has hated her enough to cut her all to pieces. If you can find out just what happened between that wedding and this murder you will have a novel for yourself and a short story for me. Go on now, take your time, and get this tragedy, as a tragedy."[1]

Steffens's call for a different kind of journalism that helps readers "to see" the story behind what happened was exactly what Truman Capote had in mind seven decades later when he stumbled over a small article buried in *The New York Times* with the headline "Wealthy Farmer, 3 of Family Slain." Capote reflected later that there was "nothing really exceptional" about the Clutter murder. "But after reading the story it suddenly struck me that a crime, the study of one such, might provide the broad scope I needed to write the kind of book I wanted to write. Moreover, the human heart being what it is, murder was a theme not likely to darken and yellow with time."

While *In Cold Blood* is probably the most famous work of American literary journalism, and the subject of at least three Hollywood films, many writers other than Wolfe and Capote were combining reporting with storytelling. John Hersey's *Hiroshima*, an account of the city's bombing as told from the point of view of six survivors, was published before Capote's nonfiction novel. Gay Talese, Joan Didion, Lillian Ross, Joseph Mitchell, Jane Kramer, and many others were writing extraordinary works of narrative journalism in the 1960s. In addition, newspaper columnists like Tom Wolfe's colleague at *The Herald Tribune*, Jimmy Breslin, were writing short narrative pieces based on street reporting, much like Crane did decades earlier.

---

[1] Thomas B. Connery, "A Third Way to Tell the Story: American Literary Journalism at the Turn of the Century." In Norman Sims, ed., *Literary Journalism in the Twentieth Century* (New York: Oxford, 1990).

Ultimately it's reporting that most distinguishes literary journalism from essay and memoir, and it's what some call "immersion reporting" that produces the richest work. Truman Capote spent a year in Holcomb, Kansas, to research *In Cold Blood*. (It took him eight years to write it.) Gay Talese spent six years following Joe Bannano, the Mafia chief who was the central character of Talese's book on the mob, *Honor Thy Father*. The result of such intensive reporting is lots of notes. Though he ultimately used only a small percentage of the material to write *In Cold Blood*, Capote claimed that his notes and research on the Clutter murders would "fill up a whole small room, right up to the ceiling." This abundance creates its own problems, aside from storage: For what and how should it be used?

John McPhee, a literary journalist whose interests in the last 30 years have included birch-bark canoes, Alaska, oranges, basin and range geology, and road kill, believes that it's impossible to manage all the material that goes into a book or article with worrying about structure very early on. McPhee keeps all his notes in three-ring binders and plays with possible sequences for the material using notecards on corkboard above his desk. One of the challenges of literary journalism is that the writer is often not the organizing subject. In essays, we have the "I-character," the author who narrates the story. It is his or her story, after all. But much narrative journalism is not reported in first person. The story, if there is one, can't be found in the writer's life but in the material he or she has collected, usually about someone else. This story is what McPhee is after, and finding the story in the material he's gathered is a motive behind the corkboard, note-cards, and three-ring binders.

Ethical Dramas

This reliance on the information gathered through reporting makes many literary journalists insist on the importance of accuracy. No one is more eloquent on this subject than Tracy Kidder, a prolific literary journalist whose first work, *The Soul of a New Machine* (1982), won the Pulitzer Prize:

> Some writers proceed by trying to discover the truth about a situation, and then invent the facts as necessary.... I take it on faith that the truth lies in the events somewhere, and that immersion in those real events will yield glimpses of that truth. I try to hew to what has begun to seem like a narrow definition of nonfiction partly in that faith, and partly out of fear. I'm afraid that if I start making things up in a story,... I'd stop believing it myself. And I imagine that such a loss of conviction would infect every sentence and make each one unbelievable.[2]

[2]Tracy Kidder, "Courting the Approval of the Dead," *TriQuarterly* 97 (1996): 43–59.

Kidder's faith that the truth lies in what actually happened seems sensible enough, but the building blocks of nonfiction narratives aren't just events but people. In news journalism, this means that writers are careful to quote their subjects fairly and accurately. In literary journalism the matter is far more complicated. Nonfiction stories, like fiction, typically rely on characters, and in some cases these are narrators of the tales. And yet, unlike fiction, these are characters who are living (or once lived), people who may or may not appreciate the kind of character the writer crafts from their story.

The literary journalist Janet Malcolm famously wrote, "Every journalist who is not too stupid or too full of himself to notice what is going on knows that what he does is morally indefensible."[3] Nonfiction writers, says Malcolm, "prey on people's vanity," and once they earn their subjects' trust, they sell them out "without remorse." It's more than that subjects feel "misrepresented," she says. It's that subjects feel duped when they realize that writing a nonfiction narrative is not a collaboration. Writers appropriate their subjects' stories and, in the end, subjects may feel deceived.

There are ethical issues that apply to all forms of creative nonfiction. But because literary journalists are often writing about living subjects and public events with which readers might be familiar, the stakes can be higher. Not only might writers' subjects feel deceived, but they might very well sue for libel, a situation that writer Joe McGinniss found himself in after he published *Fatal Vision,* the story of Dr. Jeffrey MacDonald, a convicted killer of three. Narrative journalism also needs to be accurate, not just about what a subject said or didn't say, but also about the public events that are relevant to the subject's story. After all, the situation on which the story is based—the murder, the war, the election, the mountain ascent—is made up of events about which readers may have some knowledge.

Building Blocks of Literary Journalism

The excerpts in this book conceal the ethical dramas behind their creation. What you see is a product of the writers' literary craft, and unless you look closely you may not see what holds these narratives together. Tom Wolfe wrote years ago that the "New Journalism" has four essential elements[4]:

1. Scene-by-scene construction
2. Realistic dialogue
3. "Status" details
4. Third-person point of view

[3]Janet Malcolm, *The Journalist and the Murderer* (New York: Vintage, 1990).
[4]Tom Wolfe, *The New Journalism* (New York: Harper & Row, 1973).

Wolfe believed that the third of these devices, "status" details, was the least understood. Most creative writers, fiction or nonfiction, build stories by relying on the power of particulars to say more than they say. A plumber, for example, who leaves his shiny, late-model truck idling in a customer's driveway while working says something about his character—not just his attitude about air quality or his fondness for pickups. Wolfe was particularly interested in incorporating details about the "status life" of the characters in his nonfiction, particulars that symbolize who they are (or think they are) and perhaps what they aspire to be. These may include detailed descriptions of a room or behaviors like the plumber with his idling truck. Wolfe believed that literary journalists didn't spend enough time noticing these things and writing them down. Nor did they appreciate how fundamental such observations were to crafting realistic narratives.

Third-person point of view is particularly challenging in nonfiction for obvious reasons: You can't know what characters are thinking at any given moment unless they tell you. Among the many literary accomplishments of *In Cold Blood* was Capote's ability to take the point of view not only of the living but also of the dead, something he argued was possible by interviewing people who were present when a deceased character shared what he or she was thinking or feeling. By any measure, this is extraordinary reporting. This may be one reason why many literary journalists choose not to tell a story from a character's point of view, especially in projects that aren't book length: It just takes too much research. But this may be the technique that, more than any other, makes nonfiction read like fiction and a technique that makes the work of Capote, Kidder, Kramer, Wolfe, and others so utterly compelling.

Most important, though, is that all of these writers found a story to tell, one that was inspired by something they read or experienced. Sometimes these stories are dramatic—the profile of a murderer or a Mafia boss—but even more often their subjects seem utterly ordinary, or at least they begin that way. Susan Orlean, who wrote *The Orchid Thief*, an extraordinary story of an eccentric collector of Florida orchids, notes that she's not an investigative reporter who goes out actively looking for material. Instead, she "stumbles" on story ideas, which are often focused on "the part of daily life you've never stopped to think about, and the fully realized subculture that I don't know anything about." What matters most to Orlean is that the story interests *her* and not some hypothetical reader. "I find myself talking about it to everyone I know. If I'm *not* talking about it, and am *not* able to convey my excitement, something isn't working."[5] Whether ordinary or dramatic, the literary journalists' stories must possess a quality that most news stories lack: They must have a timeless quality. All enduring literary works, fiction or nonfiction, give readers a glimpse into the human heart.

[5]Robert S. Boynton, *The New New Journalism: Conversations with America's Best Nonfiction Writers on Their Craft* (New York: Vintage, 2005).

In "The Literary Journalists," I've chosen to excerpt the work of some of the writers I mention here as well as others whose attention to craft makes them worth studying. Because a number of their pieces are long-form literary journalism, choosing a few paragraphs to look at closely was especially difficult. For one thing, there was so much to choose from. It's also impossible to appreciate from such a brief excerpt the work and skill that went into writing a book-length nonfiction narrative about a subject other than the writer. The best literary journalism, in the end, is the result of dedication to the subject. Once Truman Capote was asked how writers might improve their "technique." He said, "Work is the only device I know of." Of the three major forms of creative nonfiction featured in this book, none demand as much work as most literary journalism, and it goes beyond the demands of reporting. In essays and memoirs, writers may know—at least vaguely—what story they might tell. It is, after all, *their* story. But literary journalists often don't write about themselves. What they have to find is the story in the material they've gathered, and it may be some time before they know what that is. "I have often to wait," said Jane Kramer, "sometimes for months, or even years, before a story is ripe." As the following excerpts show, for readers as well as writers the wait is often worth it.

3.1

THE SMELL OF SWEAT

Excerpt from James Agee's
Let Us Now Praise Famous Men

This Walker Evans photo-
graph was taken inside the
Gudgers' home, one of the
tenant farmer families that
were the subject of Evans's
collaboration with the
writer James Agee. There is
some controversy about
this photograph because it
appears that Evans moved
things around in the
kitchen before taking it,
suggesting that the image is
less documentary than one
might think.

The Excerpt in Context

"Most young writers and artists roll around in description like honey-mooners on a bed," writes James Agee in his 1939 book *Let Us Now Praise Famous Men*. "It comes easier to them than anything else. In the course of years they grow or discipline themselves out of it....But I suspect that the lust for describing, and that lust in action, is not necessarily a vice." Among the many virtues of Agee's book, a collaboration with photographer Walker Evans, is the close description of the lives of three tenant cotton farmers and their families in the summer of 1936. Though Walker and Agee spent only a month with the Ricketts, the Woods, and the Gudger families, all desperately poor farm families living in an isolated part of rural Alabama, *Let Us Now Praise Famous Men* is a richly sympathetic work.

The project began as an article on tenant farming for a national magazine. It expanded into a book that is widely considered a masterpiece of nonfiction. There was a documentary impulse behind *Let Us Now Praise Famous Men*; it was an effort to record the lives of the rural poor in the thirties and to bring their living conditions to the nation's attention. But because of Agee's poetic prose style and his passion for seeing something holy in the lives of these families, *Let Us Now Praise Famous Men* is also a work of art.

It *does*, however, test the limits of descriptive writing. In one chapter, for instance, Agee lavishes 1,000 words on a description of a pair of overalls. And in the excerpt that follows, Agee tackles what is arguably the most difficult thing for a writer to capture in words: smells. Agee lived with the Gudger family for several weeks during that summer of 1936, and he renders their house in exquisite (or, depending on your point of view, excessive) detail.

The usual advice for crafting description is simple enough: Drawing on all your senses, accumulate details that, considered together, seem to say something about a particular place. In other words, description is not merely wallpaper but the walls; it's not meant to be decorative but to serve a purpose. It isn't this simple, of course. Of the many details you might use, *which* should you choose? How should they be arranged? And how, particularly in a passage like the one you're about to read, does a writer sustain reader interest in an extended description?

∾ *The Excerpt* ∾

Odors

The Gudgers' house, being young, only eight years old, smells a little dryer and cleaner, and more distinctly of its wood, than an average white tenant house, and it has also a certain odor I have never found in other such

From: James Agee and Walker Evans, *Let Us Now Praise Famous Men* (Boston: Houghton, 1960), 154–155.

houses: aside from these sharp yet slight subtleties, it has the odor or odors which are classical in every thoroughly poor white southern country house, and by which such a house could be identified blindfold in any part of the world, among no matter what other odors. It is compacted of many odors and made into one, which is very thin and light on the air, and more subtle than it can seem in analysis, yet very sharply and constantly noticeable. These are its ingredients. The odor of pine lumber, wide thin cards of it, heated in the sun, in no way doubled or insulated, in closed and darkened air. The odor of woodsmoke, the fuel being again mainly pine, but in part also, hickory, oak, and cedar. The odors of cooking. Among these, most strongly, the odors of fried salt pork and of fried and boiled pork lard, and second, the odor of cooked corn. The odors of sweat in many stages of age and freshness, this sweat being a distillation of pork, lard, corn, woodsmoke, pine, and ammonia. The odors of sleep, of bedding and of breathing, for the ventilation is poor. The odors of all the dirt that in the course of time can accumulate in a quilt and mattress. Odors of staleness from clothes hung or stored away, not washed. I should further describe the odor of corn: in sweat, or on the teeth, and breath, when it is eaten as much as they eat it, it is of a particular sweet stuffy fetor, to which the nearest parallel is the odor of the yellow excrement of a baby. All these odors as I have said are so combined into one that they are all and always present in balance, not at all heavy, yet so searching that all fabrics of bedding and clothes are saturated with them, and so clinging that they stand softly out of the fibers of newly laundered clothes. Some of their components are extremely 'pleasant,' some are 'unpleasant'; their sum total has great nostalgic power. When they are in an old house, darkened, and moist, and sucked into all the wood, and stacked down on top of years of a moldering and old basis of themselves, as at the Ricketts', they are hard to get used to or even hard to bear. At the Woods', they are blowsy and somewhat moist and dirty. At the Gudgers', as I have mentioned, they are younger, lighter, and cleaner-smelling. There too, there is another and special odor, very dry and edged: it is somewhere between the odor of very old newsprint and of a victorian bedroom in which, after long illness, and many medicines, someone has died and the room has been fumigated, yet the odor of dark brown medicines, dry-bodied sickness, and staring death, still is strong in the stained wallpaper and in the mattress. ❧

Analyzing the Craft

1. The structure of an essay is often invisible unless you're looking for it, and so is the structure of a paragraph. Each has a subtle logic. There is a logical structure to much descriptive writing as well, including the Agee excerpt. Can you explain it?

2. Narrative writers often try to create a world in their prose that surrounds their readers in ways that a good movie can—we lose ourselves in it, even if only for moments. Charles Dickens was a master at this, of course; he

was also known as a writer who lavished enormous attention on description. In the excerpt, Agee is trying to build a world, too, relying mostly on a single sense impression rather than several. Is Agee's attempt at surrounding you with a believable world convincing? Compare it with Didion's description of Southern California on page 37. What do both suggest to you about the methods of crafting a compelling world in prose?

3. A nonfiction writer should have an accountant's instinct for detail, making a complete inventory of observations, knowing that many—perhaps most—won't make it into the work. Which will you choose to use? Tom Wolfe wrote about what he called "status details," particulars that say something about someone's social position. Other writers talk about "telling" or "revealing details"—things that say more than what they say. What would you say about Agee's choices of details here? To begin with, why did he lean so heavily on the particulars of smell? And of the smells he chose, which did you find most telling? Why?

Practicing the Craft

It isn't possible to write 300 words about the smells of a single house without a nearly microscopic look at the place. Most of us are unused to looking that closely because we aren't in the habit of sustaining our gaze at any one thing for very long. But this is a good habit for writers to cultivate. Drawing on all of your senses, begin by generating a list of details about the room in which you now sit. Be as specific as you can. Here's what I notice in the office where I am typing this:

There is fine dust on the white windowsill. The weak January sun is filtered through the long horizontal blinds, leaving strips of light on the gray keyboard. The "Enter" and "Shift" and "Ctrl" keys are all momentarily bathed in this light, which brightens and fades with the movement of high clouds. It is quiet. There is the muffled hum of the hot water in the pipes—the sound is vaguely like jet turbines heard from a great distance—and then suddenly the musical grind of a pump on the floor below. It is the sound of a toiling machine past its prime, and sad somehow. It stops. There is a gold-framed mirror on the windowsill, small and arched at the top like a cathedral window. It holds the image of yellow manila folders and large brown mailing envelopes, and in the distance, a brown door. The door is closed. On the wall next to the window are two black-and-white photographs of girls, one blond and one dark, but both with magnificent eyebrows, neat hedge rows along the lower edges of two fine, clear foreheads.

Write a richly detailed sketch of the room where you are sitting, roughly the same length as mine. You might begin by simply brainstorming a list of details in your journal and then composing a sketch using the material you generated. Don't worry about coherence. Simply practice the art of looking very closely at things. You may find, as I did, the impulse to make comparisons that help to describe what you see. Also consider whether you will use first person as a means of establishing a vantage point for your description. I chose not to. Once you've crafted your sketch, consider the ways in which it might be revised to be more coherent. Might there be a pattern of seeing lurking there?

Recommended Nonfiction by James Agee

- *James Agee: Film Writing and Selected Journalism* (2005). Agee's most famous work of nonfiction was undoubtedly *Let Us Now Praise Famous Men*, from which the excerpt was selected. But the writer was also a prolific book and film reviewer and journalist. David Denby, in a 2006 *New Yorker* review of Agee's collected works, called Agee's essay "Comedy's Greatest Era," a review of humor in silent films, "one of the greatest pieces about movies ever written in this country." *James Agee: Film Writing and Selected Journalism* is one volume in a three-volume collection of Agee's complete works published by the Library of America.

THE WHEELING OF HAWKS

Excerpt from Truman Capote's
In Cold Blood

The Excerpt in Context

Truman Capote's *In Cold Blood*, the story of the 1959 murder of the Clutter family in a small Kansas town, burst on the American literary scene in 1965. It began a revolution in what some would call "New Journalism." Capote called his book a "nonfiction novel," a work of "creative reportage" that he insisted was a work of imagination as well as completely accurate. The book was based on three years of research, much of it spent interviewing the two killers responsible for the murders and the townspeople in the small Kansas town of Holcomb where the crime took place. *In Cold Blood* was first serialized in *The New Yorker* magazine and later became a national best seller.

In Cold Blood ignited a national debate about Capote's claims that this was a new genre. Capote dismissed assertions that earlier nonfiction books that had used some fictional techniques, like John Hersey's *Hiroshima*, were also works of "creative reportage." He mostly called them good reporting and argued that only fiction writers could successfully write in the new form. "It's useless for a writer whose talent is essentially journalistic to attempt creative reportage, because it simply won't work," he said.

FOUND DEAD: Herbert W. Clutter, a wealthy Kansas farmer. He, his wife and two children were found bound and shot to death.

WEALTHY FARMER, 3 OF FAMILY SLAIN

H. W. Clutter, Wife and 2 Children Are Found Shot in Kansas Home

HOLCOMB, Kan., Nov. 15 (UPI) — A wealthy wheat farmer, his wife and their two young children were found shot to death today in their home. They had been killed by shotgun blasts at close range after being bound and gagged.

Remarkably, Capote never used a tape recorder to collect the thousands of pages of material about the case, which he gathered from interviews with the criminals, townspeople, and state officials. Capote claimed that, with practice, he could remember with 95 percent accuracy everything that was said and wrote up his notes after each interview. Such a talent would have made the rendering of the following two scenes much easier than it would have otherwise been. In the excerpts that follow, following within a few pages of each other in the book, Capote describes the same scene from the point of view of each of the murderers—Dick Hickock and Perry Smith. Both are escaping the murder scene after killing the entire Clutter family, having attempted to rob a safe both Hickock and Smith believed contained a lot of money. It didn't. Ultimately, the two were convicted of murder and hung by the state of Kansas.

As I noted in "Introduction to Literary Journalism," literary journalist Tom Wolfe believed that "scene-by-scene construction" was an essential element of creative nonfiction, and he was particularly enthusiastic about entering the mind of one of his interview subjects and writing from his point of view, something that only fiction writers seemed able to do. The elements of a scene, including point of view, are similar in nonfiction and fiction except in one fundamental respect: The scene in nonfiction is not a product of the imagination but of a real place and time. It must be rendered accurately. In this excerpt, Capote borrows directly from Henry James by shifting the point of view to each one of his subjects. We don't see these scenes as Capote witnessed them but as reported by Hickock and Smith. How is this possible in nonfiction? What interview questions might have Capote asked the two to render these scenes? What are the risks for the nonfiction writer in attempting to see through the eyes of someone other than himself or herself?

The father, 48-year-old Herbert W. Clutter, was found in the basement with his son, Kenyon, 15. His wife Bonnie, 45, and a daughter, Nancy, 16, were in their beds.

There were no signs of a struggle, and nothing had been stolen. The telephone lines had been cut.

"This is apparently the case of a psychopathic killer," Sheriff Earl Robinson said.

Mr. Clutter was founder of the Kansas Wheat Growers Association. In 1954 President Eisenhower appointed him to the Federal Farm Credit Board, but he never lived in Washington.

The board represents the twelve farm credit districts in the country. Mr. Clutter served from December, 1953, until April, 1957. He declined a reappointment.

He was also a local member of the Agriculture Department's Price Stabilization Board and was active with the Great Plains Wheat Growers Association.

The Clutter farm and ranch cover almost 1,000 acres in one of the richest wheat areas.

Mr. Clutter, his wife and daughter were clad in pajamas. The boy was wearing blue jeans and a T-shirt.

The bodies were discovered by two of Nancy's classmates, Susan Kidwell and Nancy Ewalt.

Sheriff Robinson said the last reported communication with Mr. Clutter took place last night about 9:30 P.M., when the victim called Gerald Van Vleet, his business partner, who lives near by. Mr. Van Vleet said the conversation had concerned the farm and ranch.

Two daughters were away. They are Beverly, a student at Kansas University, and Mrs. Donald G. Jarchow of Mount Carroll, Ill.

∾ *The Excerpt* ∾

Hawks wheeling in a white sky. A dusty road winding into and out of a white and dusty village. Today was his second day in Mexico, and so far he liked it fine—even the food. (At this very moment he was eating a cold, oily tortilla.) They had crossed the border at Laredo, Texas, the morning of November 23, and spent the first night in a San Luis Potosí brothel. They were now two hundred miles north of their next destination, Mexico City.

"Know what I think?" said Perry. "I think there must be something wrong with us. To do what we did."

"Did what?"

"Out there."

Dick dropped the binoculars into a leather case, a luxurious receptacle initialed H.W.C. He was annoyed. Annoyed as hell. Why the hell couldn't Perry shut up? Christ Jesus, what damn good did it do, always dragging the goddam thing up? It really was *annoying.* Especially since they'd agreed, sort of, not to talk about the goddam thing. Just forget it.

"There's got to be something wrong with somebody who'd do a thing like that," Perry said.

"Deal me out, baby," Dick said. "I'm a normal." And Dick meant what he said. He thought himself as balanced, as sane as anyone, maybe a bit smarter than the average fellow, that's all. But Perry—there *was,* in Dick's opinion, "something wrong" with Little Perry. To say the least. Last spring, when they had celled together at Kansas State Penitentiary, he'd learned most of Perry's lesser peculiarities: Perry could be "such a kid," always wetting his bed and crying in his sleep ("Dad, I been looking everywhere, where you been, Dad?"), and often Dick had seen him "sit for hours just sucking his thumb and poring over them phony damn treasure guides." Which was one side; there were others. In some ways old Perry was "spooky as hell." Take, for instance, that temper of his. He could slide into a fury "quicker than ten drunk Indians." And yet you wouldn't know it. "He might be ready to kill you, but you'd never know it, not to look at or listen to," Dick once said. For however extreme the inward rage, outwardly Perry remained a cool young tough, with eyes serene and slightly sleepy. The time had been when Dick had thought he could control, could regulate the temperature of these sudden cold fevers that burned and chilled his friend. He had been mistaken, and in the aftermath of that discovery, had grown unsure of Perry, not at all certain what to think—except that he felt he ought to be afraid of him, and wondered really why he wasn't.

"Deep down," Perry continued, "way, way rock-bottom, I never thought I could do it. A thing like that."

From: Truman Capote, *In Cold Blood,* 1965. (New York: Vintage, 1993), 108–109, 110–111.

"How about the nigger?" Dick said. Silence. Dick realized that Perry was staring at him.

⁂

MOUNTAINS. Hawks wheeling in a white sky.

When Perry asked Dick, "Know what I think?" he knew he was beginning a conversation that would displease Dick, and one that, for that matter, he himself would just as soon avoid. He agreed with Dick: Why go on talking about it? But he could not always stop himself. Spells of helplessness occurred, moments when he "remembered things"—blue light exploding in a black room, the glass eyes of a big toy bear—and when voices, a particular few words, started nagging his mind: "Oh, no! Oh, please! No! No! No! No! Don't! Oh, please don't, please!" And certain sounds returned—a silver dollar rolling across a floor, boot steps on hardwood stairs, and the sounds of breathing, the gasps, the hysterical inhalations of a man with a severed windpipe.

When Perry said, "I think there must be something wrong with us," he was making an admission he "hated to make." After all, it was "painful" to imagine that one might be "not just right"—particularly if whatever was wrong was not your own fault but "maybe a thing you were born with." Look at his family! Look at what had happened there! His mother, an alcoholic, had strangled to death on her own vomit. Of her children, two sons and two daughters, only the younger girl, Barbara, had entered ordinary life, married, begun raising a family. Fern, the other daughter, jumped out of a window of a San Francisco hotel. (Perry had ever since "tried to believe she slipped," for he'd loved Fern. She was "such a sweet person," so "artistic," a "terrific" dancer, and she could sing, too. "If she'd ever had any luck at all, with her looks and all, she could have got somewhere, been somebody." It was sad to think of her climbing over a window sill and falling fifteen floors.) And there was Jimmy, the older boy—Jimmy, who had one day driven his wife to suicide and killed himself the next.

Then he heard Dick say, "Deal me out, baby. I'm a normal." Wasn't that a horse's laugh? But never mind, let it pass. "Deep down," Perry continued, "way, way rock-bottom, I never thought I could do it. A thing like that." And at once he recognized his error: Dick would, of course, answer by asking, "How about the nigger?" When he'd told Dick that story, it was because he'd wanted Dick's friendship, wanted Dick to "respect" him, think him "hard," as much "the masculine type" as he had considered Dick to be. ⁂

Analyzing the Craft

1. It's easy for a nonfiction writer to envy the ease with which a novelist can enter the mind of a character. Unfortunately, the nonfiction writer's characters are (or were) real, living human beings, and only they have ready access to their own consciousness. Obviously, to write from someone else's point of view, the literary journalist must rely heavily on interviews with a subject, interviews that pose questions we don't usually think to ask: "What were you thinking when that happened? And then what? What did you say? And then what?" As you might imagine, the technical problems in doing this well are enormous. What do you think some of these challenges might be? How would you confront them? Working backwards from these excerpts, speculate about what questions Capote might have asked both Dick and Perry that would enable Capote to craft these scenes.

2. Truman Capote was long interested in experimenting with what he called a "new art form," one that "employed all the techniques of fictional art but was nevertheless immaculately factual." The first problem was finding a subject. In the late fall of 1959, Capote found an article about the murder of a Kansas farmer and his family while browsing *The New York Times* (see reprinted article at the beginning of this chapter). This was the story he was looking for, one that "might provide the broad scope" to write a book like *In Cold Blood*. Why might this murder, of all the murders that are reported in American newspapers, have been so appealing to Capote? In what ways does it provide "broad scope?"

3. The excerpt is extraordinary not only because it convincingly portrays the thoughts of someone other than the writer, but it also captures the points of view of two characters *during the same moment and in the same scene*. Why might Capote choose to do this? How does it enhance the narrative?

Practicing the Craft

The success of *In Cold Blood* depended on remarkable reporting. Capote spent years on this project, interviewing Hickock and Smith, people in Holcomb, and police officials. He studied court transcripts and, of course, literally covered the ground on which the murders took place as well as replicated the journey the murderers took before and after the crime. In addition to all of this, Capote interviewed "quite a number of murderers" so that he could better understand their thinking. All of this reporting, as I noted earlier, was done without the benefit of a tape recorder. Capote spent years practicing transcription of passages from books read to him by friends, and claimed he finally achieved 95 percent accuracy. Even with practice, few of us could replicate Capote's note-taking skill. But with practice we *can* substantially improve, and the payoff for taking good notes is huge for a writer in any nonfiction genre.

Over the next few weeks, practice as Capote did. Spend 10 minutes a day listening to someone speak and writing down what he or she says. For the first few days ask a partner to read just a sentence or two from the newspaper. When you can write down a few sentences accurately, move to transcribing longer passages of spoken text. If you don't have a partner, navigate to an interview site on the Web that is in both text and audio. Listen and transcribe; then check for accuracy.

With a friend, partner, or other willing subject, conduct an interview that will allow you to craft a scene like Capote's, one that is written from the point of view of your interviewee. Focus your conversation on a moment—a discreet episode or event—in your subject's life that he or she felt was the beginning of something or the end of something. Alternatively, ask your partner to share a scene from the past that he or she remembers well. Ask the questions that will allow you to describe the scene from your subject's point of view, integrating, if you can, not only thoughts and feelings but dialogue as well.

Recommended Nonfiction by Truman Capote

- *The Muses Are Heard* (1956). This book recounts Capote's journey to the Soviet Union with members of the cast of the opera "Porgy and Bess" at the height of the Cold War. The piece appeared in two parts in *The New Yorker Magazine* and was considered cheeky. Capote had little patience for some aspects of Soviet culture and taste. But the writer's skill in rendering scene is as evident here as in his more famous non-fiction work, *In Cold Blood*.

3.3

MAILER'S TOWER

Excerpt from Norman Mailer's
The Armies of the Night

∾

Norman Mailer and others lead the March on the Pentagon in 1967.

The Excerpt in Context

The imaginative possibilities of literary journalism enticed novelist Norman Mailer, who gained fame in his twenties for *The Naked and the Dead,* to write a "nonfiction novel" describing his participation in a 1967 antiwar demonstration at the Pentagon. *The Armies of the Night* was so striking stylistically that one critic called it "operatic." In many ways the book *is* a public performance. Mailer, the brawling, bawdy, hard-drinking writer who was once accused of stabbing his second wife at a party with a pen knife, narrates his involvement in the protests through multiple Mailer characters, all in the third person. We get the man named Mailer but also Mailer the Novelist, the Existentialist, the Participant, and the Historian. This is more than just a narrative device. While it's obvious that

Mailer is always keenly interested in Mailer ("there are days," he told the poet Robert Lowell, who participated in the march, "when I think of myself as the best writer in America"), the shifting point of view is also a product of Mailer's interest in the reliability of historical accounts. How are we to know whom to believe? Certainly not the journalist, Mailer concludes in the excerpt that follows. Instead, he sees the nonfiction novel as the "instrument" through which we might see events most clearly.

There really hasn't been a work quite like *The Armies of the Night*, which won both the Pulitzer Prize and the National Book Award after it was published in 1968. Truman Capote, Tom Wolfe, Gay Talese, and others had certainly established the use of third-person point of view as a technique in literary journalism, but they had used it to get into the heads of characters other than themselves. Mailer seizes on the idea that the author himself might invoke multiple selves and that these can become novelistic characters. The following excerpt provides a partial explanation for why he chooses this "method"; it also shows how the author uses two Mailer characters—the Novelist and the Historian—to stand in for selves with different ways of seeing the events surrounding the March on the Pentagon. The Novelist seeks to dramatize the events, and the Historian seeks to report them.

In this pivotal passage, drawn from the opening of Book Two of *The Armies of the Night*, you can see the effect of Mailer's use of the third person as he philosophically surveys the scene of the protest. Imagine how the passage might be different had Mailer chosen the conventional first person from which to narrate. How would that have changed things? What are the advantages of this approach? The disadvantages? This excerpt, which was subtitled "A Novel Metaphor," follows Mailer's account of his arrest at the Pentagon (he failed to obey the federal marshals) and his subsequent jailing and legal challenges. As you can see, it is mostly exposition and an interesting variation on the reflective writing that is a feature common to essay and memoir.

◌⊷ *The Excerpt* ◌⊷

The Novelist in passing his baton to the Historian has a happy smile. He has been faster than you think. As a working craftsman, a journeyman artist, he is not without his guile; he has come to decide that if you would see the horizon from a forest, you must build a tower. If the horizon will reveal most of what is significant, an hour of examination can yet do the job—it is the tower which takes months to build. So the Novelist working in secret collaboration with the Historian has perhaps tried to build with his novel a tower fully equipped with telescopes to study—at the greatest advantage—our own

From: Norman Mailer, *The Armies of the Night* (New York: Plume, 1968), 219–220.

horizon. Of course, the tower is crooked, and the telescopes warped, but the instruments of all sciences—history so much as physics—are always constructed in small or large error; what supports the use of them now is that our intimacy with the master builder of the tower, and the lens grinder of the telescopes (yes, even the machinist of the barrels) has given some advantage for correcting the error of the instruments and the imbalance of his tower. May that be claimed of many histories? In fact, how many novels can be put so quickly to use? (For the novel—we will permit ourselves this parenthesis—is, when it is good, the personification of a vision which will enable one to comprehend other visions better; a microscope—if one is exploring the pond; a telescope upon a tower if you are scrutinizing the forest.)

The method is then exposed. The mass media which surrounded the March on the Pentagon created a forest of inaccuracy which would blind the efforts of an historian; our novel has provided us with the possibility, no, even the instrument to view our facts and conceivably study them in that field of light a labor of lensgrinding has produced. Let us prepare then (metaphors soon to be mixed—for the Novelist is slowing to a jog, and the Historian is all grip on the rein) let us prepare then to see what the history may disclose. ❧

Analyzing the Craft

1. Metaphors have many virtues in a piece of writing. For example, they can offer unexpected comparisons, and they can, perhaps more than most other literary devices, reveal a writer's particular way of seeing. Most of all, the right metaphor can break through to understandings of a subject that are unavailable in more straightforward exposition. How do Mailer's metaphors of the tower and the telescope fare in these respects? Do they work?

2. The default point of view for most creative nonfiction is first person. Rarely do writers employ the device of referring to themselves in the third person as Mailer does here, much less often do they divide that third person further into multiple personas—as in the Novelist and the Historian. There's probably a good reason these are unusual moves: They're hard to pull off successfully. Referring to oneself as a novelistic character can seem contrived, cute, and overly clever. What's your assessment of how the method is working in the excerpt? Why might you want to take the risk of trying this approach?

3. This brief excerpt highlights a tension between journalism and fiction, between the novel and history, that very much interested Mailer. He concludes that it is only Mailer the Novelist who is capable of providing the best "instrument" for reporting the March on the Pentagon. It isn't necessary to take sides on this issue. More interesting is what *each* genre—fiction and nonfiction—offers in getting at the truth of public events like this one. What would you say about that?

Practicing the Craft

It's odd to write about yourself in the third person. Try it. Choose one of the following sentences as an opening line for a scene about yourself in a particular situation. Refer to yourself as he (or she) throughout.

He/she sat in the car.
He/she saw this moment as the end.
He/she heard the sound.
It was a smell that he/she always remembered.

Save this scene. Then copy and paste it into a new document. Using the Find tool in your word processing program, change into first person every third-person pronoun in the scene that refers to you. Print each of these out and lay them side by side. Are they different in subtle ways? What might be some motives for crafting a work of nonfiction in one point of view or the other?

Recommended Nonfiction by Norman Mailer

- *The Executioner's Song* (1980). Although before publication Mailer asked his publisher to call the book a novel, *The Executioner's Song* is in many ways an heir to the literary tradition sparked by Capote's *In Cold Blood*. The book is an extensively researched account of the life of Gary Gilmore, a killer who was executed in the late seventies by the state of Utah. Strangely, Mailer never considered the book among his best, but it was among his most popular; the book received the Pulitzer Prize in 1980.

- "Superman Comes to the Supermarket," *Esquire Magazine* (November 1960). Mailer's piece on the Democratic convention that nominated John F. Kennedy for president was recently ranked, along with Gay Talese's "Frank Sinatra Has a Cold," one of the seven "greatest stories" in the history of *Esquire Magazine.*

- *Miami and the Siege of Chicago* (1968). On the heels of the success of *The Armies of the Night*, Mailer wrote a similar treatment of the tumultuous Democratic and Republican conventions during a political year that was to provide exactly the kind of stories that brings out Mailer's best work.

- *The Fight* (1975). George Foreman and Muhammad Ali met in Africa for what was later called the best fight in the history of boxing. Mailer, this time using the persona "Norman," covered the event with his usual style, excess, and insight, with memorable and sympathetic characterizations of both fighters.

3.4

TOO FREAKING TRUE!

Excerpt from Tom Wolfe's The Electric Kool-Aid Acid Test

∽

The scene at one of the "acid tests," haphazardly organized events that Ken Kesey and others believed would transform consciousness.

The Excerpt in Context

As Tom Wolfe tells it, the assignment that changed the way he understood the possibilities of journalism was the one when he covered a custom car show in California for *Esquire*. He was interested in doing a different kind of piece, one that didn't, as he put it, make "gentle fun" of the "eccentric creeps and kooks" who lavished extravagant attention on custom cars back then. But he couldn't write it, even with the *Esquire* editor calling him on deadline to say that they were holding the pages, that they absolutely had to have the article immediately, and

136

if Wolfe couldn't write it he should just send in his notes and they would find someone who would. So Wolfe began a memorandum, intending to get the information together, and the thing just took off. After about 24 hours of nonstop writing, Wolfe sent the memorandum, and it was published in its entirety as "The Kandy-Kolored Tangerine-Flake Streamline Baby."

The title of the piece, a breathless combination of words unique to the world of custom cars, which are both intriguing and meaningless to the rest of us, hints at what is unique about Wolfe's contribution to literary journalism. He was keenly interested in two things: drilling into the subcultures that seem to be changing America and trying to find a language that matched his encounters with the people who inhabited these often-subterranean worlds. *The Electric Kool-Aid Acid Test* (1968), one of Wolfe's most enduring contributions to what he called the "New Journalism," reflects these interests in cultural phenomena and how they might be represented in language. The book reports on Wolfe's experience with Ken Kesey and his Merry Pranksters, an irreverent, visionary, and perpetually stoned group of misfits who, Wolfe believed, were engaged in a quasireligious cultural experiment. LSD was part of it. Kesey, author of *One Flew Over the Cuckoo's Nest* and other novels, was the brilliant provocateur of the project. The so-called "Acid Test," described in the excerpt that follows, was Kesey's attempt to create public events that might "communicate the experience" of the altered states LSD and other drugs might provide. They were to be public rituals. Ultimately, only a few "Acid Tests" were held, but Wolfe's accounts of the gatherings are among the most compelling scenes in his book.

❧ The Excerpt ❧

CAN
YOU
PASS THE
ACID TEST?

Anybody who could take LSD for the first time and go through all that without freaking out... Leary and Alpert[6] preached "set and setting." Everything in taking LSD, in having a fruitful, freakout-free LSD

From: Thomas Wolfe, *The Electric Kool-Aid Acid Test* (New York: Bantam, 1969), 207–208.

[6]Dr. Timothy Leary and his collaborator Timothy Alpert cofounded the International Foundation for Internal Freedom on the Harvard University campus in 1962, an institute dedicated to researching the experience of taking LSD and its potential for changing behavior.

experience, depended on set and setting. You should take it in some serene and attractive setting, a house or apartment decorated with objects—of the honest sort, Turkoman tapestries, Greek goatskin rugs, Cost Plus blue jugs, soft light—not Japanese paper globe light, however, but untasselated Chinese textile shades—in short, an Uptown Bohemian country retreat of the $60,000-a-year sort, ideally, with Mozart's *Requiem* issuing with liturgical solemnity from the hi-fi. The "set" was the set of your mind. You should prepare for the experience by meditating upon the state of your being and deciding what you hope to discover or achieve on this voyage into the self. You should also have a guide who has taken LSD himself and is familiar with the various stages of the experience and whom you know and trust... and Fuck that! That only clamped the constipation of the past, the eternal *lags,* on something that should happen *Now.* Let the setting be as unserene and lurid as the Prankster arts can make it and let your set be only what is on your... *brain,* man, and let your guide, your trusty hand-holding, head-swaddling guide, be a bunch of Day-Glo crazies who have as one of their mottoes: "Never trust a Prankster." The Acid Tests would be like the Angels' party[7] plus all the ideas that had gone into the Dome fantasy. Everybody would take acid, any time they wanted, six hours before the Test began or the moment they got there, at whatever point in the trip they wanted to enter the new planet. In any event, they would be on a new planet.

The mysteries of the synch! Very strange... the Acid Tests turned out, in fact, to be an art form foreseen in that strange book, *Childhood's End,*[8] a form called "total identification": "The history of the cinema gave the clue to their actions. First, sound, then color, then stereoscopy, then Cinerama, had made the old 'moving pictures' more and more like reality itself. Where was the end of the story? Sure the final stage would be reached when the audience forgot it was the audience, and became part of the action. To achieve this would involve stimulation of all the senses, and perhaps hypnosis as well... When the goal was attained, there would be an enormous enrichment of human experience. A man could become—for a while, at least,—any other person, and could take part in any conceivable adventure, real or imaginary.... And when the 'program' was over, he would have acquired a memory as vivid as any experience in his actual life—indeed, indistinguishable from reality itself."

Too freaking true! ❧

---

[7]For a time, Kesey's Pranksters developed a strong relationship with the motorcycle gang Hell's Angels.
[8]A 1953 science fiction novel.

Analyzing the Craft

1. Tom Wolfe, well-known for his rakish white suits, is as interested in prose style as he is in stylish clothing. Most writers care about style, of course. But one of the things that most distinguishes *The Electric Kool-Aid Acid Test* was Wolfe's effort to find a language that would express the supposedly ineffable: in this case, the LSD experience and the Pranksters' sometimes brilliant, sometimes nutty, and often quasireligious "understandings" of their acid test project. Among other things, Wolfe frequently uses odd punctuation, especially colons (::::::::::) and ellipses, as well as repetition and abrupt transition. In an author's note at the end of the book, Wolfe writes that he has "tried not only to tell what the Pranksters did but to recreate the mental atmosphere or subjective reality of it." He pushed language in an attempt to capture that "subjective reality." What is your impression of how Wolfe manipulated style in the passage, and what effect do you think it had?

2. In his famous essay, "The New Journalism," Wolfe says that there are four elements essential to the form: scene-by-scene construction, realistic dialogue, third-person point of view, and "status" details, or particulars about characters that "express their position in the world or what they think it is or they hope it to be." Analyze the excerpt by applying Wolfe's four devices.

3. Both Norman Mailer (see page 132) and Tom Wolfe wrote about American subcultures; Mailer focused on the antiwar movement and Wolfe focused on prophets of the psychedelic experience. Each writer began with this question: How will I narrate this story? And each writer answered that question differently. Mailer narrated his story from Mailer's point of view, told from the third person. For the most part, Wolfe narrated *Acid Test* from his subjects' points of view, especially Ken Kesey's. When writing as an outsider of the group that is your subject, what are the risks and benefits of each approach?

Practicing the Craft

How do you punctuate thoughts? In what ways can style represent experience? These are some of the questions at the heart of *The Electric Kool-Aid Acid Test* and much of Wolfe's nonfiction. With brilliant playfulness, he deploys punctuation to capture the wildly fragmentary nature of thought, as in this sentence:

> They would take wax pencils, different colors, and scrawl out symbols for each other to improvise on: Sandy the pink drum strokes there, and he would make a sound like *chee-oonh-chunh, chee-oonh-chunh,* and so forth, and

Kesey the guitar arrows there, *broinga broinga brang brang,* and Jane Burton the bursts of scat vocals there, and Bob Stone the Voice Over stories to the background of the Human Jazz—all of it recorded on the tape recorder—and then all soaring on—what?—acid, peyote, morning-glory seeds, which were very hell to choke down, billions of bilious seeds mulching out in sodden dandelions in your belly, bloated—but soaring!—...

Write to the edge of your own prose style for a moment.

- Think about an experience that took five minutes or less—a first kiss, a near-drowning experience, the first moments you watched the Trade Center Towers fall on TV, a skiing accident;;;;;;;;;;;;whatever;;;;;;;;;; you;;;;;;;;;;;remember (or think you remember);;;;;;well.....that,,,,,,,,,,,, made you feel!!!!!!!!!!!!something.

- In your journal, write fast for three or four minutes in the present tense, putting yourself back into that moment. Don't bother providing backstory. Just jump into the moment.

- Now rewrite the material into a paragraph that attempts to use style as a way of representing how it felt, what you thought, and how you saw that moment as you experienced it. Think about this as an experiment in using language to capture, in some small way, your own consciousness. Play with punctuation, especially.

Recommended Nonfiction by Tom Wolfe

- *The Right Stuff* (1979). While *Acid Test* will always be remembered as the book that established Wolfe's credentials as a literary journalist, *The Right Stuff*, a look into the American space program, is arguably Wolfe's most critically acclaimed work of creative nonfiction. Unlike his method for much of his earlier work, for *The Right Stuff* Wolfe relied less on immersion reporting; instead, he researched events that had already occurred.

- "The New Journalism" (1973). This landmark essay, the introduction to an anthology Wolfe edited with E. W. Johnson with the same title, is a must-read for writers who want to understand Wolfe's argument that journalism could compete with the novel as a genre of literary realism.

3.5

A FINE, SOLEMN SWAGGER

Excerpt from Jane Kramer's
The Last Cowboy

Gary Cooper in the 1952 film High Noon. *Both the actor and the film inspired Henry Blanton, the man who Jane Kramer profiled in* The Last Cowboy.

The Excerpt in Context

One of the great mysteries and marvels of Jane Kramer's portrait of a man she called Henry Blanton is how successfully she insinuated herself into the man's life. The author of *The Last Cowboy* and the man she profiled could not have been more different. Blanton was a 40-year-old Texas cowboy who admitted that "cowboys don't like the company of women much," and Kramer was a New Yorker and, of course, a woman. Yet it's obvious from her rich and sympathetic story of Blanton that he must have allowed her extraordinary access to his life. The profile genre is a common magazine feature, often brief enough to require a single interview, but Kramer's book-length masterpiece on Henry Blanton demanded the kind of "immersion reporting" that is only possible by spending considerable time with the interview subject and others who knew him. It also demands extraordinary note-taking skills. *The Last Cowboy* features, for instance, moments of interior monologue with not only Blanton but also his wife, Betsy, and extended conversations between Blanton and fellow cowboys while they castrate and dehorn cattle. This is more than good journalism. What makes Kramer's book a literary accomplishment is her success in creating in Blanton a complex character that is as good as any in the best fiction.

The Last Cowboy follows Blanton as he performs his duties as a ranch manager on a large spread near Amarillo and as he gets into trouble in town. The narrative is interrupted with digressions about Blanton's background as well as the historic changes that were taking place in the ranching business at the time, including the shift in ownership from long-time ranching families to young businessmen in air-conditioned Buicks. Cowboys were still essential for these modern operations, but with the rise of feedlots, there was little time on the range. Blanton grieved these changes, and he found solace in knocking back whiskey and knocking heads. Kramer's book is about a very ordinary and flawed man. He is, as you will see in the following excerpt, prone to sentimental, even naïve, ideas about himself and the life he leads. But he is also tough and principled in a way that is easy to admire. Part of Kramer's purpose is to give us the man but also to dramatize the mythology that surrounds men like him. Reality and myth collide in *The Last Cowboy*, and Henry Blanton humanizes this tragedy in ways that make it meaningful and often moving. Virtually all profiles, long or short, feature a description of their subject. This excerpt is the first extended look at Blanton, appearing within the first 20 pages of the book, and it creates an impression that lasts in the many pages that follow. Jane Kramer's carefully crafted description of the cowboy is a textbook case in how to put details and narrative to work in the service of creating a dominant impression of someone.

❧ *The Excerpt* ❧

Henry liked wearing black. The Virginian, he had heard, wore black, and so had Gary Cooper in the movie "High Noon," and now Henry wore it with a kind of innocent pride, as if the color carried respect and a hero's stern, elegant qualities. Once, Betsy discovered him at the bathroom mirror dressed in his black gear, his eyes narrowed and his right hand poised over an imaginary holster. She teased him about it then—at least, until he got so mad that he stayed out half the night in town drinking—but a few weeks later she took a snapshot of him in that same gear and sent it to the Philip Morris company, with a note saying that in her opinion Henry Blanton was much more impressive as a cowboy than the people they used to advertise their Marlboro cigarettes. Henry was, in fact, a handsome man. He was tall and rugged, and ranch life had seasoned the smooth, round face that grinned, embarrassed, in the tinted wedding picture that Betsy kept on the upright piano in her parlor. There was a fine-lined, weathered look about Henry at forty. Too much bourbon and beer had put a gut on him, but his gray eyes were clear and quick most days, and often humorous, and his sandy hair had got thick and wiry as it grayed—a little rumpled and overgrown, because he hated haircuts, though never long enough to cause comment in a cowboy bar. He had a fine, solemn swagger. Saturday nights at the country-and-Western dance in Pampa, he thumped around the floor, serious and sweating, and the women liked to watch him—there was something boyish and charming about his grave self-consciousness. When he was younger, he used to laugh and bow and shake hands with everybody after a good polka. Now, more often than not, he blinked and looked around, suddenly embarrassed, and his laugh was loud and nervous, and made the women who had been watching him uncomfortable. ❧

Analyzing the Craft

1. The visual equivalent to a character profile is the portrait. A face fills the frame, and there is no doubt at all about what (or who, in this case) the subject is. When we describe someone in writing, the task is both easier and harder than taking a photographic portrait. It is easier because we don't have to rely on a single moment to capture our subject, and it's harder because we must do with language what the camera does with an image—help others *see* someone. There is so much we might say. What

From: Jane Kramer, *The Last Cowboy*, 1977 (London: Pimlico, 1998) 17–18.

do we choose and how do we choose it? What do you infer from the excerpt about how Kramer answered this question?

2. A physical description of someone is *rendered*; that is, a writer doesn't simply list details—this is what he looked like, this is how he moved, and this is how he talked—but shapes and shaves the material to create a dominant impression. In a few words, what is your dominant impression of Henry Blanton, and what one detail speaks to you most in influencing that impression? Why?

3. What might be the logic behind the way Kramer organized the material in the excerpt?

Practicing the Craft

He had a strange taste in clothes.
Henry valued authority.
She often kidnapped silence.

Each of these is a particular rendering of a character, just one of many things that might be said about someone. In fiction, this rendering is invented to serve the story in some way; in nonfiction, characterization still serves the story, but it must be based on what you have learned about the person you're writing about. The evidence you gather must convince you that this impression is truthful. What kinds of evidence might you gather? The excerpt suggests some—physical description, anecdote, secondhand impressions and observations, and telling details. A good literary journalist studiously collects all this information and then selects from it to craft a particular way of seeing a person.

Get some practice with this. Craft a sketch about someone, roughly the length of the Kramer excerpt, that begins with a sentence like the three examples—some interpretation or dominant impression around which you organize the material. Do this about someone you've interviewed for a minimum of 30 minutes. This can be anyone. When you do the interview and draft your sketch, do the following:

- Take extensive notes, gathering the kind of evidence that will help you write the sketch: anecdotes, physical descriptions, self-descriptions, observations, and so on.

- If possible, interview others who know your subject, and collect information on their impressions.

- Immediately following your interview, fastwrite in your notebook for four or five minutes about your own initial impressions of your subject. What was most memorable?

- Write your character sketch in the past tense, as Kramer did.
- Work toward focusing your sketch on *a single idea* you have about your subject: a dominant impression, a quality that seems representative of a larger group to which the subject identifies (e.g., Henry is a remnant of cowboy culture in the modern era), or a comment about why your subject is worthy of a profile.

Recommended Nonfiction by Jane Kramer

- *The Lone Patriot* (2003). This book draws on many of the gifts that Kramer demonstrates in *The Last Cowboy*—a keen eye, elegant prose, incisive characterization, and dedication to her subject. *The Lone Patriot* tells the story of John Pitner, who was a leader in the right-wing militia movement in Washington state. The group cultivates conspiracy theories and festering hatred for minorities, which is both sad and serious. On the other hand, the militiamen prove so ineffectual that the story is at times comic.
- *Whose Art Is It?* (1994). First published in *The New Yorker*, the magazine with which Kramer has served as a staff writer for 40 years, "Whose Art Is It?" won the National Magazine Award in 1993. It is an extraordinarily readable and intelligent exploration of how one "public art" project in New York became a case study for the question that is the book's title.

3.6

CLAUSTROPHOBIA

Excerpt from Erik Larson's
The Devil in the White City

❧

While Chicago celebrated the success of its 1893 World Exposition at the quickly erected White City, pictured here, Dr. H. H. Holmes was engaged in a killing spree that claimed as many as 27 lives.

The Excerpt in Context

Erik Larson's bestselling *The Devil in the White City* (2003) tells two parallel stories: the realization of the dreams of leading Chicagoans who planned to host the 1893 World's Fair, and the calculations of a serial murderer named Dr. H. H. Holmes, a psychopath who used the fair to further his macabre purposes. In this meticulously researched book, Larson shifts back and forth between the two narratives, the one describing the efforts of some of the late nineteenth century's leading architects and developers who create a "Great White City" by the lake and the other describing the dark heart of a methodical and charming killer.

Larson's work is both a historical and literary triumph. He finds in the story of the Chicago World's Fair insight into the ambitions of Americans on the threshold of a new century, anticipating the wonders of new technology and worshipping wealth like never before. As a work of nonfiction literature, *The Devil in the White City* is a compelling story, and the symbolism of Holmes's dark deeds next to the rise of the white city resonates throughout the narrative. While the book may read at times like a novel, Larsen insists on its authenticity. "However strange or macabre some of the following incidents might seem," he writes, "this is *not* a work of fiction."

As you know, there is a great deal of controversy among readers and writers of nonfiction about what constitutes "truth-telling" in the form. We usually assume, of course, that if we're reading nonfiction, the events described actually happened; but do we agree that the details of those events should be accurate down to the color of the yellowed wallpaper? What's at stake here for readers of nonfiction? Even less understood, what's at stake for *writers* of nonfiction when they flirt with telling lies in their work—even small ones? In this excerpt, Larson describes the murder of Anna, the sister of a woman named Minnie, to whom Harry Holmes is briefly married. The three of them—Anna, Minnie, and Holmes—were to travel together; instead, Holmes murders both women.

The excerpt is an exquisitely rendered series of scenes and includes interior monologues from both Anna and Holmes. Typically, these monologues are only possible in nonfiction through interview, but in the case of these historical figures, Larson is forced to be more speculative. In his endnotes, Larson explains that this version of Anna's murder is based in part on another writer's speculation in a previously published biography of the killer. This account suggested that Holmes "led her toward the vault" on the pretense of needing a forgotten document. "Something like this might have occurred," writes Larson, "although I think my proposal that Holmes sent her into the vault on a false errand . . . would have suited more closely his temperament." In news journalism, this kind of speculation would be unacceptable. But what about literary journalism? Does Larson err when he assumes that, in the service of the story, he can use such speculation to construct a scene presented implicitly as fact? There is no easy answer to these questions, nor is there a correct one. What does seem clear, however, is how effectively Larson uses what he *does* know about both Holmes and Anna to craft a dramatic moment in the story he tells.

❧ *The Excerpt* ❧

Holmes knew that most if not all of his hotel guests would be at the fair. He showed Anna the drugstore, restaurant, and barbershop and took her up to the roof to give her a broader view of Englewood and the pretty, tree-shaded neighborhood that surrounded his corner. He ended the tour at his office, where be offered Anna a seat and excused himself. He picked up a sheaf of papers and began reading.

Distractedly, he asked Anna if she would mind going into the adjacent room, the walk-in vault, to retrieve for him a document he had left inside.

Cheerfully, she complied.

Holmes followed quietly.

∿∿∿∿

At first it seemed as though the door had closed by accident. The room was utterly without light. Anna pounded on the door and called for Harry. She listened, then pounded again. She was not frightened, just embarrassed. She did not like the darkness, which was more complete than anything she had ever experienced—far darker, certainly, than any moonless night in Texas. She rapped the door with her knuckles and listened again.

The air grew stale.

∿∿∿∿

Holmes listened. He sat peacefully in a chair by the wall that separated his office and the vault. Time passed. It was really very peaceful. A soft breeze drifted through the room, cross-ventilation being one of the benefits of a corner office. The breeze, still cool, carried the morning scent of prairie grasses and moist soil.

∿∿∿∿

Anna removed her shoe and beat the heel against the door. The room was growing warmer. Sweat filmed her face and arms. She guessed that Harry, unaware of her plight, had gone elsewhere in the building. That would explain why he still had not come despite her pounding. Perhaps he had gone to check on something in the shops below. As she considered this, she became a bit frightened. The room had grown substantially warmer. Catching a clean breath was difficult. And she needed a bathroom.

From: Erik Larson, *The Devil in the White City* (New York: Vintage, 2003), 294–295.

He would be so apologetic. She could not show him how afraid she was. She tried shifting her thoughts to the journey they would begin that afternoon. That she, a Texas schoolmarm, soon would be walking the streets of London and Paris still seemed an impossibility, yet Harry had promised it and made all the arrangements. In just a few hours she would board a train for the short trip to Milwaukee, and soon afterward she, Minnie, and Harry would be on their way to the lovely, cool valley of the St. Lawrence River, between New York and Canada. She saw herself sitting on the spacious porch of some fine riverside hotel, sipping tea and watching the sun descend.

She hammered the door again and now also the wall between the vault and Harry's breeze-filled office. ✎

Analyzing the Craft

1. Here's one way to think about the difference between description and scene: One is static, and the other is dynamic. Something usually *happens* in a scene, though it isn't necessarily dramatic. People do things. We know that prose action is powered by verbs, and not just any will do. Underline the verbs in the excerpt. As you look at them together, what do you notice about the kinds of verbs Larson chose and the characters' movements in the scene, in order, that the verbs enact. When you visualize this movement, what do you notice?

2. In the first section, consider the following sentence: "A soft breeze drifted through the room, cross-ventilation being one of the benefits of a corner office. The breeze, still cool, carried the morning scent of prairie grasses and moist soil." Remember that Larson could not be physically present in Holmes's office at this moment. How then could he have written these two sentences? Does this raise any ethical issues? What other lines or passages might be contested in terms of accuracy or truthfulness?

3. The scene is rendered in separate segments, each shifting point of view from one character to the other. Alternatively, Larson could have written the scene more conventionally, in a more continuous narrative without the breaks. Why might he have chosen not to do this?

Practicing the Craft

Erik Larson relied heavily on archival material to tell his story, a common source of information for the writer of historical narratives. For crafting a scene like the one in the excerpt, a character's first-person account of what happened and, if possible, what he or she was thinking when it occurred is obviously most reliable. However, a secondhand account, particularly if the observer talked to the character about the event, can be an excellent substitute.

Try your hand at crafting a scene using archival material.

In 1927, the famous slugger Babe Ruth was poised to break his own home-run record of 59 in a season. On September 30th, in the eighth inning of a game between the New York Yankees—Ruth's team—and the Washington Senators, Ruth was at bat against pitcher Tom Zachary. It was the second-to-last game of the season. When the count was two balls and one strike, Ruth connected and hit the ball far into the right-hand bleachers. He sauntered nonchalantly around the bases, tipping his hat to the exuberant crowd in Yankee stadium, and then planted his foot on home base. It was a record that would stand for 34 years.

The following passage is an account of that moment by Ruth's second wife, Clair Ruth, who attended the game. Use this material to craft a scene of the event *from Babe Ruth's point of view*. You can also find additional material—including a video of Ruth hitting the home run—if you search online.

> The pennant race was over by September, but Babe was fighting to break his 59 home-run record. He needed 17 to do it in the last month, or better than one every two days. He did it of course. The 60th was made in Yankee Stadium against Washington. Tom Zachary, a left-hander, was the pitcher, and the homer came in the final game.
>
> The Babe had smashed out two home runs the day before to bring his total to 59 for the season, or the exact equal of his 1921 record. He had only this game to set a new record. Zachary, a left-hander, was by the nature of his delivery a hard man for the Babe to hit. In fact, the Babe got only two homers in all his life against Tom.
>
> Babe came up in the eighth inning and it was quite probable that this would be his very last chance to break his own record. My mother and I were at the game and I can still see that lovely, lovely home run. It was a tremendous poke, deep into the stands. There was never any doubt that it was going over the fence. But the question was, would it be fair? It was fair by only six glorious inches!
>
> The Babe later professed himself to be unimpressed and unexcited and certainly not surprised by the blow. "I knew I was going to hit it," he insisted. I didn't, although I was now used to his rising to occasions.
>
> What delighted him as much, more than the homer, was the spectacle of his pal, Charlie O'Leary, jumping and screaming on the coaching lines, his bald head glinting in the falling sun. Charlie had thrown away his cap in jubilation when the umps signaled the ball fair.
>
> Babe knew the extent of Charlie's joy because he knew his little friend was almost psychopathic about his bald dome. They didn't play the "Star-Spangled Banner" before every game then, only on festive occasions. On these occasions

Charlie would hide. The baring of Charlie's gleaming head was an appreciated tribute to the popularity of that historic homer.[9]

An exercise like this is great practice for your own work, for which you might use primary and secondary sources to craft a scene that you couldn't have witnessed firsthand. This is an essential skill for writers of historical narratives like Larsen but is relevant to essays and memoirs as well. For example, I can do more than simply imagine what my father was thinking when he was in his final days of alcohol rehab in Hazelden, Minnesota, because I have his journal entries and other first-person accounts of the treatment regime there. I also can find a photograph of the facility in the 1970s. However, it is impossible to be completely certain about what a person thought or felt without asking him or her, but there is always a perfectly acceptable hedge: *perhaps.*

The Babe at bat

Recommended Nonfiction by Erik Larson

- *Isaac's Storm* (1999). Larson brought his considerable narrative and research skills to another historical event—the Galveston hurricane in 1900—a storm that is still considered one of the nation's worst natural disasters. The book's title refers to Isaac Cline, a meteorologist who dismissed the danger and who stands in for the larger theme of American hubris at the turn of the century.

[9]This eyewitness account appears in the following books: Mrs. Babe Ruth with Bill Slocum, *The Babe and I* (1959); Robert Creamer, *Babe: The Legend Comes to Life* (1974); Marshall Smelser, *The Life That Ruth Built: A Biography* (1975).

3.7

A FOOD FOR WHAT AILS YOU

An Excerpt from Joseph Mitchell's
Old Mr. Flood

For 183 years, New York City's Fulton Fish Market was one of the largest wholesale fish markets on the East Coast and hosted characters like this one, pictured at about the time that the writer Joseph Mitchell haunted the docks. In 2005, the fish market was closed and moved to a new location.

The Excerpt in Context

Decades before the advent of the "New Journalism," Joseph Mitchell was crafting long works of nonfiction about "low-life" characters in New York City that relied on scene, dialogue, and strong characterization—the qualities we often associate with good fiction. Mitchell, a newspaper reporter, joined *The New Yorker* staff in its heyday, sharing an office with E. B. White, forging a lifelong friendship with A. J. Liebling, and being edited by the magazine's founder, Harold Ross. Mitchell was considered "the finest writer" on *The New Yorker* staff, according to Brendan Gill, who also wrote for the magazine. Literary critic Malcolm Cowley called Mitchell "the best reporter in the country" and compared his work in quality and subject matter to the best novels of Charles Dickens.

It's striking that such a pioneer of literary journalism is largely unknown to students of the genre. Mitchell's *New Yorker* essays were later published as books, including *McSorley's Wonderful Saloon* (1943), *The Bottom of the Harbor* (1960), and *Old Mr. Flood* (1948). All of them were successful, but after the publication of his last work in 1964, *Joe Gould's Secret,* Mitchell never published another piece, though he diligently returned to his desk at *The New Yorker* until he died in 1996. "The city changed on me.... I can't seem to get anything finished anymore," Mitchell offered as a possible explanation for this long silence. "The hideous state the world is in just defeats the kind of writing I used to do." The kind of writing Mitchell used to do was profiles of people like the man he called Mr. H. G. Flood, a 92-year-old former contractor who lived in an old hotel near Fulton Fish Market in New York City and spent his days drinking whiskey and hunting down fresh fish for his next meal. Flood vowed to live until July 27, 1965, when he would turn 115. His fish-only diet would be the reason for his longevity, he said.

It is no coincidence that July 27, 1965, was Mitchell's own birthday. Old Mr. Flood was a composite character, not a real person. "Mr. Flood is not one man," Mitchell wrote in an introduction to the story, "combined in him are aspects of several old men who work or hang out in Fulton Fish Market, or who did in the past. I wanted these stories to be truthful rather than factual, but they are solidly based on facts." The composite character in nonfiction is troubling to some who believe it crosses over the blurry genre line and into fiction. But for Mitchell it was a practical solution to a real problem: None of the Fish Market men would fully cooperate with him on a profile, so Mitchell's editor at *The New Yorker*, William Shawn, suggested the composite.

The excerpt that follows appears a few pages into Mitchell's profile of Mr. Flood, the last few paragraphs of a rich characterization of the man. The opening of the piece focuses on Mr. Flood's fondness for seafood, especially the fish parts most other people won't eat—"fried cod tongues, cheeks, and sounds, sounds being the gelatinous air bladders along the cod's backbone." Eating something that "most people would edge away from," says Mr. Flood, makes him feel "superior," and he insists on the simplest preparation. Fish cooks can be drunk, but "they have to be old," Mr. Flood adds. "It takes almost a lifetime to learn how to do a thing simply."

◌ *The Excerpt* ◌

Mr. Flood doesn't think much of doctors and never goes near one. He passes many evenings in a comfortable old spindle-back chair in the barroom of the Hartford House, drinking Scotch and tap water and arguing, and sometimes late at night he unaccountably switches to brandy and wakes up next morning with an overwhelming hangover—what he calls a katzenjammer. On these occasions he goes over to S. A. Brown's, at 28 Fulton Street, a highly aromatic little drugstore which was opened during President Thomas Jefferson's second term and which specializes in outfitting medicine chests for fishing boats, and buys a bottle of Dr. Brown's Next Morning, a proprietary greatly respected in the fish market. For all other ailments, physical or mental, he eats raw oysters. Once, in the Hartford barroom, a trembly fellow in his seventies, another tenant of the hotel, turned to Mr. Flood and said, "Flood, I had a birthday last week. I'm getting on. I'm not long for this world."

Mr. Flood snorted angrily. "Well, by God, I am," he said. "I just got started."

The trembly fellow sighed and said, "I'm all out of whack. I'm going uptown and see my doctor."

Mr. Flood snorted again. "Oh, shut up," he said. "Damn your doctor! I tell you what you do. You get right out of here and go over to Libby's oyster house and tell the man you want to eat some of his big oysters. Don't sit down. Stand up at that fine marble bar they got over there, where you can watch the man knife them open. And tell him you intend to drink the oyster liquor; he'll knife them on the cup shell, so the liquor won't spill. And be sure you get the big ones. Get them so big you'll have to rear back to swallow, the size that most restaurants use for fries and stews; God forgive them, they don't know any better. Ask for Robbins Islands, Mattitucks, Cape Cods, or Saddle Rocks. And don't put any of that red sauce on them, that cocktail sauce, that mess, that gurry. Ask the man for half a lemon, poke it a time or two to free the juice, and squeeze it over the oysters. And the first one he knifes, pick it up and smell it, the way you'd smell a rose, or a shot of brandy. That briny, seaweedy fragrance will clear your head; it'll make your blood run faster. And don't just eat six; take your time and eat a dozen, eat two dozen, eat three dozen, eat four dozen. And then leave the man a generous tip and go buy yourself a fifty-cent cigar and put your hat

From: Joseph Mitchell, "Old Mr. Flood," Up in the Old Hotel (New York: Vintage, 1993), 378–379.

on the side of your head and take a walk down to Bowling Green. Look at the sky! Isn't it blue? And look at the girls a-tap-tap-tapping past on their pretty little feet! Aren't they just the finest girls you ever saw, the bounciest, the rumpiest, the laughingest? Aren't you ashamed of yourself for even thinking about spending good money on a damned doctor? And along about here, you better be careful. You're apt to feel so bucked-up you'll slap strangers on the back, or kick a window in, or fight a cop, or jump on the tailboard of a truck and steal a ride." ❧

Analyzing the Craft

1. When I was writing about Mr. Flood in the introduction to the excerpt, I couldn't shake the knowledge that he was a composite character. I was tempted to call him "Mr. Flood" (with the quotation marks) to signal that perhaps the name shouldn't be taken literally—this man with that name never really walked this earth. Did your awareness that Mitchell crafted this character from more than one person affect your reading of the excerpt? Does it matter?

2. In more than half of this excerpt, we hear Mr. Flood talk, and the passage ends with a long, unbroken monologue. This kind of extended quotation is a little unusual, though the literary journalist John McPhee uses it frequently. What do you think of the technique? You can imagine that it requires the writer to take excellent notes, lean heavily on a recorder, or both. Why might it be worth all that work to craft a monologue like the one in the Mitchell excerpt?

3. Mr. Flood is an ordinary person and a literary character. Obviously, the convergence of those two things—a literary profile and a subject who happens to be fascinating or unusual—isn't that common. People are much more likely to be ordinary, knowing little, say, about the curative powers of Saddle Rock or Mattituck oysters. Is this true, and if it is, is this a problem? In other words, can any character be as interesting as a Mr. Flood?

Practicing the Craft

Mitchell's success with these pieces, like Truman Capote's with *In Cold Blood*, depended on his empathy with the people he wrote about, a keen eye for detail, and a tremendous amount of time listening. We all want to be listened to, which is one reason why people, despite their initial reservations, are usually delighted to be interviewed. The stories of older people like Mr. Flood can be particularly compelling, perhaps because the stories they choose to tell may very well be those that most define their character.

The Veterans History Project, a program of the Library of Congress, offers writers a rich online database of interviews with survivors of the last century's major wars: World War II, the Korean War, and the Vietnam War. This material provides excellent listening practice and a chance to try to see a character in the story he or she tells. You can find the Veterans History Project at the following URL: http://www.loc.gov/vets/.

From the home page, you can find audio (and sometimes video) files of veterans talking about their war experiences. Choose a few to listen to or watch (the link to "featured interviews" can be a good place to start). Listen to all or a portion of the audio, and then focus on four or five minutes that you find most compelling. Take notes.

Drawing on this material, craft a long paragraph like the following example that I wrote using material from the site. Your short piece should tell a revealing story about your subject and its historical context. Because you are writing about people who participated in public events—battles overseas or service back home—you may find information online that will help you write this flash profile. But especially work with the material the subjects provide in their interviews, and actively look for opportunities to incorporate their voices.

> Dan Akee remembers stepping over the bodies, so numerous and so randomly scattered that they seemed like "trash." After the third day, it broke him. "I was getting tired of all the battles I went through," Akee said. "I was scared." By the time the five marines and one navy corpsman raised the flag on Mt. Suribachi in the famous photograph, Iwo Jima was littered with the dead, and Akee was not among them. One reason, perhaps, is that when he went crazy after hours of Japanese shelling, Akee did not run out of his foxhole. He imagined it. "I felt like I was running. We should go, that's on my mind. But somehow I left there. I was out of my mind. Before I left... the foxhole, I sat down, and I said 'God help me. I'm too young to die.'"

Recommended Nonfiction by
Joseph Mitchell

- *Up in the Old Hotel* (1993). This extraordinary collection of Mitchell's work draws on over 50 years of his *New Yorker* pieces, all of which were published in four earlier books: *McSorely's Wonderful Saloon* (1943), *Old Mr. Flood* (1948), *The Bottom of the Harbor* (1960), and *Joe Gould's Secret* (1964). For Mitchell fans, *Up in the Old Hotel* is a constant source of delight and a little sadness, too, because his published work came to an abrupt halt after *Joe Gould's Secret*. For decades, however, he went to work at his *New Yorker* office anyway, and if Mitchell was writing, we may yet see more from this lion of literary journalism.

3.8

A LIGHT TOUCH OF THE LIPS

Excerpt from Diane Ackerman's
A Natural History of the Senses

∾

Photographer Alfred Eisenstaedt's picture, "V-J Day in Times Square" is one of the more famous kissing images. Diane Ackerman suggests in A Natural History of the Senses *that kissing is as much about "inhaling scent" as it is about touching lips.*

The Excerpt in Context

There are four sources of information for nonfiction writing: memory, observation, interview, and reading. Conventional schooling in writing often misleads novice writers into thinking each of these is directly related to certain forms of nonfiction writing. For instance, some assume the personal essay draws exclusively from memory and never from research, and think the profile is based only on interviews and never on memory. While it's true that certain forms of writing are loosely related to particular sources of information, most nonfiction writers don't think much about that relationship. Most writers simply discover questions that interest them, and then cast a wide net for information—any kind of information—that will help them explore those questions. You will find, for example, that a personal essay by Annie Dillard might include information from a scientific article on weasels, or an essay on the social habits of ants by Lewis Thomas might include his personal observations of scientists at a professional meeting in Atlantic City.

Diane Ackerman's nonfiction exemplifies how a writer's sense of wonder can lead her to draw from many wells. Her most famous early work, *A Natural History of the Senses*, combines personal experience and observation, interview, and extensive research. The book takes each of the five senses in turn, and in a final chapter explores *synesthesia*, or how the senses stimulate each other. In the excerpt that follows from the chapter on touch, Ackerman opens with a personal anecdote about summer camp, but then she arcs away into exposition about the cultural origins of kissing—prose that could easily be burdened by the weight of fact. Though Ackerman's nonfiction is often heavily researched, it never reads like a research paper. This isn't easily accomplished. We are drawn to the power of story and hesitate to turn narratives toward fact because we know the risk: Exposition can be dull. Somehow the best nonfiction writers—Diane Ackerman, John McPhee, Susan Orlean, Tracy Kidder, Lewis Thomas, and others—manage to avoid this.

Diane Ackerman is also a poet, and certainly her grace with words distinguishes this excerpt, a passage that forms a tight weave of personal experience, biblical history, anthropology, and biology. A close analysis of her writing, especially in the final paragraph of the passage, yields insight into how a skilled nonfiction writer's turn to research seems a natural move. Ackerman's work teaches that temporarily abandoning narrative for exposition is not as risky as it often seems.

⚜ *The Excerpt* ⚜

When I was in high school in the early sixties, nice girls didn't go all the way—most of us wouldn't have known how to. But man, could we kiss! We kissed for hours in the busted-up front seat of a borrowed Chevy, which, in motion, sounded like a broken dinette set; we kissed inventively, clutching our boyfriends from behind as we straddled motorcycles, whose vibrations turned our hips to jelly; we kissed extravagantly beside a turtlearium in the park, or at the local rose garden or zoo; we kissed delicately, in waves of sipping and puckering; we kissed torridly, with tongues like hot pokers; we kissed timelessly, because lovers throughout the ages knew our longing; we kissed wildly, almost painfully, with tough, soul-stealing rigor; we kissed elaborately, as if we were inventing kisses for the first time; we kissed furtively when we met in the hallways between classes; we kissed soulfully in the shadows at concerts, the way we thought musical knights of passion like The Righteous Brothers and their ladies did; we kissed articles of clothing or objects belonging to our boyfriends; we kissed our hands when we blew our boyfriends kisses across the street; we kissed our pillows at night, pretending they were mates; we kissed shamelessly, with all the robust sappiness of youth; we kissed as if kissing could save us from ourselves.

Just before I went off to summer camp, which is what fourteen-year-old girls in suburban Pennsylvania did to mark time, my boyfriend, whom my parents did not approve of (wrong religion) and had forbidden me to see, used to walk five miles across town each evening, and climb in through my bedroom window just to kiss me. These were not open-mouthed "French" kisses, which we didn't know about, and they weren't accompanied by groping. They were just earth-stopping, soulful, on-the-ledge-of-adolescence kissing, when you press your lips together and yearn so hard you feel faint. We wrote letters while I was away, but when school started again in the fall the affair seemed to fade of its own accord. I still remember those summer nights, how my boyfriend would hide in my closet if my parents or brother chanced in, and then kiss me for an hour or so and head back home before dark, and I marvel at his determination and the power of a kiss.

A kiss seems the smallest movement of the lips, yet it can capture emotions wild as kindling, or be a contract, or dash a mystery. Some cultures just don't do much kissing. In *The Kiss and Its History,* Dr. Christopher Nyrop refers to Finnish tribes "which bathe together in a state of complete nudity," but regard kissing "as something indecent." Certain African tribes, whose lips are decorated, mutilated, stretched or in other ways deformed,

From: Diane Ackerman, *A Natural History of the Senses* (New York: Random House, 1990), 109–110.

don't kiss. But they are unusual. Most people on the planet greet one another face to face; their greeting may take many forms, but it usually includes kissing, nose-kissing, or nose-saluting. There are many theories about how kissing began. Some authorities, as noted, believe it evolved from the act of smelling someone's face, inhaling them out of friendship or love in order to gauge their mood and well-being. There are cultures today in which people greet one another by putting their heads together and inhaling the other's essence. Some sniff each other's hands. The mucous membranes of the lips are exquisitely sensitive, and we often use the mouth to taste texture while using the nose to smell flavor. Animals frequently lick their masters or their young with relish, savoring the taste of a favorite's identity.[10] So we may indeed have begun kissing as a way to taste-and-smell someone. According to the Bible account, when Isaac grew old and lost his sight, he called his son Esau to kiss him and receive a blessing, but Jacob put on Esau's clothing and, because he smelled like Esau to his blind father, received the kiss instead. In Mongolia, a father does not kiss his son; he smells his son's head. Some cultures prefer just to rub noses (Inuits, Maoris, Polynesians, and others), while in some Malay tribes the word for "smell" means the same as "salute." Here is how Charles Darwin describes the Malay nose-rubbing kiss: "The women squatted with their faces upturned; my attendants stood leaning over theirs, and commenced rubbing. It lasted somewhat longer than a hearty handshake with us. During this process they uttered a grunt of satisfaction." ◌

Analyzing the Craft

1. The conventions of academic writing, as you know, require citations whenever you use an outside source. While this often seems an annoying and arbitrary obligation, there is a logic to it: Scholars are grafting new knowledge onto the branches of what is already known, and citations tell this story. However, in creative nonfiction and other forms of popular writing that use research, writers rarely use formal citations, yet they do make a variety of moves to signal that the information they share is not their own. Where does Ackerman make these moves in the excerpt? Examine other excerpts or other published work that use research, and describe how writers acknowledge their sources.

2. We typically experience dialogue as the fastest prose form to read and factual exposition as among the slowest. This helps explain why some writers of narrative worry about whether informative stretches of writing might put the brakes on the forward motion of the story. In

---

[10]Not only humans kiss. Apes and chimps have been observed kissing and embracing as a form of peacemaking.

her lengthy paragraph of exposition about kissing, does Ackerman manage to avoid this problem? How, exactly, does she manage to keep the information about the history of kissing compelling?

3. Closely examine the language Ackerman uses in the first paragraph. One technique that she uses is recurrence—the repetition of certain words or phrases that might seem unnecessary if they weren't so affecting. "We kissed for hours," she writes, "we kissed extravagantly," and "we kissed furtively." She repeats the phrase "we kissed," paired with a different adverb, *15 times* in a single paragraph. Why might Ackerman choose to do this? What affect is she after? In general, how might recurrence serve the stylistic purposes of a writer?

Practicing the Craft

Diane Ackerman reminds us that creative nonfiction writers, unlike academics, are free to roam from discipline to discipline and field to field as we research our subject. Each provides a different perspective that gives us, finally, a more comprehensive look. Practice this technique by choosing your own subject and researching it from at least three different disciplinary perspectives. For example, a subject like Ackerman's study of the senses lends itself to historical, cultural, scientific, literary, political, sociological, psychological, and artistic ways of seeing. This wandering across fields of study isn't difficult to do. Consider, for instance, a headache:

> Some experts believe that prehistoric people got them, and suspected that headaches were caused by "demons and evil spirits" that had to be removed by drilling a hole in the skull. It is not clear what tool was used for this delicate procedure. Contemporary physicians are much more likely to reach for a pill rather than a drill because the most common headaches are caused by the much more treatable modern demon—stress. Ironically, *The New York Times* reported that one fourth of all headaches might actually be caused by the pills people take to relieve them. Called the "rebound effect," overuse of painkillers is especially common among migraine sufferers. "Overuse has less to do with how many pills you take to relieve a single headache than with how often you take them," said headache expert Dr. Robert Kunkel. "If you get more than two headaches a week and take pain pills for them, you're at risk." Jane Cave Winscom, the unofficial poet of the headache, might have welcomed the modern painkiller despite its risks. In "The Head-Ach," the eighteenth-century British poet wrote the following lines about her own suffering:
>
>> Through ev'ry particle the torture flies,
>> But centres in the *temples, brain,* and *eyes*;
>> The efforts of the hands and feet are vain,

While bows the head with agonizing pain;
While heaves the breast with th' unutterable sigh,
And the big tear drops from the languid eye.

Try your hand at this. Choose a similar commonplace subject—houseflies, baseball bats, Cheetos, a shovel—as a focus for some flash research, drawing information from three or more different fields. Then write a sketch like the one I wrote about headaches. You may later develop this into an essay or article.

Recommended Nonfiction by
Diane Ackerman

- *A Natural History of Love* (1995). After the extraordinary success of *A Natural History of the Senses*, Ackerman turned her attention to a related subject—love—and brings to it the same poetic prose and research savvy of the earlier book. *A Natural History of Love* examines the history of love, its rituals, and its kinds. I found her exploration of the chemistry of love particularly fascinating.

- *The Zookeeper's Wife* (2007). This is a compelling story about a pair of Polish zookeepers, Jan and Antonina Zabinski, who harbored Jews from the Nazis in empty cages during World War II. Writers will appreciate how skillfully Ackerman weaves a narrative from a wide range of sources—newspaper clippings, interviews, photographs, letters, diaries, historical archives, and so on.

Part 4
A Brief Anthology

❦❦❦

Introduction

In this final section of *Crafting Truth* the window opens wider. Rather than looking through the sliver of two or three paragraphs of a longer work of creative nonfiction, we'll examine complete essays and partial chapters from memoirs and literary journalism. Here you can see narratives unfold and watch how the parts we've analyzed in the previous three sections of the book put those stories into motion. Apply what you've learned about the machinery of craft, and you'll deepen your understanding of well-written creative nonfiction, knowledge that you can bring to your own work.

In choosing selections for this anthology, I had three things in mind. First, I wanted to bring in voices that we hadn't yet heard from—outstanding writers like Susan Orlean and John Edgar Wideman. But I was also interested in perhaps less well-known contemporary nonfiction writers, especially authors who are experimenting with the genre (or in some cases, writing against it)—lyric essayists like Lia Purpura and memoirist Lauren Slater. I've also chosen authors whose gift for storytelling has made their work not just a critical success but a popular one as well. For example, I've included a portion of a chapter from H. G. Bissinger's *Friday Night Lights*, an engrossing look at high school football in a Texas town that was later made into a television series. Finally, I wanted to include some student work. I've been lucky to work with some wonderful young writers over the years, and in the classes we've had together I watched Andrea Oyarzabal become a versatile, talented nonfiction writer. Her radio essays are especially compelling. Andrea agreed to share an early essay draft of an essay she's working on, in the beginning of this anthology.

Because I wanted to keep the emphasis on learning from excerpts rather than full-length work in *Crafting Truth*, the anthology is relatively brief, with two examples of each creative nonfiction form—essay, memoir, and literary journalism. I think that's plenty to work with, particularly if you take the time to explore some of the recommended nonfiction writing by the excerpted authors listed at the end of each chapter. Above all, I hope that your reading of these selections inspires you to return to your own writing with a renewed sense of possibility. Though it has a long tradition, this is a vibrant time for creative nonfiction. Throw open the window, admire the view, and then get to work. Write.

STUDENT ESSAY

4.1

MATH, METAMORPHOSIS, AND MONARCHS

by Andrea Oyarzabal

Student Draft: A Personal Essay in the Making

My wife cringes every time I propose to glue a broken plate or cup because it ultimately looks like crap and she's never certain it won't fall apart in her hands. I resent this, of course, but she is right—my first try is a bit sloppy with globs of glue, and often the seams show. My writing—most anyone's writing—is often quite like this when in early drafts, and revision is a process of finding the right pieces and integrating them more seamlessly into the piece. Personal essays are especially difficult to revise. Why? For one thing, perhaps more than any other writers, essayists are interested in discovering what they think by *following* language rather than wrestling it into submission. It's easier to get down what you already know rather than chase words that might lead you astray. But it's those unplanned digressions that might lead to surprises, to what you didn't know you knew. While it offers the promise of discovery, an essay draft is often a mess—pointless, baggy, heading off in too many directions. Revising an essay is like being a spectator at a horse race of meaning; you're pretty sure one idea is a winner when another suddenly emerges from the pack. In the beginning, all bets are off. It's hard to overstate how hard it is to revise a personal essay and how satisfying it can be.

In the essay that follows, Andrea Oyarzabal invites us to watch as she struggles with the third draft of an essay. The piece began, as essays often

164

do, with a memory that puzzled her: Why did she resent an old math teacher so? And why did being singled out as "smart" in the third grade feel wrong? By the third draft, she's beginning to understand what the essay is really about, but the seams still show. Follow her as she draws on her knowledge of craft to find ways to remake her essay in the fourth draft.

                                                    ❧❧❧

When I was nine years old and in the third grade at Pierce Park Elementary, my classroom was one of three portables, glorified trailers, placed outside because the school didn't have enough room to house all of the students inside the building. In addition to mine, there were two more third grade classes held in the adjacent two portables. Each student had a homeroom teacher, and in an unprecedented experimental program, during the afternoons each student went to a teacher that specialized in a different difficulty level of a certain subject—math, reading, and social studies. This program was initially designed to put the accelerated students with accelerated students and the dumb kids with dumb kids. I've always questioned the intentions of those who developed the program. Was it so dumb students had more time to work at their own pace? No matter how well-intentioned, even nine-year-olds knew what it felt like to be labeled dumb or smart—both of which became labels for me that year.[1]

That year, the school sent a letter to my mother, a single parent who constantly struggled financially and emotionally. School officials wanted to test my IQ, and if my score was high enough, they wanted to enroll me in special classes—a program called G.A.T.E. (Gifted and Talented Education). My mother agreed, and I remember the day I was tested, walking from my classroom, the cream-colored portable on the far left, to the south, across the blacktop, to an identical cream-colored building with a brown roof, and a gray, sand-paper textured ramp leading up to it. Of the questions I was asked that day, I remember these: How many days are in a year? How many weeks are in a year? How many feet are in a yard?[2] As I remember, I passed with

---

[1] I feel like this beginning is really lacking. While I don't want to give away too much information at the beginning, so as to create tension, I feel like I have to give enough setting description so my reader knows where the story takes place. As *Crafting Truth* states "A good lead, like the stem of an old watch, puts tension on the spring that drives the work forward and keeps readers engaged because they wonder what will happen next." I guess a reader may be curious about where I am headed after reading this, but I don't know if my first lines do enough work in this lead.

[2] Memory can be questioned easily here, as memory is fallible, and this happened over 20 years ago. However, I know for certain that I was asked these questions. I omitted the other questions because I don't remember them, and this felt like I made a good effort at getting to the "truthful" details.

flying colors, and the woman testing me, who I believe now to have been a school counselor,[3] seemed impressed while I indignantly answered the questions, as they seemed like such silly ones.

In the three afternoon classes, reading, math, and social studies, I was in the advanced group for both reading and social studies. Mrs. Ware, the reading teacher, was a roly-poly woman with a bad perm. The books we read were part of a series of anthologies called The Junior Reader series[4]— my three books, the smart kid books, were yellow with blue writing and blue borders and featured greats like Roald Dahl. In private, I squeezed the books between my fingers out of excitement, feeling the thickness of each volume—A, B, and C—and released pent up squeals of delight at the anticipation of reading the stories within the bound pages.

I think the social studies teacher's first name was Susan. She had short hair, big glasses, even bigger teeth that shined from too much saliva, and was in her fifties. Her mouth was full of dental work—partials and bridges or maybe it was a set of adult braces. We watched the fall of the Berlin Wall in class in 1989 on the old TV atop the metal rolling TV cart while in social studies. While at the time I understood the event was significant, as were all major historical events aired on the TV, I was too young to understand the importance or implications of what was going on in the world. And as I look back now, I realize what exactly this says about who I was at the time: At nine, my microcosm was school. What happened in Germany didn't matter to me.[5] School and learning was my world—it set me apart from the others. The other kids were good at sports and had siblings and parents to go home to. For the most part, I was left at home alone, my mom at work, my older siblings not at home. Knowledge was my closest

---

[3]I don't know for certain who the woman who tested me was. If I said she was the school counselor, I would be lying. That is why I said, I "believe" her to be—*believe* and *is* as word choices have two very different meanings. "Perhaps" is another word that gives nonfiction writers wiggle room with the truth.

[4]A detail I couldn't remember for certain was the title of the anthology series we used for class. I vaguely remember the series having "Junior" in the title. This is an instance where I researched the series to validate my memory, much as Bruce talks about doing in his essay about the eclipse in *Crafting Truth*.

[5]While the detail of the fall of the Berlin Wall is not significant to the story, it helps the readers gain a sense of time for the rest of the story or, as *Crafting Truth* says, of framing a story within the context of nonfiction: "It is frequently framed by time and place—something happened somewhere and then it was over—and the nonfiction scene is observed from a consistent perspective." Also, the detail of the Berlin Wall not only gives time perspective, 1989, but I think it gives perspective about time in children's lives and illuminates how children think. The Berlin Wall collapse was a major historical event, but to the "then" me, it was insignificant compared to what was happening in my world. Reflecting now, I remember feeling that such events were a nuisance, interrupting my regularly scheduled programming, and this illustrates a child's naïveté.

friend and surrogate mother. Being smart was important to me—learning was the gratification I needed, the pat on the back that wasn't there when I got home from school on most afternoons.

I didn't mind reading or social studies. When it came to math, however, I was a dumb kid. In some ways, I am still the dumb kid in math. As an adult, numbers still make me cry and sweat. In college, a teacher asked us to write down a goal for the semester. I wrote, "I don't want to cry in front of the other students." Not a lot has changed since I was nine.

When you're young, being a smart kid gets you harassed for being a geek, but as an adult, it's okay—geeks succeed. When you're a dumb adult, however, it gets you nowhere. And while being labeled dumb or smart really shouldn't matter, it does. It's society's way of separating blue collar from white collar, the poor from the rich, the advantaged from the disadvantaged, the struggling from the stressless. Being called smart isn't so bad: It's a compliment. Being called dumb, on the other hand, can lead to years of resentment and anguish.

My anguish came at the hands of Mrs. Jayo, my math and homeroom teacher. She was, by far, the youngest and most attractive of the three teachers. She was petite with chin-length curly blond hair. Her face escapes me now, although in my mind's eye, she looks like Amy Sedaris, though I know this wasn't what she really looked like.[6]

I don't know if I would recognize Mrs. Jayo if I saw her again, but if I did, I would tell her she may be the root of all my math ills. As an adult, I understand it doesn't make sense to blame one person for my problems, but it seems that the childlike me still infiltrates my adult mind, needling my emotional center each time I think of Mrs. Jayo. Maybe it's not just math I blame her for.

The day was a dreary one, cold, dark, cloudy, probably damp.[7] The teachers held an ice cream social at lunchtime as a reward for memorizing our times tables. The problem being, I didn't memorize mine. While the others celebrated with their ice cream and toppings, Mrs. Jayo made me go outside, alone. Even Sary Anderson, the girl who owned rats and kept them in a bathtub at her house, and in adult life was on Judge Judy, got to go to the ice cream social.

This has always seemed a great injustice to me—something in my brain made me smarter than the rest of the kids, so much so that I was deemed gifted; yet, that same brain couldn't figure out numbers. These diametrically opposed brains—one that knew words and one that didn't

[6] I have toyed with taking out the part about how I see Amy Sedaris's face when I think of Mrs. Jayo, but I think it speaks to our desire for people to have a face when we are writing. When our memory fails us, we assign somebody else's face, though we know it isn't the right one.

[7] This sentence, "The day was a dreary one, cold, dark, cloudy, and probably damp," is trying to build tension. I suspect readers at this point know something important is coming.

know numbers—never placed me in the middle, where people seem to be left alone.[8] Average kids don't get picked on as much as the ones who stick out. Instead, they fade into the background. The other injustice, though, is making a nine-year-old feel so left out that she remembers it for the next twenty years, never to forget it. I was damned if I was smart, and I was damned if I was dumb. Being left out of the ice cream social is the first day in my life I remember feeling weird and different, the only kid on the playground, ostracized. Maybe Mrs. Jayo thought I was already too pudgy, I didn't need any more ice cream, my little chubby cheeks and chubby body indicating I ate enough ice cream already. Or maybe she just didn't know any better, ascribing to teaching methods that had been used for years without realizing their implications.

I learned my times tables though—no thanks to Mrs. Jayo or the experimental system that segregated the dumb kids from the smart ones. I learned my times tables the next year, during the fourth grade, at a different school, Cole Elementary, a school that's been torn down. I learned my times tables from Mrs. Sutherland, the butterfly lady of Idaho.

Mrs. Sutherland wore matching polyester pantsuits, had large glasses, and wore her dark hair in a style that seemed as though she curled the sides of her hair and her bangs in one fell swoop of her curling iron, never bothering to brush the hair out, the curls retaining their unity. As I think back now, it seemed as though Mrs. Sutherland was 80 years old, but when I looked her up, I found she was only 62 when she was my elementary school teacher—not much older than my own mother is now.

Mrs. Sutherland was a passionate woman who devoted her life to not only school children and her family, but also to monarch butterflies. She studied monarchs and taught her students about them for about 30 years.[9] Each year, she brought cages into the classroom containing monarch butterfly larvae, and the students watched the butterflies' metamorphosis process from caterpillars to green chrysalises to stunning bright orange and black monarchs. Once the butterflies emerged, and their wings dried and strengthened, we soaked cotton balls in a solution of honey and water, mimicking the nectar that monarchs eat, and placed the balls in the cages for the monarchs to feed on. In an effort to track the migratory habits of the monarchs, Mrs. Sutherland

---

[8]I have always really liked this section, and I feel like I did a lot of work to get it to where it is now. I think it adds a certain amount of tension: dumb me versus smart me—the two me's juxtaposed.

[9]I remember Mrs. Sutherland well, and I remember working on the butterfly project in her classroom. I might like to add more about that here, but I don't know how relevant the information is other than showing my relationship with her. I asked a former classmate about our work in the class with the monarchs, and she gave me some details, but her memory was limited. It would be nice to actually ask Mrs. Sutherland, but she was someone I researched, too, and I found that she had passed away. However, her obituary gave me great details about her character in regard to her personal life.

tagged them, and each year she released the tagged monarchs to start their migratory journey to the overwintering habitats in coastal California and, for some, the Sierra Madres in Mexico. In recent years, monarch numbers have declined by almost 60 percent, devastated by the recent harsh and long winters. Mrs. Sutherland developed a project for her fourth grade class to learn about the government and sought legislation to make the monarch butterfly the Idaho State Insect. In 1993, she succeeded.[10]

I don't know how Mrs. Sutherland helped me or how I eventually learned my times tables, but I remember piles and piles of worksheets, and going over the numbers again and again. Maybe Mrs. Sutherland was more patient or she saw a part of herself in me, a woman so eccentric that she devoted her life to insects. Maybe she recognized that much like the monarchs, everyone's metamorphosis process differs. Maybe it was her tender nature, realizing that everything in this world is sensitive—monarchs and humans alike—and in her understanding of this, she made calculated efforts to treat everything with nurturing and compassion because she realized that life is about balance—no one extreme. To her there was no smart or dumb.

When I finally conquered the times tables, beating the other students at the chalkboard in a competition, I was elated and shocked. But there was another feeling, too. I recognize it now as one of loathing for Mrs. Jayo, though I know this is present-day me loathing her, maybe unfairly, because adult me is stuck in 1989 wandering around the playground alone and dejected, wondering where I went wrong, thinking I am defective.[11]

I was saddened to learn that Mrs. Sutherland died earlier this year. I am sorry I didn't think of her more often before her death. Mrs. Jayo almost ruined it all, filling space in my memory with the resentment I feel for her, almost pushing Mrs. Sutherland out. But maybe without the Mrs. Jayos of the world, the Mrs. Sutherlands wouldn't be able to correct the world's delicate balance.[12]

---

[10]There is definitely more room for research here, and I wish I could find some element about the monarchs that I can compare to Mrs. Sutherland, but I don't know if this would be getting too far away from the heart of the essay. Bruce says that his mentor, the writer Donald Murray, once handed out laminated cards to his writer friends printed with the acronym S.O.F.T.— "Say One F—ing Thing"—which he believed was one of the best pieces of advice he could pass along about essay writing." I always fear that I am on the verge of violating the S.O.F.T. rule.

[11]I think this is a good example of "now" me reflecting on "younger" me, or as *Crafting Truth* says, "There are two narrators, essentially, the one to whom things happened and the one who is beginning to understand what it means."

[12]I like this as a last line, and no matter what else happens in the rest of the piece, I think I would like to keep it. It juxtaposes two divergent teachers, the different ideas about education, and how society is always comfortable relying on extremes. I think this holds a good amount of tension for the piece, and the statement slows the reader down, making him or her pause to think about the statement and, ultimately, the whole essay.

ESSAY

4.2

AUTOPSY REPORT

by Lia Purpura

❧

This essay is from *On Looking*, a 2006 collection of lyric essays by Lia Purpura. Her sharp, often-startling imagery and graceful language betrays the eyes and ears of a poet, so Purpura comes to the lyric essay naturally. But it's too simple to say that the lyric essay is a hybrid between prose and poetry. Martha Ronk wrote that the form has the qualities of a constellation; it may start with a discrete experience but instead of moving toward "narrative or fact," it "spins out" into analogy, "a free movement away from the main event as each star is simultaneously far-flung" but also "a part of" the whole constellation.

❧❧❧

> *I wish I understood the beauty in leaves falling. To whom are we beautiful as we go?*
>
> —David Ignatow

I shall begin with the chests of drowned men, bound with ropes and diesel-slicked. Their ears sludge-filled. Their legs mud-smeared. Asleep below deck when a freighter hit and the river rose inside their tug. Their lashes white with river silt.

❧❧❧

I shall stand beside sharp pelvic bones, his mod hip-huggers stretched tightly between them. His ribs like steppes, ice-shelves, sandstone. His wide-open mouth, where a last breath came out. And there at his feet, the stuff of his death: a near-empty bottle of red cough syrup, yellow-labeled and bagged by police.

❧❧❧

I shall touch, while no one is looking, the perfect cornrows, the jacket's wet collar. Soaked black with blood, his stiffening sleeve. And where the bullets passed neatly through, the pattern when his shirt's uncrumpled: four or five holes like ragged stars, or a child's cut-out snowflake.

❧❧❧

I shall note the blue earring, a swirled, lapis ball in the old, yellowed man's ear, his underwear yellowed, his sunken face taut. The amber and topaz half-empty fifths his landlord found and gave to police.

❧❧❧

The twenty-year alcoholic before us, a businessman. All the prescriptions for his hypertension, bagged and unused near his black-socked, gold-toed foot. The first button open on his neat, white shirt and, I shall confirm, the requisite pen in the pocket neatly clamped in.

❧❧❧

"Oh no," an assistant says. The gospel station's softly on, floaty in its mild joy; it's 7:45 on a rainy Sunday morning and so far I'm the only visitor. Turning briefly to me, he asks, "What did you come here for?"

Then, "Oh no," he says again, "no more eighteen-year-olds," as he stops at the first body, surveying. Soon, the doctors gather in the hall, finish their donuts, scrub, suit up, begin to read from the police reports, the facts meditative as any rote practice, marking and measuring, preparing ritual ground: *The last person to see him alive was his girlfriend. History: bipolar. Suspected: OD, heroin.* "Something too pure is killing these kids in the county," the doctor says. Of the boy's house, the report states "nice," "middle class" and "the deceased's bedroom is cluttered and dirty." Multiple generations at home. Bottle caps with resin in the trash. And here is a silver soup spoon, blue-black from the flame, encrusted where he cooked the stuff, its graceful stem embellished for nothing. As his body is—beautiful now, for nothing. Is olive-skinned, muscled, nicely proportioned. No, I shall say it, is stunning, as it turns to marble before us.

We walk back to the first body, unmingling stories. They divide up the bodies. They take the clothes off.

What I thought before seeing it all: *never again will I know the body as I do now.*
And how, exactly, is that?

Have I thought of the body as sanctuary? A safe, closed place like the ark from which the Torah is taken and laid out on a table to be unscrolled. The two sides parted, opened like, soon I'd know, a rib cage, that a hand with a sharp-tipped pointer might lead the way over, reading toward depth.
Here's the truth: when I first saw the bodies, I laughed out loud. The laugh burst forth, I could not stop it. *Forgive me,* I thought even then, but the scene, the weird gestures looked entirely staged. Such a response is sure measure of expectations; sure proof I held other images dear: shrouds, perhaps? Veils? A pall hanging (and though I've never seen a pall, I know it is "cast over," that it shadows all that it touches). Had I assumed crisp sheets drawn up, as in surgery, to section off an operating theater around the site of death? Had somewhere an ideal been lodged: arms at sides in the position of sleep (not so birdlike, jutting, rigid); faces placid (mouths not slack, not black, empty sockets, dry shafts down, archeological, beckoning, unquiet).
Was I awaiting some sign of passage, the strains of ceremony slapping in its wake? (There was the dime the police searched for, evidence caught in the body bag, bright and mud-smeared, I didn't point out. How meager against the royal cats, well-fed and gold-haltered, the canopic jars holding royal organs, the granaries built for the beautiful pharaohs... *leave the dime in, I thought, that the boatman might row him across.*)
Did I expect, finally, the solemnity of procession? Death gowned and dancing, scythe raised and cape blowing, leading the others, at dusk, over a mountain. In silhouette. Fully cinematic.

And now that I've admitted laughing, I shall admit this, more unexpected, still:
When the assistants opened the first body up, what stepped forth, unbidden, was calm.
It was in the assistants' manner of touching their material, their work, that delicacy. The precise, rote gestures feeling space and resistance; adjusting the arc of a blade to the bodies' proportions; cupping and weighing, knowing the slippage, anticipating it; the pressure, the estimate, the sure, careful exchange of hand and knife, the gesture performed so efficiently it looked like habit: easy, inevitable.
The calm came to me while the skin behind the ears and across the base of the skull was cut from its bluish integument. While the scalp was folded

up and over the face like a towel, like a compress draped over sore eyes. While the skull was sawed open and a quarter of it lifted away, dust flying, the assistants working without masks. It was calm that came forth while the brain was removed, while the brain, heavy and gray and wet, was fileted with an enormous knife, one hand on top to keep it from jiggling. While the doctor found the ragged lesion in the thalmus and ruled the cause of death hypertension—not alcoholism. Calm, while the brain was slipped into a jar, and the skull refitted, the skin pulled back over to hold it all in again.

I suppose they expected queasiness, fear, short, labored breath—all death's effect. That I'd back away. That after the first, I'd have seen enough. Or the tears that followed fast, after the laughter—for the waste, the fine bones, because these were sons or fathers or would never be fathers—perhaps they expected the tears to return?

But when the bodies were opened up—how can I say this? The opening was familiar. As if I'd known before, this...what? Language? Like a dialect spoken only in childhood, for a short time with old-world relatives, and heard again many years later, the gist of it all was sensible. And though I couldn't reply, meanings hung on. A shapeliness of thought was apparent, all inflection and lilt and tonal suggestion.

Nothing was too intimate: not the leaves stuck to the crewman's thigh, and higher up, caught in the leg of his underwear; the captain's red long johns and soaked, muddy sock. Their big stomachs and how reliably strong they still looked. Not the diesel fuel slicking their faces, stinking the building, dizzying us, nor the pale, wrinkled soles of one's foot, water-logged. Not the hair braided by some woman's hands, her knuckles hard against his head. The quarter-sized hole in his twisted, gray sweat sock, sock he pulled on that morning, or afternoon, or whenever he rose while he lived and dressed without a thought to dressing.

Not the dime the police found and bagged. The buckshot pock-marking his face, his young face, the buccal fat still high, rounded and thick. Nothing was unfamiliar in the too-bright room. Not the men's nakedness, although I have never seen twelve men, naked, before me. Not the method by which the paths of bullets were measured: rods of different lengths pushed through each hole—I had to stop counting there were so many—until one came out the other side.

Not the phrase "exit wound."

And though I'd never seen a bullet hole, of course it would be shallow as the tissue underneath swelled uselessly back together. Of course blood pooled each blue-burnt circumference. *Of course*, I remember thinking.

The purpose the work comprised, the *opening*, was familiar.

It was familiar to see the body opened.

Because in giving birth, I knew the body opened beyond itself?

Because I have been opened, enough times now in surgery, once the whole length of me, and there are hundreds of stitches?

Then, when everything was lifted out—the mass of organs held in the arms, a cornucopia of dripping fruits hoisted to the hanging scale—there was the spine. I could look straight through the empty body, and there, as if buried in wet, red earth, there was the white length of spine. Shields of ribs were sawed out and saved to fix back into place. There were the yellow layers of fat, yellow as a cartoon sun, as sweet cream butter, laid thinly on some, in slabs on others. There were the ice-blue casings of large intestines, the small sloshing stomach, transparent, to be drained. The bladder, hidden, but pulled into view for my sake and cupped in hand like a water balloon. Cracks and snappings. The whisking and shushing of knives over skin, a sound like tearing silk. The snipping. The measuring jars filled with cubed liver. The intercostal blood vessel pulled out like a basted hem. The perforating branches of the internal thoracic artery leaving little holes behind in the muscle like a child's lace-up board. The mitral valves sealing like the lids of ice cream cups. And heavy in the doctor's hand, the spleen, shining, as if pulled from a river.

How easily the body opens.

How with difficulty does the mouth in awe, in praise. For there are words I cannot say.

If looking, though, is a practice, a form of attention paid, which is, for many, the essence of prayer, it is the sole practice I had available to me as a child. By seeing I called to things, and in turn, things called me, applied me to their sight and we became each as treasure, startling to one another, and rare. Among my parents' art, their work, I moved in fields of color and gesture, cut parts built to make up wholes: mannequin heads adorned with beads; plaster food so real, so hard the mashed potatoes hurt, and painted sandwiches of sponge grew stiff and scratched. Waxed fibers with feathers twisted into vessels. Lips and mouths and necks of clay were spun and pulled into being in air. With the play of distance, with hues close up, paintings roughened with weaves, softened with water, oil, turpentine, greens, fleshes, families of shapes grew until—better than the bodies of clouds, these forms stayed put—forms spoke, bent toward, nodded so that they came to happen again and again, and I played among them in their sight. And what went on between us was ineffable, untold and this was *the silent part of my life as a child.*

I never thought to say, or call this "God," which even then sounded like shorthand, a refusal to be speechless in the face of occurrences, shapes, gestures happening daily, and daily reconstituting sight. "God," the very attitude of the word—for the lives of words were also palpable to me—was pushy. Impatient. Quantifiable. A call to jettison the issue, the only issue as I understood it: the unknowable certainty of being alive, of being a body untethered from origin, untethered from end, but also so terribly *here.*

And *here*—for we went out to see often—was once constituted by enormous, black, elegaic shapes closed between black gashes or bars. And in the same day, *here* was also curved, colored shapes, airborne and hung from wire, like, ah! muted, lobed organs, so that *here* could be at once a gesture of mourning and a gesture of ease.

I went home and showered, showered and scrubbed in hottest water and threw away the old shoes I'd worn. Later that day, at the grocery store among the other shoppers, I saw all the scalps turned over faces, everyone's face made raw and meatlike, the sleek curves of skulls and bony plates exposed. I saw where to draw the knife down the chest to make the Y that would reveal.

I'd seen how easily we open, our skin not at all the boundary we're convinced of as we bump into each other and excuse ourselves. I'd seen how small a thing gone wrong need be: one sip, just one too many, mere ounces of water in the lungs too much. And the woman in front of me on the check-out line, the pale tendons in her neck, the fibers of muscle wrapping bone below her wool collar, her kidneys backed against my cart—how her spleen, so unexpectedly high in the body, was marked precisely by the orange flower on her sweater! And after seeing the assistants gather the organs up in their arms and arrange them on the aluminum table, after seeing such abundance there—here, too, was abundance: pyramids of lemons, red-netted sacks of oranges and papery onions, bananas fitting curve to curve, the dusty skins of grapes, translucent greens, dark roses, heavy purples.

Then, stepping out into the street with my bags, everything fresh and washed in the cold March rain, there was that scent hanging in the air—a fine film of it lingered, and I knew it to be the milky blueness I saw, just hours ago, cut free and swaying, barest breath and tether. That scrim, an opacity, clung to everyone, though they kept walking to cars, lifting and buckling children in. Packing their trunks, returning their carts. Yes, everything looked as it always had—bright and pearly, lush and arterial after the rain.

4.3

THANKS FOR THE MEMOREX

by Sarah Vowell

∾

In the digital age, mixing a cassette tape for a special someone is old-fashioned. People don't have cassette players anymore unless they have a car from the nineties. But Sarah Vowell's essay isn't about technology. It's about trying to script someone else's soundtrack—coming up with a playlist of songs that will say just the right thing to that person while remaining faithful to one's own musical tastes, a nearly impossible task that says a lot about the fickle nature of sentiment, among other things. Sarah Vowell, along with David Sedaris, who appears earlier in this book, is a regular contributor to the radio program *This American Life*. Much of her work is—at least initially—written to be *heard* rather than read, and this strongly influences her narrative style.

∾∾∾

Long distance love affair by cassette tape: It happened to me. While digital romances grow increasingly common, our strange fling was quaintly analog. We talked on the phone for hours and enjoyed the occasional mushy rendezvous in the flesh at airports and bookstores and bars. But mostly, we wore out the heads on our respective tape decks compiling Memorex mash notes. I'm not really the scented envelope kind of girl, preferring instead to send yellow Jiffylite mailers packed with whatever song is on my mind.

The most interesting thing about the correspondence was that we rarely agreed. While we cared for each other, we cared little for each other's taste in music. I sent him lovey-dovey lullabies like Blondie's "In the Flesh" and he sent me back what could have been field recordings of amplified ant farms by bands with names like Aphex Twin and Jarboe. I sent him the Jonathan Richman song that goes "If the music's gonna move me it's gotta be action-packed," but he didn't take the hint, sending back music that was almost uniformly action-*lacked*. I think my scrappy little pop songs got on his nerves, and his techno-ambient soundscapes left me impatient for something, *anything*, to happen. Still, I gritted my teeth through them all,

176

groaning over every last spacy synth jam as if I were doing him some kind of personal favor. Since he went to the trouble of making the tape, the least I could do was sit there and take it.

I liked picturing him in his little house, flipping through records and putting them on, taking them off and timing out the cassette so he could fill it up as much as possible but still avoid those immoral endings in which the sound gets cut off in the middle. Just as I liked running around my little apartment trying to remember, say, every rock song that ever had an accordion in it and whether the keyboardless concertina counts.

After a while, the question we asked each other about the tapes we sent wasn't "Did you like it?" The question was "Did you *get* it?" Because receipt ultimately took on more importance than pleasure, and that was perhaps the most telling note. Not that I miss those "songs" of his since we parted ways—not by a long shot. (The letters were good. Those I miss. He quoted James Baldwin a lot. And the phone calls were sweet. I fell in love with him on the phone. He had a soothing voice. A couple of times he called the second he'd finished reading a novel and just had to tell me about it, and I know it sounds hokey and librarianish to say so, but I just *swooned* when he did that.)

That music of his did not bother me when we were making out on a bench in front of the La Brea Tar Pits or the alley behind my favorite Chicago bar. It bothered me in those ponderous solitary moments when I asked myself if I could really love a man who did not think, as I do, that a band with two drummers playing two drum sets was some kind of mortal sin, just as I'm sure he asked himself if such a free-wheeling, free-jazz, open mind as himself could really fall for such an oldfangled, verse-chorus-verse relic like me. Which might be shallow, but our incompatible music pointed to incompatible world views. He was the ocean, preferring waves of sound to wash over him with no beginning, middle, or end. I'm more of a garden hose, fancying short bursts of emotion that are aimed somewhere and get turned on and off real quick.

A couple of days after the last time I saw him, I got a typically well-written postcard. He said that after he kissed me goodbye at LAX he was driving away and turned on the radio. Elvis was singing "It's Now or Never." In my personal religion, a faith cobbled together out of pop songs and books and movies, there is nothing closer to a sign from God than Elvis Presley telling you "tomorrow will be too late" at precisely the moment you drop off a girl you're not sure you want to drop off. Sitting on the stairs to my apartment, I read that card and wept. It said he heard the song and thought about running after me. But he didn't. And just as well—those mixed-faith marriages hardly ever work. An Elvis song coming out of the radio wasn't a sign from God to him, it was just another one of those corny pop tunes he could live without.

What I did get out of the entire sad situation, besides big phone bills, a box of cassettes I'll never touch again, and a newfound appreciation for the short stories of Denis Johnson—especially the sentence in *Jesus' Son* that says, "The cards were scattered on the table, face up, face down, and they seemed to foretell that whatever we did to one another would be washed away by liquor or explained away by sad songs," which was pretty prophetic considering that the two men I took up with after my heart was broken were Jack Daniel and Neil Young—was a lingering sentimentality about the act of taping itself. A homemade tape is a work of friendship, an act of love.

I was reminded of that when I was reading Nick Hornby's novel *High Fidelity*. One of the subtexts of his story is the emotional complexities of the taping ritual. Much of the book takes place in a London record store. Clerks Barry and Dick are emotional cripples stuck in that mostly male pop culture circle of hell in which having seen a film (the right kind) or owning a record (ditto) acts as a substitute for being able to express what these things mean to them. Since they are incapable of really talking about human feelings, they get by on standing next to each other at rock shows and making each other complicated tapes of obscure songs.

Rob, their boss at the record store, met his girlfriend Laura when he was a DJ at a dance club. She first approached him because she liked a song he was playing called "Got to Get You Off My Mind." Rob woos Laura by making her a compilation tape, claiming, "I spent hours putting that cassette together. To me, making a tape is like writing a letter—there's a lot of erasing and rethinking and starting again. A good compilation tape, like breaking up, is hard to do. You've got to kick off with a corker, to hold the attention (I started with 'Got to Get You Off My Mind,' but then realized that she might not get any further than track one, side one if I delivered what she wanted straightaway, so I buried it in the middle of side two), and then you've got to up it a notch, or cool it a notch, and you can't have white music and black music together, unless the white music sounds like black music, and you can't have two tracks by the same artist side by side, unless you've done the whole thing in pairs and...oh, there are loads of rules."

While I was reading Hornby's book, I happened to glance at an ad in *San Francisco Weekly* that read, "I'll tape record albums for you. Reasonable rates, excellent service. Pick-up available. Bob." And it gave a phone number. Prostitution! That's what I thought, anyway. Paying someone to make a tape for you seems a whole lot like paying someone for a kiss. It is traditional to cover for one's inability to articulate feelings of love through store-bought greeting cards. It's another thing entirely to pass off a purchased compilation tape, a form which is inherently amateur and therefore more heartfelt. To spend money on such a tape would be a crime against love. Aphrodite herself might rise from the ocean to conk such a criminal on the head with the seashell she rode in on.

I asked Hornby what his music-mad record clerks would think if they saw Bob's ad in the paper. "Their public view would be that it's a terrible, awful job for a grown man to do, and why haven't all these people got their own turntables? But I think maybe they'd think secretly it was kind of a neat job and they'd like to sit at home all day taping other people's records."

I called the number in the ad and talked to Bob, a very nice, sane person actually. I expressed my reservations about his work using subtle, professional phrases such as "What a weird job!" Bob explains that by taping his clients' old Dottie West and Frank Sinatra Jr. records, he "brings to life something that was essentially lying dormant in their life. I see it as providing a service that people are happy to pay for. They think it's worth the money. I feel great, make a little money on the side. No problem."

So Bob's business is much more businesslike than I imagined. He doesn't make the kind of painstaking mix tapes you make for someone you have a crush on. "Actually," Bob points out, "people call me and they're so delighted that this service exists that they're super happy and almost not even that price sensitive." His rates vary depending on the quantity of taping his clients demand. He says each tape costs, on average, about ten dollars. Hardly prostitution, more like giving it away.

Still, I remained fascinated by the unsavory if fictional idea that someone might be willing to pay someone else good money to make a compilation tape for his or her loved one. I decided I wanted the job. I had heard that my friend Dave has a new lady in his life, so I roped him into hiring me to make a tape for her.

"It honestly would be a good idea," said my client during our first consultation.

"You're at the tape stage?"

"Well, it could use a spark."

"So tell me about her. Let's try and get at who she is. Is she a femme fatale kind of girl, or more of a my funny valentine?"

He cringed. "Oh God. In sort of a scary way, she's maybe too much of a carbon copy of me."

"And are you a femme fatale, Dave?"

"No. I wouldn't say either one of those. It's not a saccharine, sweet thing. It's kind of low-key."

I wanted to know how intense he feels about this girl, hoping that the term "low-key" wouldn't come up again. I ran some iconic song titles by him so he can decide how far to go with his musical expression of love and/or like. He said that he's okay with "I Wanna Hold Your Hand"; "Let's Spend the Night Together" by the Rolling Stones "has been done"; "Kiss" by Prince is "nice"; though Frank Sinatra singing "Love and Marriage" is nixed because their relationship is "not sentimental. The I-love-you, I-need-you genre would be out. It would be more upbeat, fun stuff than 'Love Me Tender' kind of stuff at this point."

I thought making the tape was going to be easy. If Dave was calling his romance "not sentimental," then he was not having a romance. Thus anything was going to be an improvement. But once I started making Dave's tape, I discovered something I hadn't suspected.

Choosing the songs and their order was sweaty, arduous toil. Making a mix tape isn't like writing a letter, it's like having a job. Without love as the engine of my labor, it was unpleasant. And I discovered something else. I did not want to follow Dave's instructions. Sure, I had worked in the service industry before. I understood its abiding principle, "the customer is always right." At first, I was committed to following Dave's wish not to get too sentimental. I don't know if he's listened to much popular music recorded in the last, oh, half century, but it's pretty gushy stuff. Even though Dave hired me to choose love songs which didn't say I love you, there aren't that many out there. And even if there were, I'm fully confident that his desire for them is dead wrong. My reasoning? He's a boy. I'm a girl. I know better.

Certainly in making the tape I exercised restraint. After all, they've only been together two months. My role in their relationship is important, perhaps pivotal, and I take that responsibility seriously. I want to reassure her, not scare her off. I steered clear of the heavies, avoiding the serious courtship crooner Al Green. I vetoed Elvis, who should, in my opinion, only be employed when you *really* mean it. And when I did invoke Sinatra, I played it safe: not "Taking a Chance on Love" or even "I've Got a Crush on You," but picking instead cheerful, subtle "Let's Get Away from It All" as a low-key, you-and-me-baby, just-the-two-of-us-out-of-town sort of thing. Cole Porter's "Let's Do It" found a place, too. But I went with urbane jokester Noël Coward's live in Las Vegas rendition, in which he moons, "Each man out there shooting craps does it / Davy Crockett in that dreadful cap does it." Still, despite Dave's request to hold the sugar, the word "love" must pop up something like ninety-eight times over the course of the tape.

So I dropped off the tape at his house and the next day we got together to talk about it.

"I like the tape a lot," he says cheerfully. "There isn't anything that I don't really like."

"I don't know if you noticed or not, but I sort of ditched your instructions. Because you told me not to be too sentimental, and to keep it light and upbeat."

"I thought it was light."

"The word 'love' is bandied about, let's say. Yesterday, you said, the 'I-love-you, I-need-you' genre would be out."

"I did. I don't know where they say that in this tape. Do they?"

"Well, 'I love you' is certainly in there."

"I don't think it is."

But the Raspberries' "Go All the Way" (with the climax, "I need you! I love you! I need you!") is on the tape. Along with Chic's "Give Me the Lovin'" and James Brown's "Hot (I Need to Be Loved Loved Loved)." Can the differences between the way he heard the songs and the way I heard them be attributed to something as cheap and clumsy as a gender cliche? That Dave hears them as songs about sex and I hear them as songs about love? Maybe. But it's not as if I've wanted to marry every man I ever slept with. And since Dave is such a good friend to have, a rememberer of birthdays even, I know firsthand he's not without a certain softness. If we both like the tape, if we both think the tape would make a nice gift for his sweetheart, could the impasse be in the way we're talking about the tape? This being my story, however, I get to like the way I talk about it better. Even if James Brown hollers the verb "love" as a radio-friendly way of saying "fuck" I don't think he means it unsentimentally. James Brown is not, and never was, "low-key."

Anyway, the argument might be moot.

"We got into some sort of fight this morning," he confesses.

"So now you need a tape."

"Yeah. Maybe. I don't know what's up, actually."

I know exactly what's up. Dave has a problem that all the love songs in the world couldn't solve. Dave has a problem that could not be solved even by a one-hundred-minute, Chet Baker/Al Green/Elvis Presley medley recorded on a master-quality, super low-noise, high-bias, five-dollar cassette played in the moonlight as he asks her to dance. His love affair was too far gone before I ever pushed record and play on his behalf. It isn't that Dave is necessarily unsentimental. It's that he's unsentimental about her. He liked the songs I picked. He just didn't mean what the songs said. I can make a tape of "I Believe in Miracles" but I cannot perform miracles.

MEMOIR

4.4

LYING

by Lauren Slater

❧

The reader is on guard from the beginning. The sentence "I exaggerate" is Chapter One in Lauren Slater's memoir, *Lying*. Just that one sentence. Within a few paragraphs, in the second chapter, we wonder whether Slater does—or does not—have epilepsy. This provocative memoir is as much about the truth as it is a window into the author's life, and it is an excellent specimen of the "mongrel form." It is what David Shields argues is the future of nonfiction in his book *Reality Hunger: A Manifesto*. "To be alive," he writes, "is to travel ceaselessly between the real and the imaginary." This is the journey that Slater begins in this excerpt of the first two chapters of her memoir. It is not a journey that readers of nonfiction are used to.

❧❧❧

Chapter 1

I exaggerate.

Chapter 2

Three Blind Mice

The summer I turned ten I smelled jasmine everywhere I went. At first I thought the smell was part of the normal world, because we were having a hot spell that July, and every night it rained and the flowers were in full bloom. So I didn't pay much attention, except, after a while, I noticed I smelled jasmine in the bath, and my dreams were full of it, and when, one day, I cut my palm on a piece of glass, my blood itself was scented, and I started to feel scared and also good.

That was one world, and I called it the jasmine world. I didn't know, then, that epilepsy often begins with strange smells, some of which are pleasant, some of which are not. I was lucky to have a good smell. Other people's epilepsy begins with bad smells, such as tuna fish rotting in the sun, dead shark, gin and piss; these are just some of the stories I've heard.

My world, though, was the jasmine world, and I told no one about it. As the summer went on, the jasmine world grew; other odors entered, sometimes a smell of burning, as though the whole house were coming down.

Which, in a way, it was. There were my mother and my father, both of whom I loved—that much is true—but my father was too small, my mother too big, and occasionally, when the jasmine came on, I would also feel a light headedness that made my mother seem even bigger, my father even smaller, so he was the size of a freckle, she higher than a house, all her hair flying.

My father was a Hebrew School teacher, and once a year he took the *bimah* on Yom Kippur: My mother was many things, a round-robin tennis player with an excellent serve, a hostess, a housewife, a schemer, an ideologue, she wanted to free the Russian Jews, educate the Falashas, fly on the Concorde, drink at the Ritz. She did drink, but not at the Ritz. She drank in the den or in her bedroom, always with an olive in her glass.

I wanted to make my mother happy, that should come as no surprise. She had desires, for a harp, for seasonal seats at the opera, neither of which my father could afford. She was a woman of grand gestures and high standards and she rarely spoke the truth. She told me she was a Holocaust survivor, a hot-air balloonist, a personal friend of Golda Meir. From my mother I learned that truth is bendable, that what you wish is every bit as real as what you are.

I have epilepsy. Or I feel I have epilepsy. Or I wish I had epilepsy, so I could find a way of explaining the dirty, spastic glittering place I had in my mother's heart. Epilepsy is a fascinating disease because some epileptics are liars, exaggerators, makers of myths and high-flying stories. Doctors don't know why this is, something to do, maybe, with the way a scar on the brain dents memory or mutates reality. My epilepsy started with the smell of jasmine, and that smell moved into my mouth. And when I opened my mouth after that, all my words seemed colored, and I don't know where this is my mother or where this is my illness, or whether, like her, I am just confusing fact with fiction, and there is no epilepsy, just a clenched metaphor, a way of telling you what I have to tell you: my tale.

The summer of the smells was also the summer of new sounds. There were the crickets, which I could hear with astonishing clarity each evening, and the rain on the roof, each drop distinct. There was the piano, which my mother did not tell us about, her secret scheme, delivered one day in ropes and pulleys, its forehead branded "Lady Anita."

"Return it," my father said.

"I can't," she said. "I've had it engraved."

"Anita," he said. We were standing in the living room.

"Anita, there's no room to move with this Steinway in here."

"Since when do you move anyway?" my mother said.

"You play pinochle. You pray. You are not a man who requires room."

I never witnessed one of their fights. My father was, by nature, private and shy. My mother, though flamboyant, did not display emotion in public. Whenever a fight came up I was banished to my room. I, however, had long ago discovered that if I put my head in the upstairs bathroom toilet bowl, I could hear everything through the pipes.

"We can't afford this," I heard my father say.

"You," my mother said, "had the chance to partner up in Irving Busney's bakery business."

And so it went from there, as it always did, fights containing words like *you*, and *you*, fights about bills and house repairs, vacations and cars, fights with false laughs—ha! and ha! and sometimes crashing glass, and other times, like this time, such silence.

⁓⁓⁓

And in the silence—a silence of moments, hours, days—my mother started to play. A strange thing happened then. I could see the sounds she made, the high piano notes pink and pointed, the low notes brown and round. I don't mean this metaphorically. I watched the colors and I watched my mother. She had no talent, but she didn't stop. A driven woman, my mother never knew the way time might slow in a tub, the pleasure of a stretch. I watched her hands arched, her neck stiff, and I felt my eyes go fuzzy and saw spectrums in the room, colors much more beautiful than the sounds from which they sprang, her repetitive rhythms, twinkle twinkle little star, and three blind mice, bonking and chasing their tails.

And then one day, as the mice were being blind, I went with them. My sight shut down; it was black; I could not see.

"Mom," I said. I held on tight to the side of the piano.

"I'm practicing," I heard her say.

"Mom," I said. "I can't see."

She stopped. "Of course you can see," she said. "You have two eyes. You can see."

"It's dark," I shouted.

"How many fingers am I holding up?" she asked.

"I can't see your fingers," I said.

"Of course you can see my fingers," she said. "You have two eyes. Now look."

I felt her grip my chin, force my face toward her. "How many fingers? *Think*."

I heard some panic in her voice now, but not a lot, because my mother believed you could conquer anything through will.

"Two," I said, a total guess.

"Exactly," she said, triumphant.

And just like that, I started to see again. She said *exactly* and the angles came back, as though her words determined the truth and not the other way around, the way it should be: something solid.

⧉⧉⧉

I could see again, most of the time fine, but not always. First I smelled jasmine, and then I had whole moments when the world went watery, when I saw the air break apart and atomize into dozens of glittering particles. Ahead of me shapes and colors suggested the billowing sails of a ship, or a zebra floating, when in reality it was just a schoolgirl in the crosswalk. I had not known, until then, that beauty lived beneath the supposedly solid surface of things, how every line was really a curve uncreased, how every hill was smoke.

At first the vision problems frightened me because I thought I was going blind, but as weeks went by, I settled in. I thought of the vision the same way I thought of the smells, as a secret world. I became dreamy, sometimes hours and hours passing, and afterward, although I hadn't been asleep, I would feel I was waking, and my head hurt.

This is how epilepsy begins. It begins beautifully, and with only slight pain.

"Lazy," my mother said.

The colors cleared and she was standing over me, frowning. "Stop staring into space," she yelled. "Get out there and do something."

What she meant was do something gorgeous with your life. "Work," she said, and Latin and Greek, and math to master my wandering mind, hers was a household of dream and muscle both.

I went into the woods a lot that summer. The woods were cool, and I could close my eyes, and if colors came when the birds cooed or the oak trees creaked, I didn't have to worry; I could drift. And if the colors didn't come, and the world smelled only of itself, then I could play. I found toads in those woods, and Indian arrowheads. I cut a worm in half and made two worms. I got blood beneath my fingernails and bird dirt on my palms.

"You," she said, when I came home one day, "are filthy."

She slapped me, hard, across the cheek.

I hate to say it, but it's true.

My cheek.

And then, she reached across the piano keys, a longing in her look now, and smudged her pinkie to my soiled face.

Looked at the dirt I'd transferred to her finger like it was chocolate. Oh, that she could sink so low. Oh, that she, like me, could sleep.

Put your finger in your mouth, Mom, go on.

This, the gift I gave her.

෴

Even before the smells and sights and, later, the terrible slamming seizures, even before all this, my mother thought I was doomed, which, in her scheme of things, was much better than being mediocre. I was disobedient and careless, I climbed with boys, I ran with boys, and where, she wanted to know, where would this end? I would surely become a street girl, and wind up being shipped to a filthy brothel crawling with hairy tropical bugs in Buenos Aires. For my part, her predictions confused me, because they didn't seem to match the facts of my mundane life—the facts, the facts, they probe at me like the problem they are—I was, I thought, it seemed, mildly curious, fond of red-eared turtles, good at reading but bad at math, with teeth a tad bit yellow. For her part, her predictions seemed to excite her, because when she spoke of them her words had a certain slinky sound, a lush quality to the consonants, *filthy* she would say like a hungry person pronounces *chocolate, brothel* she would say, like, well, like someone longing for and scared of sex.

෴

I wanted to get my mother a gift. I scratched at the ground with sticks, split the milkweed pods. Not this, no. Not that, no. I went to the store in town—Accents Unlimited—and roamed amongst vanilla-scented candles, heart-shaped pillows, but I knew none of it would do.

The year I turned ten, the year of what I called my colored hearing and my smells, my father gave her his surprise. I think he loved her, or, like me, her unhappiness was his. He partnered up with Irving Busney in the bakery business, and now we had toppling apple muffins in the mornings and a double salary from a double job—prayer man and business man—and so he announced a vacation.

We went to Barbados. We flew. We flew! I had never been on a plane before. I loved the bubble windows, and the stewardesses who wore wings on their busts.

I loved Logan Airport, in Boston, from which we departed on a snowy day, a typical New England winter day when the trees were in ice and the old slush stank and everyone was grumpy. We left early in the morning, when the air was blue and only a few lights flickered in our neighbors' windows. We were extremely excited. On the island, we were going to stay in a place called the Princess Hotel. My mother had brought me to Decelles the week before, and the saleslady took us to the Winter Cruise Section, and I got to buy a bikini with dots on it. I got sandles with turquoise stones studded along them. I got white gloves—*for dinners*, my mother said—and crisp white dresses and also shorts.

And we left Boston on a snowy dawn, dark airport, smell of grime and fuel, and I drank chocolate milk as the plane went up. And a wonderful, ecstatic feeling came over me, a feeling which I attributed to the plane, but which I now know happens to some epileptics when the altitude changes, like you are getting closer to God, and gold, and sweet and smells, and I saw the sun rising in the sky from a whole new vantage point. The tawny sun rose like a lazy lion, all hot fur in a pink safari sky. The plane roared, and then was quiet, and I said to my father, "Are we flying?"

And then we landed, and just like that the world was different. The ecstasy passed. Fear came, a distinct sense that something horrible would happen soon. A stewardess leaned close and said, "It's not the jungle here, you know, it's a lovely island," and I said, "Yes," but the fear, which I now know, like the ecstasy, is also a part of the preseizure state, wouldn't pass.

We went down the plane's steep stairs. "Please, God," I was saying to myself, "please, God, let her like this." If you had asked me then just why I was afraid, I would have told you, *My mother my mother please let her be pleased my mother*. I would not have told you about the epileptic's electrical arousal in the brain's emotional centers, how the fear and joy, the intense prismatic sharpness of things, all come from something as small as a single cortical spark. That was not my story then, and it is not my story now, although it is the right story, the true story, not my mother but matter more basic still; or is it?

Here's what was true. Barbados. Palm trees with leaky coconuts, the humid wind that blew in our faces as we walked across the runway. There were a lot of black people, and no snow. Outrageous flowers, redder than crayons, waved in the wind. A cab took us to our hotel. The Princess Hotel. Would this, finally, be what it was she wanted?

What we did. Deep-sea fishing on a glass-bottomed boat. Caves, where Basien bats hung upside down. Piña coladas, plums in sauce, raw sugar sucked straight from the cane. This is what I remember best about Barbados. The sugarcane. Everywhere we drove there were fields and fields of it, stalks harvested under hot sun by men with small machetes. Chop chop. Castles of sugar and sweat. The sun always shone, except for the squalls that scrabbled across the sky, opened up on us, and then departed, leaving the sugar mounds damp and pooled in places. I loved those hills of sugar. There, the fear went away. Wet from the ocean, wet from sweat, I rolled in the mounds and came to her like candy.

I watched her. *Please please let her be pleased.* When the captain pointed out the coral, I looked for the movements of pleasure in her mouth, but found none. I watched her like I should have watched my sinking sickening self. I watched her like I now, an amateur gardener, watch the weather when it might be bad. Clear sky, clouds to the left? Force of the wind? Bring in the seedlings? Sudden frost? Rising heat? What?

✿✿✿

Here were my clues. Her postcards home. She bought postcards every day and scripted out messages, her handwriting a series of careful curves. "Lovely time," she wrote to a woman named Nance. "Dear Nance, lovely time. Lovely island. We're purchasing a second home here." Or, "Emma, I'm painting every day, the colors are magnificent." And yet, I'd never seen her paint, and I'd heard nothing of a second home, but then again, what did I know? Did she paint in private? Was there a second home my parents might reveal to me? It could have all been fact. It could have all been fiction. I looked at the names on my mother's postcards—Nance, Emma, Shelly, Judith, Lil, and said those names over and over to myself, like a song. Like words might make it real.

We were to leave the island on New Year's Day. We were to celebrate on New Year's Eve, at the hotel, where the chefs were putting on quite a feast. Three whole days before the New Year's Eve feast, management posted the menu in all the prominent places, appetizers, sherbet to clear the palate, crusty rolls, and the main course, lobster.

My father said, "I think that's going too far, Anita."

She said, "We never keep kosher outside the house. We haven't kept kosher the whole time we've been here."

"But shellfish," my father said.

"A fish with a shell," she said. "It's no different than fish without a shell, which God knows we eat enough of."

"I don't like it," he said, but you could tell, anyone could tell, he didn't know how to stand up to her. I hate to say it, it's so politically incorrect, but I think if he'd been brutish, my father, she may have learned to love him.

"Lobster," she went around saying. "Have you ever had lobster? Dipped in butter?"

She said it while staring up at my father, daring him to leap into the ring with her, but he wouldn't. He had fair skin, freckled everywhere, and he spent a lot of time in the hotel, where the air conditioners shuddered and the sun came through the slats in bright chinks.

The morning of the feast I woke early. I often did. I liked the sugar hills best at dawn. This particular morning, though, I stopped by my parents' hotel room door. There were no sounds coming from the room, so I don't know why I was drawn. I never went into their bedroom at home without permission. Perhaps, here, it was the quality of the silence, silence as sharp as a shout. Their room was connected to mine, and so they hadn't locked up. I turned the handle.

It was early, maybe 6:00 A.M. They were lying on their separate sides of the bed. My mother was curled on her side, my father on his back in boxer shorts. What was it that gave this moment its particular horror for me? They were two people in bed, bored in bed, hardly a tragedy, nothing like Northern Ireland, or Panama. But I froze. I saw the spongy pouf of my father's stomach, my mother's arms where the blue veins had an ethereal glow. The room was still dawn-dark, and bottles of gin stood sweating in the cooler. The room, despite her perfumes, had a sour smell, and the air-conditioning unit banged above them. The heavy hotel curtains moved in the false breeze. Slowly, my mother turned, opened her eyes. She seemed to be entirely awake, as though she'd been waiting for me. She seemed monstrous. She did not say a word. Just saw me standing there and stared, and stared, as if to say, "So now you see," and I, well, I stepped back.

❧❧❧❧

We didn't have our lobster. It required bibs and tongs, scraping green gunk from dark places, and my mother, it turned out, couldn't lower herself to partake. I could tell she wanted to, though, the same way I could tell she secretly longed to walk with me in the woods, to take in soil, to sleep the heavy, sweaty sleep of the rude and the relaxed. Instead she watched from the polite sidelines as men and women at other tables cracked open the casing and speared the white meat, holding it up like a tiny trophy before popping it in their mouths.

No, in the end, my mother couldn't allow herself that lobster. We ate chicken instead. There was dancing and colored lights in all the trees, and the patio stones were freshly washed. And maybe because it was the New Year, my brain gave me not only jasmine that night but many other wonderful nameless odors, so strong I felt sick in a sweet way.

There was liquor galore. My mother had a thirst, she drank and drank. The pianist played many lovely songs, and she, elegant, waltzed from table to table, making comments. "His pianissimo's a little off," she said a little too loudly.

"He doesn't have much Mozart in him," she announced at the end of an aria.

"Anita, be quiet," my father hissed, a chicken bone in his mouth.

I, for my part, was mortified, because she was such a big woman with a big voice, and everyone on the patio could hear her.

Including the poor pianist.

"Play 'Gay Tarantella,'" she shouted out.

He did and when it was over she sighed and said, "Such heavy hands."

A few people tittered.

"Music," my mother announced to the patio, "is a delicate art form. It should breathe."

"Anita, we're going," my father said, spitting out his chicken bone.

Everyone was listening.

"Do you play, ma'am?" the pianist said, glaring at her. "Perhaps you could do a better job?"

"Do I play?" she said, laughing. "What a sweet question. You are a sweet," she said to the musician, who, by the by, was black. "You are a sweet man with many sweet things in you, but with no thunder. A man should have thunder," she said, glancing at my father.

"Do you play, ma'am?" the pianist said again. He was still glaring. "Would you like to play some thunder for the crowd?"

All the waiters had stopped, and all the people had stopped eating, and the patio looked like a frozen place, a garish game of freeze tag.

"I have my own Steinway at home," she said.

"How nice," the pianist said.

"And I've played," she said, and paused. "I've played in...many situations."

"Do take a seat," he said, standing up from the bench and gesturing to his place.

And then she went forward. I stopped being mortified and started being proud. Or, I was proud and mortified both, and my own dizziness was getting worse. She had balls, and she had vodka. She never stumbled or slurred, though: You could only tell if you knew her, from the metal smell of her breath.

She pushed out the seat and sat down to take it. She made a big show of positioning her hands and straightening her shoulders, just like she had practiced all those hours at home. The party waited, waited for a symphony. Waited for the maestro she'd claimed herself to be. I know I could not have seen her face—her back was to me—but I have such a clear memory, a clear dream of my mother's face as she sat at the peak of a promise she'd made, stuck in a lie, three blind mice all she knew. *Just play it, Mom,* I thought. *Three blind mice, see how they run, just play it and get it over with.* I think she stared down at the ivory keys, the bared teeth, and all things sober passed across her face, because she did not know. She must have known she did not know. Somewhere in the world, if you pressed the right keys, or the right combination of keys, there would be thunder and Mozart, and more; there would be all you'd craved but been too clenched to take, soft songs you could sleep to, chords like a hammock, maybe, and a hand to hold, the way time slows in a tub. If you knew the right notes. Which she didn't.

You could've heard a pin drop. You could've heard the petals fall from a flower while we waited, and waited. Her hands poised over the keys. Sobering up. "I suppose not," she finally said, and stood, and carefully, carefully walked away.

That night, I had my first seizure.

∞∞∞∞∞

At the school where I later went to learn about my illness, I saw movies, so I know what it is; it is not careful. You grit your teeth, you clench, a spastic look crawls across your face, your legs thrash like a funky machine, you hit hard and spew, you grind your teeth with such a force you might wake up with a mouth full of molar dust, tooth ash, the residue of words you've never spoken, but should have. You bite your mouth—I do at least—chew it to pieces from the inside out, a mythical hunger, my whole self jammed into my jaw.

When I woke up my father was bending over me and then a doctor came, a guest of the hotel. He did not seem impressed. "Seizure," he pronounced. "Rather common in young ones," and then he left.

I can dimly recall seeing my father's face in the background of the hotel room, pale and shocked. My mother, as it turns out, missed that first seizure. She had fallen into one of her restless sleeps, a sleep so fractured and tentative she always had a veil of exhaustion in her glittery eyes. Sometime during the night my father must have told her; he must have woken her and said, "She's had a seizure," and so I waited, but she never appeared to nurse me that night, and this is a grudge I still hold.

We flew back to Boston the next day. How did I feel? Shrinks have been asking me that question for decades now, as though the origin of whatever mental miseries I might have are linked to that first fall down. How did I feel, the shrinks ask, and offer me some Dilantin; you must be depressed, the shrinks say, and proffer me some Prozac. How did I feel? I'll tell you. We were in a plane, going backward. Before, I had watched the tawny sun lionize the sky, and now, through the Boeing's bubble windows, I watched it set; I watched it soil the sky and burn up a bird and take every cloud and taint it. We zoomed through the air, held up by nothing but hope, and at any moment, I knew, we could crash.

Also, my head throbbed. Someone was playing the piano in my head, and the wooden notes kept bonging my brain.

I puked in a bag and that gave me some relief.

My mother must have heard me puking, and said, from the seat in front of me, "Just give the waste to the stewardess, Lauren."

We landed in the dark. We took a taxi home in the dark. That night, finally, she came to me. She stood over me in my bed for a while, and she seemed entranced. Or maybe it was I who was entranced. No, I think it was her, actually. She stood over me, her eyes roving me from head to foot—this daughter of hers, this grand mal, this big badness—and then, finally, she touched my head like it was hot.

✺✺✺

In Beth Israel Hospital, where my mother took me the next day, I sat in a small room and drew clocks, and houses, and put together red cubes to make red-and-white patterns. "What happened?" my pediatrician, Dr. Patterson, asked.

"I smelled something funny," I said. "I remember, before I fell, I smelled a funny thing."

"What was it?" he said.

I searched for the words. Now I know that, prior to seizures, in states called auras, people frequently smell strange things. I've been in seizure support groups and heard the wackiest olfactory tales, the woman who was hounded by the smell of charred steak, another by the odor of a past lover's shampoo. The smells live, and though doctors claim they are purely physiological phenomena, without mental meaning, I cannot help but think the smells have significance; we smell what we want, or cannot allow ourselves to want; we smell our own stink, we smell our sin, we smell the tang of an unspoken hope.

"Lobster," I said.

"You smelled lobster," the doctor repeated, writing it down.

"Lobster?" my mother said. She raised an eyebrow. She was holding her square purse to her chest.

"Yes," I said. "I smelled the lobster. I smelled salty lobster and butter."

"Lobster and butter, what a meal that would've been," my mother said.

The doctor looked up, confused. "Excuse me?" he said.

I giggled.

"And the green gunk too, I smelled that."

"That's enough, Lauren," my mother said. "You're losing your credibility."

But she had a small smile on her face, and, well, just for the sake of the story let's say she even licked her lips a little bit, and that was the first time I realized how, through illness, I might be able to give her good food.

There were a lot of tests—the Wada Test, the Ray Figure Drawing Test, the Wechsler Memory Scales Test, the Digit Span Test. I took an IQ test, where, according to my mother, I scored in the genius range, but we all know she never told the truth. I had an electroencephalogram, little suckers hooked up to my head and my brain waves rolling out of a machine like a receipt from a cash register. Ribbons and ribbons of brain waves, and later, when the doctor showed them to us, we could see, my mother and I, how in some places the waves were smooth, but in others, spiky as stiletto heels, and in still others, a series of rapid round *u*'s, like this—*UUUUUUUUUU*—a language gone awry.

"She has epilepsy," I heard her whisper to someone on the phone, Nance, maybe, or Emma. "She has epilepsy, but so did van Gogh, you know."

She asked for a clipping of my brain waves and took them home, and a change came over her. She seemed to almost like the illness. She seemed disgusted, which I would have expected, but then a moment later, I saw her looking at me with wishes in her eyes, as though she, too, might like to drop and thrash, to break the brittle caul of cleanliness and artifice.

"Will, Lauren," she said to me, "use your will to get you out of this." She practiced the piano and, even with my seizures, took me skating so I could be a skating star. One morning, though, before we dressed to go out to the pond, I saw her tracing my brain's undulations, those sleepy dips, those troughs filled with earth and snooze, sex and spasm, and I'd say she smiled then.

"You," she said to me, all sternness, "need to learn to pull yourself together."

But she touched my head gently now, like it was hot, like it was cold, like it was warm, like it was whatever she was not, a wild and totally true world in there, a place she had forsaken for artifice, etiquette, marriage, mediocre love, and which I had returned to her; here, Mom; have my head.

She was right. A lot of famous people have had epilepsy. Take Dostoevski, for instance. He had a serious case of it. Saint Paul probably had epilepsy, and from its craziness he crafted a world religion. Van Gogh, of course, had epilepsy, which may be why he is the van Gogh we know, a painter of tilted stars, low-hanging moons, fields full of flowers and blue vortexes that take all sensible shape away. If you look at a van Gogh painting, you might get a sense of what the world looks like as you go down. In the weeks that followed, it kept happening to me. I was a wrong girl, I flamencoed on the floor, feathers came out of my ears, and my body made music, made thunder and sleep, made Mozart, my hands curled into lobster claws.

Epilepsy shoots your memory to hell, so take what I say, or don't. This I think I recall. One week after Barbados, after her failed music, the vodka, her empty eyes in the hotel room, I woke from a long seizure on the floor. Every muscle ached. There was blood in my mouth. I opened my eyes and saw her standing above me, staring at me, probably, for a long long time, as just a few days earlier, in the Basien dawn, I had stared at her. I had looked into that hotel room and seen how all her energy was really deadness; not me. I was a girl in motion. I was wrong and dark and full of smells. When a seizure rolled through me, it didn't feel like mine; it felt like hers—her ramrod body sweetening into spasm. She gave it all to me, and I returned it all to her, this wild, rollicking, hopeful life, this Chuck Berry blast, all striving sunk to the bottom of the brain's deep sea; crack a claw, Mom.

Rest with me when it's over.

This, the gift I gave you.

How we held each other.

4.5

BROTHERS AND KEEPERS

by John Edgar Wideman

In 1979, novelist John Edgar Wideman's brother, Robby, was convicted of murder and sentenced to life in prison in Pittsburgh's Western Penitentiary. Several years later, the two brothers began a collaboration on a book, *Brothers and Keepers,* and the result is a sometimes raw, often insightful story about two men—and two brothers—who manage to rediscover each other in a most unlikely place. Though published 30 years ago, *Brothers and Keepers* is an important book. The Widemans, who grew up in Pittsburgh's tough Homewood neighborhood in the late sixties, shared the desire to rise from poverty and racism in the turmoil of white flight, the sudden flood of cheap street heroin, and increasingly militant politics. One stayed in the neighborhood and the other went off to the university. *Brothers and Keepers* is also an extraordinary work of nonfiction. As you will see from the following excerpt, drawn from the middle of the book, Wideman uses alternating points of view—his brother's and his own—an enormously difficult technique in nonfiction. But he does it convincingly.

That day six years later, I talked with Robby three hours, the maximum allotted for weekday visits with a prisoner. It was the first time in life we'd ever talked that long. Probably two and a half hours longer than the longest, unbroken, private conversation we'd ever had. And it had taken guards, locks, and bars to bring us together. The ironies of the situation, the irony of that fact, escaped neither of us.

I listened mostly, interrupting my brother's story a few times to clarify dates or names. Much of what he related was familiar. The people, the places. Even the voice, the words he chose were mine in a way. We're so alike, I kept thinking, anticipating what he would say next, how he would say it, filling in naturally, easily with my words what he left unsaid. Trouble was our minds weren't interchangeable. No more than our bodies. The guards wouldn't have allowed me to stay in my brother's place. He was the

195

criminal. I was the visitor from outside. Different as night and day. As Robby talked I let myself forget that difference. Paid too much attention to myself listening and lost some of what he was saying. What I missed would have helped define the difference. But I missed it. It was easy to half listen. For both of us to pretend to be closer than we were. We needed the closeness. We were brothers. In the prison visiting lounge I acted toward my brother the way I'd been acting toward him all my life, heard what I wanted to hear, rejected the rest.

When Robby talked, the similarity of his Homewood and mine was a trap. I could believe I knew exactly what he was describing. I could relax into his story, walk down Dunfermline or Tioga, see my crippled grandmother sitting on the porch of the house on Finance, all the color her pale face had lost blooming in the rosebush beneath her in the yard, see Robby in the downstairs hall of the house on Marchand, rapping with his girl on the phone, which sat on a three-legged stand just inside the front door. I'd slip unaware out of his story into one of my own. I'd be following him, an obedient shadow, then a cloud would blot the sun and I'd be gone, unchained, a dark form still skulking behind him but no longer in tow.

The hardest habit to break, since it was the habit of a lifetime, would be listening to myself listen to him. That habit would destroy any chance of seeing my brother on his terms; and seeing him in his terms, learning his terms, seemed the whole point of learning his story. However numerous and comforting the similarities, we were different. The world had seized on the difference, allowed me room to thrive, while he'd been forced into a cage. Why did it work out that way? What was the nature of the difference? Why did it haunt me? Temporarily at least, to answer these questions, I had to root my fiction-writing self out of our exchanges. I had to teach myself to listen. Start fresh, clear the pipes, resist too facile an identification, tame the urge to take off with Robby's story and make it my own.

I understood all that, but could I break the habit? And even if I did learn to listen, wouldn't there be a point at which I'd have to take over the telling? Wasn't there something fundamental in my writing, in my capacity to function, that depended on flight, on escape? Wasn't another person's skin a hiding place, a place to work out anxiety, to face threats too intimidating to handle in any other fashion? Wasn't writing about people a way of exploiting them?

A stranger's gait, or eyes, or a piece of clothing can rivet my attention. Then it's like falling down to the center of the earth. Not exactly fear or panic but an uneasy, uncontrollable momentum, a sense of being swallowed, engulfed in blackness that has no dimensions, no fixed points. That boundless, incarcerating black hole is another person. The detail grabbing me functions as a door and it swings open and I'm drawn, sucked, pulled in head over heels till suddenly I'm righted again, on track again and the peculiarity, the ordinariness of the detail that usurped my attention becomes a window, a way of seeing out of another person's eyes, just as for a second it had been my way in. I'm scooting along on short, stubby legs and the legs are not anybody else's and certainly not mine, but I feel for a second what it's like to motor through the world atop those peculiar duck thighs and foreshortened calves and I know how wobbly the earth feels under those run-over-at-the-heel, split-seamed penny loafers. Then just as suddenly I'm back. I'm me again, slightly embarrassed, guilty because I've been trespassing and don't know how long I've been gone or if anybody noticed me violating somebody else's turf.

Do I write to escape, to make a fiction of my life? If I can't be trusted with the story of my own life, how could I ask my brother to trust me with his?

The business of making a book together was new for both of us. Difficult. Awkward. Another book could be constructed about a writer who goes to a prison to interview his brother but comes away with his own story. The conversations with his brother would provide a stage for dramatizing the writer's tortured relationship to other people, himself, his craft. The writer's motives, the issue of exploitation, the inevitable conflict between his role as detached observer and his responsibility as a brother would be at the center of such a book. When I stopped hearing Robby and listened to myself listening, that kind of book shouldered its way into my consciousness. I didn't like the feeling. That book compromised the intimacy I wanted to achieve with my brother. It was as obtrusive as the Wearever pen in my hand, the little yellow sheets of Yard Count paper begged from the pad of the guard in charge of overseeing the visiting lounge. The borrowed pen and paper (I was not permitted into the lounge with my own) were necessary props. I couldn't rely on memory to get my brother's story down and the keepers had refused my request to use a tape recorder, so there I was. Jimmy Olson, cub reporter, poised on the edge of my seat, pen and paper at ready, asking to be treated as a brother.

We were both rookies. Neither of us had learned very much about sharing our feelings with other family members. At home it had been assumed that each family member possessed deep, powerful feelings and that very little or nothing at all needed to be said about these feelings because we all were stuck with them and talk wouldn't change them. Your particular feelings were a private matter and family was a protective fence around everybody's privacy. Inside the perimeter of the fence each family member resided in his or her own quarters. What transpired in each dwelling was mainly the business of its inhabitant as long as nothing generated within an individual unit threatened the peace or safety of the whole. None of us knew how traditional West African families were organized or what values the circular shape of their villages embodied, but the living arrangements we had worked out among ourselves resembled the ancient African patterns. You were granted emotional privacy, independence, and space to commune with your feelings. You were encouraged to deal with as much as you could on your own, yet you never felt alone. The high wall of the family, the collective, communal reality of other souls, other huts like yours eliminated some of the dread, the isolation experienced when you turned inside and tried to make sense out of the chaos of your individual feelings. No matter how grown you thought you were or how far you believed you'd strayed, you knew you could cry *Mama* in the depths of the night and somebody would tend to you. Arms would wrap round you, a soft soothing voice lend its support. If not a flesh-and-blood mother then a mother in the form of song or story or a surrogate, Aunt Geral, Aunt Martha, drawn from the network of family numbers.

Privacy was a bridge between you and the rest of the family. But you had to learn to control the traffic. You had to keep it uncluttered, resist the temptation to cry wolf. Privacy in our family was a birthright, a union card granted with family membership. The card said you're one of us but also certified your separateness, your obligation to keep much of what defined your separateness to yourself.

An almost aesthetic consideration's involved. Okay, let's live together. Let's each build a hut and for security we'll arrange the individual dwellings in a circle and then build an outer ring to enclose the whole village. Now your hut is your own business, but let's in general agree on certain outward forms. Since we all benefit from the larger pattern, let's compromise, conform to some degree on the materials, the shape of each unit. Because symmetry and harmony please the eye. Let's adopt a style, one that won't crimp anybody's individuality, one that will buttress and enhance each member's image of what a living place should be.

So Robby and I faced each other in the prison visiting lounge as familiar strangers, linked by blood and time. But how do you begin talking about blood, about time? He's been inside his privacy and I've been inside mine, and neither of us in thirty-odd years had felt the need to exchange more than social calls. We shared the common history, values, and style developed within the tall stockade of family, and that was enough to make us care about each other, enough to insure a profound depth of mutual regard, but the feelings were undifferentiated. They'd seldom been tested specifically, concretely. His privacy and mine had been exclusive, sanctioned by family traditions. Don't get too close. Don't ask too many questions or give too many answers. Don't pry. Don't let what's inside slop out on the people around you.

The stories I'd sent to Robby were an attempt to reveal what I thought about certain matters crucial to us both. Our shared roots and destinies. I wanted him to know what I'd been thinking and how that thinking was drawing me closer to him. I was banging on the door of his privacy. I believed I'd shed some of my own.

We were ready to talk. It was easy to begin. Impossible. We were neophytes, rookies. I was a double rookie. A beginner at this kind of intimacy, a beginner at trying to record it. My double awkwardness kept getting in the way. I'd hidden the borrowed pen by dropping my hand below the level of the table where we sat. Now when in hell would be the right moment to raise it? To use it? I had to depend on my brother's instincts, his generosity. I had to listen, listen.

Luckily there was catching up to do. He asked me about my kids, about his son, Omar, about the new nieces and nephews he'd never seen. That helped. Reminded us we were brothers. We got on with it. Conditions in the prisons. Robby's state of mind. The atmosphere behind the prison walls had been particularly tense for over a year. A group of new, younger guards had instituted a get-tough policy. More strip searches, cell shakedowns, strict enforcement of penny-ante rules and regulations. Grown men treated like children by other grown men. Inmates yanked out of line and punished because a button is undone or hair uncombed. What politicians demanded in the free world was being acted out inside the prison. A crusade, a war on crime waged by a gang of gung-ho guards against men who were already certified casualties, prisoners of war. The walking wounded being beaten and shot up again because they're easy targets. Robby's closest friends, including Cecil and Mike, are in the hole. Others who were considered potential troublemakers had been transferred to harsher prisons. Robby was warned by a guard. We ain't caught you in the shit yet, but we will. We know what you're thinking and we'll catch you in it. Or put you in it. Got your buddies and we'll get you.

The previous summer, 1980, a prisoner, Leon Patterson, had been asphyxiated in his cell. He was an asthma sufferer, a convicted murderer who depended on medication to survive the most severe attacks of his illness. On a hot August afternoon when the pollution index had reached its highest count of the summer, Patterson was locked in his cell in a cellblock without windows and little air. At four o'clock, two hours after he'd been confined to the range, he began to call for help. Other prisoners raised the traditional distress signal, rattling tin cups against the bars of their cells. Patterson's cries for help became screams, and his fellow inmates beat on the bars and shouted with him. Over an hour passed before any guards arrived. They carted away Patterson's limp body. He never revived and was pronounced dead at 10:45 that evening. His death epitomized the polarization in the prison. Patterson was seen as one more victim of the guards' inhumanity. A series of incidents followed in the ensuing year, hunger strikes, melees between guards and prisoners, culminating in a near massacre when the dog days of August hung once more over the prison.

One of the favorite tactics of the militant guards was grabbing a man from the line as the prisoners moved single-file through an archway dividing the recreation yard from the main cell blocks. No reason was given or needed. It was a simple show of force, a reminder of the guards' absolute power, their right to treat the inmates any way they chose, and do it with impunity. A sit-down strike in the prison auditorium followed one of the more violent attacks on an inmate. The prisoner who had resisted an arbitrary seizure and strip search was smacked in the face. He punched back and the guards jumped him, knocked him to the ground with their fists and sticks. The incident took place in plain view of over a hundred prisoners and it was the last straw. The victim had been provoked, assaulted, and surely would be punished for attempting to protect himself, for doing what any man would and should do in similar circumstances. The prisoner would suffer again. In addition to the physical beating they'd administered, the guards would attack the man's record. He'd be written up. A kangaroo court would take away his *good time,* thereby lengthening the period he'd have to wait before becoming eligible for probation or parole. Finally, on the basis of the guards' testimony he'd probably get a sixty-day sojourn in the hole. The prisoners realized it was time to take a stand. What had happened to one could happen to any of them. They rushed into the auditorium and locked themselves in. The prisoners held out till armed state troopers and prison guards in riot gear surrounded the building. Given the mood of that past year and the unmistakable threat in the new warden's voice as he repeated through a loudspeaker his refusal to meet with the prisoners and discuss their grievances, everybody inside the building knew that the authorities meant business, that the forces of law and order would love nothing better than an excuse to turn the auditorium into a shooting gallery. The strike was broken. The men filed out. A point was driven home again. Prisoners have no rights the keepers are bound to respect.

That was how the summer had gone. Summer was bad enough in the penitentiary in the best of times. Warm weather stirred the prisoners' blood. The siren call of the streets intensified. Circus time. The street blooming again after the long, cold winter. People outdoors. On their stoops. On the corners. In bright summer clothes or hardly any clothes at all. The free-world sounds and sights more real as the weather heats up. Confinement a torture. Each cell a hotbox. The keepers take advantage of every excuse to keep you out of the yard, to deprive you of the simple pleasure of a breeze, the blue sky. Why? So that the pleasant weather can be used as a tool, a boon to be withheld. So punishment has a sharper edge. By a perverse turn of the screw something good becomes something bad. Summer a bitch at best, but this past summer as the young turks among the guards ran roughshod over the prisoners, the prison had come close to blowing, to exploding like a piece of rotten fruit in the sun. And if the lid blew, my brother knew he'd be one of the first to die. During any large-scale uprising, in the first violent, chaotic seconds no board of inquiry would ever be able to reconstruct, scores would be settled. A bullet in the back of the brain would get rid of troublemakers, remove potential leaders, uncontrollable prisoners the guards hated and feared. You were supremely eligible for a bullet if the guards couldn't press your button. If they hadn't learned how to manipulate you, if you couldn't be bought or sold, if you weren't into drug and sex games, if you weren't cowed or depraved, then you were a threat.

Robby understood that he was sentenced to die. That all sentences were death sentences. If he didn't buckle under, the guards would do everything in their power to kill him. If he succumbed to the pressure to surrender dignity, self-respect, control over his own mind and body, then he'd become a beast, and what was good in him would die. The death sentence was unambiguous. The question for him became: How long could he survive in spite of the death sentence? Nothing he did would guarantee his safety. A disturbance in a cell block halfway across the prison could provide an excuse for shooting him and dumping him with the other victims. Anytime he was ordered to go with guards out of sight of other prisoners, his escorts could claim he attacked them, or attempted to escape. Since the flimsiest pretext would make murdering him acceptable, he had no means of protecting himself. Yet to maintain sanity, to minimize their opportunities to destroy him, he had to be constantly vigilant. He had to discipline himself to avoid confrontations, he had to weigh in terms of life and death every decision he made; he had to listen and obey his keepers' orders, but he also had to determine in certain threatening situations whether it was better to say no and keep himself out of a trap or take his chances that this particular summons was not the one inviting him to his doom. Of course to say no perpetuated his reputation as one who couldn't be controlled, a bad guy, a guy you never turn your back on, one of the prisoners out to get the guards. That rap made you more dangerous in the keepers' eyes and therefore increased the likelihood they'd be frightened into striking first. Saying no put you in no less jeopardy than going along with the program. Because the program was contrived to kill you. Directly or indirectly, you knew where you were headed. What you didn't know was the schedule. Tomorrow. Next week. A month. A minute. When would one of them get itchy, get beyond waiting a second longer? Would there be a plan, a contrived incident, a conspiracy they'd talk about and set up as they drank coffee in the guards' room or would it be the hair-trigger impulse of one of them who held a grudge, harbored an antipathy so elemental, so irrational that it could express itself only in a burst of pure, unrestrained violence?

If you're Robby and have the will to survive, these are the possibilities you must constantly entertain. Vigilance is the price of survival. Beneath the vigilance, however, is a gnawing awareness boiling in the pit of your stomach. You can be as vigilant as you're able, you can keep fighting the good fight to survive, and still your fate is out of your hands. If they decide to come for you in the morning, that's it. Your ass is grass and those minutes, and hours, days and years you painfully stitched together to put off the final reckoning won't matter at all. So the choice, difficult beyond words, to say yes or say no is made in light of the knowledge that in the end neither your yes nor your no matters. Your life is not in your hands.

The events, the atmosphere of the summer had brought home to Robby the futility of resistance. Power was absurdly apportioned all on one side. To pretend you could control your own destiny was a joke. You learned to laugh at your puniness, as you laughed at the stink of your farts lighting up your cell. Like you laughed at the seriousness of the masturbation ritual that romanticized, cloaked in darkness and secrecy, the simple, hungry shaking of your penis in your fist. You had no choice, but you always had to decide to go on or stop. It had been a stuttering, stop, start, maybe, fuck it, bitch of a summer, and now, for better or worse, we were starting up something else. Robby backtracks his story from Garth to another beginning, the house on Copeland Street in Shadyside where we lived when he was born.

∿∿∿

I know that had something to do with it. Living in Shadyside with only white people around. You remember how it was. Except for us and them couple other families it was a all-white neighborhood. I got a thing about black. See, black was like the forbidden fruit. Even when we went to Freed's in Homewood, Geraldine and them never let me go no farther than the end of the block. All them times I stayed over there I didn't go past Mr. Conrad's house by the vacant lot or the other corner where Billy Shields and them stayed. Started to wondering what was so different about a black neighborhood. I was just a little kid and I was curious. I really wanted to know why they didn't want me finding out what was over there. Be playing with the kids next door to Freed, you know, Sonny and Gumpy and them, but all the time I'm wondering what's round the corner, what's up the street. Didn't care if it was *bad* or good or dangerous or what, I had to find out. If it's something bad I figured they would have told me, tried to scare me off. But nobody said nothing except, No. Don't you go no farther than the corner. Then back home in Shadyside nothing but white people so I couldn't ask nobody what was special about black. Black was a mystery and in my mind I decided I'd find out what it was all about. Didn't care if it killed me, I was going to find out.

One time, it was later, I was close to starting high school, I overheard Mommy and Geraldine and Sissy talking in Freed's kitchen. They was talking about us moving from Shadyside back to Homewood. The biggest thing they was worried about was me. How would it be for me being in Homewood and going to Westinghouse? I could tell they was scared. Specially Mom. You know how she is. She didn't want to move. Homewood scared her. Not so much the place but how I'd act if I got out there in the middle of it. She already knew I was wild, hard to handle. There'd be too much mess for me to get into in Homewood. She could see trouble coming.

And she was right. Me and trouble hooked up. See, it was a question of being somebody. Being my own person. Like youns had sports and good grades sewed up. Wasn't nothing I could do in school or sports that youns hadn't done already. People said, Here comes another Wideman. He's gon be a good student like his brothers and sister. That's the way it was spozed to be. I was another Wideman, the last one, the baby, and everybody knew how I was spozed to act. But something inside me said no. Didn't want to be like the rest of youns. Me, I had to be a rebel. Had to get out from under youns' good grades and do. Way back then I decided I wanted to be a star. I wanted to make it big. My way. I wanted the glamour. I wanted to sit high up.

Figured out school and sports wasn't the way. I got to thinking my brothers and sister was squares. Loved youall but wasn't no room left for me. Had to figure out a new territory. I had to be a rebel.

Along about junior high I discovered Garfield. I started hanging out up on Garfield Hill. You know, partying and stuff in Garfield cause that's where the niggers was. Garfield was black, and I finally found what I'd been looking for. That place they was trying to hide from me. It was heaven. You know. Hanging out with the fellows. Drinking wine and trying anything else we could get our hands on. And the ladies. Always a party on the weekends. Had me plenty sweet little soft-leg Garfield ladies. Niggers run my butt off that hill more than a couple times behind messing with somebody's piece but I'd be back next weekend. Cause I'd found heaven. Looking back now, wasn't much to Garfield. Just a rinky-dink ghetto up on a hill, but it was the street. I'd found my place.

Having a little bit of a taste behind me I couldn't wait to get to Homewood. In a way I got mad with Mommy and the rest of them. Seemed to me like they was trying to hold me back from a good time. Seemed like they just didn't want me to have no fun. That's when I decided I'd go on about my own business. Do it my way. Cause I wasn't getting no slack at home. They still expected me to be like my sister and brothers. They didn't know I thought youns was squares. Yeah. I knew I was hipper and groovier than youns ever thought of being. Streetwise, into something. Had my own territory and I was bad. I was a rebel. Wasn't following in nobody's footsteps but my own. And I was a hip cookie, you better believe it. Wasn't a hipper thing out there than your brother, Rob. I couldn't wait for them to turn me loose in Homewood.

Me being the youngest and all, the baby in the family, people always said, ain't he cute. That Robby gon be a ladykiller. Been hearing that mess since day one so ain't no surprise I started to believing it. Youns had me pegged as a lady's man so that's what I was. The girls be talking the same trash everybody else did. Ain't he cute. Be petting me and spoiling me like I'm still the baby of the family and I sure ain't gon tell them stop. Thought I was cute as the girls be telling me. Thought sure enough, I'm gon be a star. I loved to get up and show my behind. Must have been good at it too cause the teacher used to call me up in front of the class to perform. The kids'd get real quiet. That's probably why the teacher got me up. Keep the class quiet while she nods off. Cause they'd listen to me. Sure nuff pay attention.

Performing always come natural to me. Wasn't nervous or nothing. Just get up and do my thing. They liked for me to do impressions. I could mimic anybody. You remember how I'd do that silly stuff around the house. Anybody I'd see on TV or hear on a record I could mimic to a T. Bob Hope, Nixon, Smokey Robinson, Ed Sullivan. White or black. I could talk just like them or sing a song just like they did. The class yell out a famous name and I'd do the one they wanted to hear. If things had gone another way I've always believed I could have made it big in show business. If you could keep them little frisky kids in Liberty School quiet you could handle any audience. Always could sing and do impressions. You remember Mom asking me to do them for you when you came home from college.

I still be performing. Read poetry in the hole. The other fellows get real quiet and listen. Sing down in there too. Nothing else to do, so we entertain each other. They always asking me to sing or read. "Hey, Wideman. C'mon man and do something." Then it gets quiet while they waiting for me to start. Quiet and it's already dark. You in your own cell and can't see nobody else. Barely enough light to read by. The other fellows can hear you but it's just you and them walls so it feels like being alone much as it feels like you're singing or reading to somebody else.

Yeah I read my own poems sometimes. Other times I just start in on whatever book I happen to be reading. One the books you sent me, maybe. Fellows like my poems. They say I write about the things they be thinking. Say it's like listening to their own self thinking. That's cause we all down there together. What else you gonna do but think of the people on the outside. Your woman. Your kids or folks, if you got any. Just the same old sad shit we all be thinking all the time. That's what I write and the fellows like to hear it.

Funny how things go around like that. Go round and round and keep coming back to the same place. Teacher used to get me up to pacify the class and I'm doing the same thing in prison. You said your teachers called on you to tell stories, didn't they? Yeah. It's funny how much we're alike. In spite of everything I always believed that. Inside. The feeling side. I always believed we was the most alike out of all the kids. I see stuff in your books. The kinds of things I be thinking or feeling.

Your teachers got you up, too. To tell stories. That's funny, ain't it.

❧❧❧❧

I listen to my brother Robby. He unravels my voice. I sit with him in the darkness of the Behavioral Adjustment Unit. My imagination creates something like a giant seashell, enfolding, enclosing us. Its inner surface is velvet-soft and black. A curving mirror doubling the darkness. Poems are Jean Toomer's petals of dusk, petals of dawn. I want to stop. Savor the sweet, solitary pleasure, the time stolen from time in the hole. But the image I'm creating is a trick of the glass. The mirror that would swallow Robby and then chime to me: You're the fairest of them all. The voice I hear issues from a crack in the glass. I'm two or three steps ahead of my brother, making fiction out of his words. Somebody needs to snatch me by the neck and say, Stop. Stop and listen, listen to him.

The Behavioral Adjustment Unit is, as one guard put it, "a maximum-security prison within a maximum-security prison." The "Restricted Housing Unit" or "hole" or "Home Block" is a squat, two-story cement building containing thirty-five six-by-eight-foot cells. The governor of Pennsylvania closed the area in 1972 because of "inhumane conditions," but within a year the hole was reopened. For at least twenty-three hours a day the prisoners are confined to their cells. An hour of outdoor exercise is permitted only on days the guards choose to supervise it. Two meals are served three hours apart, then nothing except coffee and bread for the next twenty-one. The regulation that limits the time an inmate can serve in the BAU for a single offense is routinely sidestepped by the keepers. "Administrative custody" is a provision allowing officials to cage men in the BAU indefinitely. Hunger strikes are one means the prisoners have employed to protest the harsh conditions of the penal unit. Hearings prompted by the strikes have produced no major changes in the way the hole operates. Law, due process, the rights of the prisoners are irrelevant to the functioning of this prison within a prison. Robby was sentenced to six months in the BAU because a guard suspected he was involved in an attempted escape. The fact that a hearing, held six months later, established Robby's innocence, was small consolation since he'd already served his time in the hole.

Robby tells me about the other side of being the youngest: Okay, you're everybody's pet and that's boss, but on the other hand you sometimes feel you're the least important. Always last. Always bringing up the rear. You learn to do stuff on your own because the older kids are always busy, off doing their things, and you're too young, left behind because you don't fit, or just because they forget you're back here, at the end, bringing up the rear. But when orders are given out, you sure get your share. "John's coming home this weekend. Clean up your room." Robby remembers being forced to get a haircut on the occasion of one of my visits. Honor thy brother. Get your hair cut, your room rid up, and put on clean clothes. He'll be here with his family and I don't want the house looking like a pigpen.

I have to laugh at the image of myself as somebody to get a haircut for. Robby must have been fit to be tied.

LITERARY JOURNALISM

4.6

BOOBIE

by H. G. Bissinger

❧

Fifty years ago, Truman Capote was looking for the true story that would fulfill his aspirations to experiment with the "nonfiction novel." He found it buried in *The New York Times*, a single-column article about the murder of the Clutter family in Holcomb, Kansas. H. G. Bissinger's story about the Permian High School football team, a state championship contender from the hard-luck town of Odessa, Texas, is as interesting and timeless as Capote's. There is the cult-like Texas obsession with football. There are the politics of race in rural America. There are the high expectations that high school teenagers put on with their shoulder pads. Bissinger, like Capote, saw the richness of the story, and *Friday Night Lights* tells it with skillful writing and reporting. In the following excerpt from the third chapter of the book, "Boobie," an extraordinary black running back for the team learns of an injury that may shatter his dreams.

❧❧❧

The pre-season scrimmage in the late August twilight had barely started when Boobie peeled off a run that gave glimpses of why the college recruiters were after him, why Texas A & M and Nebraska and Houston and all the others routinely crammed his mailbox with heady testimonials to his magnificence.

You have been recommended to us as an outstanding prospective major college student-athlete.

You had an outstanding junior year at Permian and I am sure your senior year will be even better. You are in a situation that many young athletes dream about.

The entire Houston Cougar football staff has been in the process of putting together the top list of high school senior football players in Texas.... Booby, we feel that you are one of these few select players.

James—we are in New York preparing for the kickoff classic and enjoying the sights. Good luck in your first game. Looking forward to watching you play later this season.

They weren't interested in him just because he was big and looked imposing in a football uniform. There were a thousand kids in Texas who fit that description. It was something else, more than just strength or speed, a kind of invincible fire that burned within him, an unquenchable feeling that no one on that field, *no one*, was as good as he was. "Miles had the *attitude*," said former teammate Art Wagner with admiration. "He thought he was the *best*."

He had played his junior year with a kind of seething emotion that sometimes dissolved into quick frustration and discouragement. He easily got rattled, particularly when things weren't going well, and there were times on the field when he seemed as frazzled as a child. But there were other times when that emotion made him spellbinding and untouchable.

It had been there during the Abilene High game when he gained 232 yards on eight carries and scored touchdowns of 62 yards, 80 yards, and 67 yards. His father, who lived in Houston, had been in the stands that night. They had been separated for some time, and it was the first time James senior had ever seen his son play football at Permian. He was almost unprepared for what it felt like to watch his own flesh and blood out there on that field. "Oh, man," he remembered. "The first I seen him carry that ball, he busted that line for eighty yards. Do you know how you feel when you see your son doin' good, doin' somethin' special? It kind of put a lump in your throat. Man, that boy ran that ball that night!"

The fire had been there during the Arlington game in the playoffs, after he had come off the field with tears in his eyes because one of the opposing players had called him a nigger. Gaines tried to comfort him and told him the other team only wanted to get him worked up so he would get himself kicked out of the game. And then he saw a change come over Boobie as if something had snapped, the hurt and humiliation giving way to a raging anger. He only carried the ball twelve times that day for forty-eight yards, but it was his savage blocking that made the recruiters up in the stands take notice, the way he went after the Arlington defenders with uncontrolled vengeance, the way he flattened a linebacker and rendered him semi-unconscious. It proved to them that Boobie had more than just the requisite size and speed to play big-time college ball. He had the rawness, the abandon, the unbridled meanness.

"He's strong as snot," Mike Winchell said of him.

"He's the best football player I've ever seen," said Jerrod McDougal.

Boobie himself was well aware that all eyes were poised on him this season, and while he luxuriated in it, he seemed almost carefree about it. Holding court in the trainer's room shortly after the practices had begun in the August heat, he bantered with the nine-year-old son of one of the coaches as if they were best pals in grade school together, calling him "waterbug head," asking him if he had a girlfriend, grabbing his head and giving him a noogie, telling him that when it came to "the shoe," Adidas would never hold a nickel next to the almighty Nike. He lay on one of the brown trainer's tables, but it was impossible for him to keep still. With his head hanging over the table, he ran his fingers along one of the crevices in the wall and started to do a rap tune.

He asked one of the student trainers to dial the phone for him and call his girlfriend. The student held the phone out as Boobie, shaking with laughter, yelled from across the room, "What's the deal, what's the holdup on comin' to the house?" When Trapper walked in, Boobie called him "cuz" and "cat-daddy." A few minutes later he was handed a list of defensive plays to study. He looked at it for several seconds, the droning terminology of numbers and letters as appealing as Morse Code, and started to read it aloud in rap to give it a little flavor, a little extra pizzazz.

He continued to play with the wall and then turned onto his stomach before flipping over again on his back. He spoke in little snatches.

"My last year . . . I want to win State. You get your picture took and a lot of college people look at you.

"When you get old, you say, you know, I went to State in nineteen eighty-eight."

He dreamed of making it to the pros, just as long as it wasn't the New York Jets because he didn't like the color green. And as he flipped onto his stomach one more time, he said he couldn't ever, ever imagine a life without football because it would be "a big zero, 'cause, I don't know, it's just the way I feel. If I had a good job and stuff, I still wouldn't be happy. I want to go pro. That's my dream . . . be rookie of the year or somethin' like that."

He moved off the line against the Palo Duro Dons and everything was in pulsating motion, the legs thrust high, the hips swiveling, the arms pumping, the shoulder pads clapping wildly up and down like the incessant beat of a calypso drum.

He went for fifteen yards and it was only a scrimmage but he wanted more, he always wanted more when he had the ball. Near the sidelines he planted his left leg to stiff-arm a tackler. But the leg got caught in the artificial turf and then someone fell on the side of it and when he got up he was limping and could barely put any pressure on it at all.

The team doctor, Weldon Butler, ran his fingers up and down the leg, feeling for broken bones. Then he moved to the knee.

Boobie watched the trail of those fingers, his eyes ablaze and his mouth slightly open. With the tiny voice of a child, he asked Butler how serious it was, how long he would be out.

Butler just kept staring at his knee.

"You might be out six, eight weeks," he said quietly, almost in a whisper.

Boobie jolted upright, as if he was wincing from the force of a shock.

"Oh fuck, man!"

"We won't know until we X-ray it. It may be worse if you don't stop moving that leg."

"You can't be serious, man! You got to be full of shit, man!"

Butler said nothing.

"Man, *I know you're not talking about any six to eight weeks.*"

Boobie was placed on the red players' bench behind the sideline and his black high tops were slowly untied. The leg was placed in a black bag filled with ice to help stop the swelling. He turned to Trapper.

"Is it gonna fuck up my season, man?" he asked in a terrified whisper.

"I sure hope not," said Trapper.

But privately, Trapper's assessment was different. As a trainer he dealt with knee injuries all the time. His gut told him it was something serious, an injury that might prevent Boobie from ever playing football again the way he once had.

Boobie lay down and several student managers took off his pads. In his uniform, with all the different pads he fancied, he looked a little like Robo Cop. But stripped of all the accoutrements, reduced to a gray shirt soaked with sweat, he had lost his persona. He looked like what he was—an eighteen-year-old kid who was scared to death.

"I won't be able to play college football, man," said Boobie in a whisper as the sounds of the game in the gauzy light—the bits, the whistles of the officials, the yells of the coaches—coated over him, had no effect on him anymore. "It's real important. It's all I ever wanted to do. I want to make it in the pros.

"All I wanted to do," he repeated again. "Make it to the pros." When the injury occurred, L. V. could only watch with silent horror. He had stayed frozen in the stands, not wanting to accept it or confront it, hoping that it would go away after a few nervous moments. But there were too many people around Boobie looking at his knee as if it were a priceless vase with a suddenly discovered crack that had just made it worthless.

He had always feared that Boobie would be seriously injured one day, but not like this, not in a scrimmage that didn't count for a single statistic, not when he was about to have it all.

He had pushed Boobie in football and prodded him and refused to let him quit. He did it because he loved him. And he also did it because he saw in his nephew the hopes, the possibilities, the dreams that he had never had in his own life when he had been a boy growing up in West Texas, back in a tiny town that looked like all the other tiny towns that dotted the plains like little bottlecaps, back in the place the whites liked to call Niggertown.

4.7

THE AMERICAN MAN AT AGE TEN

by Susan Orlean

∾

Susan Orlean's work, and particularly this piece, proves once again that it isn't necessary for a literary journalist to cover a war, investigate a murder, or profile a president in order to tell a good story. All you need is a ten-year-old boy named Colin and some time in his company. Years ago, former Chicago newspaper columnist Bob Greene wrote an essay, "Fifteen," in which he tailed two boys for an afternoon at a local mall. Orlean's "The American Man at Age Ten" is a similar story, and yet it's also a richer work because, unlike Greene, she is part of the narrative. From the beginning, we imagine her in conversation with Colin, an adult eagerly trying to enter his world. She writes with great sympathy and curiosity, qualities that are apparent not just in this essay but in everything she writes.

∾∾∾

If Colin Duffy and I were to get married, we would have matching super-hero notebooks. We would wear shorts, big sneakers, and long, baggy, T-shirts depicting famous athletes every single day, even in the winter. We would sleep in our clothes. We would both be good at Nintendo Street Fighter II, but Colin would be better than me. We would have some home-work, but it would never be too hard and we would always have just fin-ished it. We would eat pizza and candy for all of our meals. We wouldn't have sex, but we would have crushes on each other and, magically, babies would appear in our home. We would win the lottery and then buy land in Wyoming, where we would have one of every kind of cute animal. All the while, Colin would be working in law enforcement—probably the FBI. Our favorite movie star, Morgan Freeman, would visit us occasionally. We would listen to the same Eurythmics song ("Here Comes the Rain Again") over and over again and watch two hours of television every Friday night. We would both be good at football, have best friends, and know how to drive, we would cure AIDS and the garbage problem and everything that hurts animals. We would hang out a lot with Colin's dad. For fun, we

210

would load a slingshot with dog food and shoot it at my butt. We would have a very good life.

Here are the particulars about Colin Duffy: He is ten years old, on the nose. He is four feet eight inches high, weighs seventy-five pounds, and appears to be mostly leg and shoulder blade. He is a handsome kid. He has a broad forehead, dark eyes with dense lashes, and a sharp, dimply smile. I have rarely seen him without a baseball cap. He owns several, but favors a University of Michigan Wolverines model, on account of its pleasing colors. The hat styles his hair into wild disarray. If you ever managed to get the hat off his head, you would see a boy with a nimbus of golden-brown hair, dented in the back, where the hat hits him.

Colin lives with his mother, Elaine; his father, Jim; his older sister, Megan; and his little brother, Chris, in a pretty pale blue Victorian house on a bosky street in Glen Ridge, New Jersey. Glen Ridge is a serene and civilized old town twenty miles west of New York City. It does not have much of a commercial district, but it is a town of amazing lawns. Most of the houses were built around the turn of the century and are set back a gracious, green distance from the street. The rest of the town seems to consist of parks and playing fields and sidewalks and backyards—in other words, it is a far cry from South-Central Los Angeles and from Bedford-Stuyvesant and other, grimmer parts of the country where a very different ten-year-old American man is growing up today.

There is a fine school system in Glen Ridge, but Elaine and Jim, who are both schoolteachers, choose to send their children to a parents' cooperative elementary school in Montclair, a neighboring suburb. Currently, Colin is in fifth grade. He is a good student. He plans to go to college, to a place he says is called Oklahoma City State College University. OCSCU satisfies his desire to live out west, to attend a small college, and to study law enforcement, which OCSCU apparently offers as a major. After four years at Oklahoma City State College University, he plans to work for the FBI. He says that getting to be a police officer involves tons of hard work, but working for the FBI will be a cinch, because all you have to do is fill out one form, which he has already gotten from the head FBI office. Colin is quiet in class but loud on the playground. He has a great throwing arm, significant foot speed, and a lot of physical confidence. He is also brave.

Huge wild cats with rabies and gross stuff dripping from their teeth, which he says run rampant throughout his neighborhood, do not scare him. Otherwise, he is slightly bashful. This combination of athletic grace and valor and personal reserve accounts for considerable popularity. He has a fluid relationship to many social groups, including the superbright nerds, the ultrajocks, the flashy kids who will someday become extremely popular and socially successful juvenile delinquents, and the kids who will be elected president of the student body. In his opinion, the most popular boy in his class is Christian, who happens to be black, and Colin's favorite television character is Steve Urkel on *Family Matters*, who is black, too, but otherwise he seems uninterested in or oblivious to race. Until this year, he was a Boy Scout. Now he is planning to begin karate lessons. His favorite schoolyard game is football, followed closely by prison dodgeball, blob tag, and bombardo. He's crazy about athletes, although sometimes it isn't clear if he is absolutely sure of the difference between human athletes and Marvel Comics action figures. His current athletic hero is Dave Meggett. His current best friend is named Japeth. He used to have another best friend named Ozzie. According to Colin, Ozzie was found on a doorstep, then changed his name to Michael and moved to Massachusetts, and then Colin never saw him or heard from him again.

He has had other losses in his life. He is old enough to know people who have died and to know things about the world that are worrisome. When he dreams, he dreams about moving to Wyoming, which he has visited with his family. His plan is to buy land there and have some sort of ranch that would definitely include horses. Sometimes when he talks about this, it sounds as ordinary and hard-boiled as a real estate appraisal; other times it can sound fantastical and wifty and achingly naive, informed by the last inklings of childhood—the musings of a balmy real estate appraiser assaying a wonderful and magical landscape that erodes from memory a little bit every day. The collision in his mind of what he understands, what he hears, what he figures out, what popular culture pours into him, what he knows, what he pretends to know, and what he imagines makes an interesting mess. The mess often has the form of what he will probably think like when he is a grown man, but the content of what he is like as a little boy.

He is old enough to begin imagining that he will someday get married, but at ten he is still convinced that the best thing about being married will be that he will be allowed to sleep in his clothes. His father once observed that living with Colin was like living with a Martian who had done some reading on American culture. As it happens, Colin is not especially sad or worried about the prospect of growing up, although he sometimes frets over whether he should be called a kid or a grown-up; he has settled on the word *kid-up*. Once, I asked him what the biggest advantage to adulthood will be, and he said, "The best thing is that grown-ups can go wherever they want." I asked him what he meant, exactly, and he said, "Well, if you're grown up, you'd have a car, and whenever you felt like it, you could get into your car and drive somewhere and get candy."

Colin loves recycling. He loves it even more than, say, playing with little birds. That ten-year-olds feel the weight of the world and consider it their mission to shoulder it came as a surprise to me. I had gone with Colin one

Monday to his classroom at Montclair Cooperative School. The Co-op is in a steep, old, sharp-angled brick building that had served for many years as a public school until a group of parents in the area took it over and made it into a private, progressive elementary school. The fifth-grade classroom is on the top floor, under the dormers, which gives the room the eccentric shape and closeness of an attic. It is a rather informal environment. There are computers lined up in an adjoining room and instructions spelled out on the chalkboard—BRING IN: (1) A CUBBY WITH YOUR NAME ON IT, (2) A TRAPPER WITH A 5-POCKET ENVELOPE LABELED SCIENCE, SOCIAL STUDIES, READING/LANGUAGE ARTS, MATH, MATH LAB/COMPUTER; WHITE LINED PAPER; A PLASTIC PENCIL BAG; A SMALL HOMEWORK PAD, (3) LARGE BROWN GROCERY BAGS—but there is also a couch in the center of the classroom, which the kids take turns occupying, a rocking chair, and three canaries in cages near the door.

It happened to be Colin's first day in fifth grade. Before class began, there was a lot of horsing around, but there were also a lot of conversations about whether Magic Johnson had AIDS or just HIV and whether someone falling in a pool of blood from a cut of his would get the disease. These jolts of sobriety in the midst of rank goofiness are a ten-year-old's specialty. Each one comes as a fresh, hard surprise, like finding a razor blade in a candy apple. One day, Colin and I had been discussing horses or dogs or something, and out of the blue he said, "What do you think is better, to dump garbage in the ocean, to dump it on land, or to burn it?" Another time, he asked me if I planned to have children. I had just spent an evening with him and his friend Japeth, during which they put every small, movable object in the house into Japeth's slingshot and fired it at me, so I told him that I wanted children but that I hoped they would all be girls, and he said, "Will you have an abortion if you find out you have a boy?"

At school, after discussing summer vacation, the kids began choosing the jobs they would do to help out around the classroom. Most of the jobs are humdrum—putting the chairs up on the tables, washing the chalkboard, turning the computers off or on. Five of the most humdrum tasks are recycling chores—for example, taking bottles or stacks of paper down to the basement, where they would be sorted and prepared for pickup. Two children would be assigned to feed the birds and cover their cages at the end of the day.

I expected the bird jobs to be the first to go. Everyone loved the birds; they'd spent an hour that morning voting on names for them (Tweetie, Montgomery, and Rose narrowly beating out Axl Rose, Bugs, Ol'Yeller, Fido, Slim, Lucy, and Chirpie). Instead, they all wanted to recycle. The recycling jobs were claimed by the first five kids called by Suzanne Nakamura, the fifth-grade teacher; each kid called after that responded by groaning, "Suzanne, aren't there any more recycling jobs?" Colin ended up with the job of taking down the chairs each morning. He accepted the task with a sort of resignation—this was going to be just a job rather than a mission.

On the way home that day, I was quizzing Colin about his worldviews.

"Who's the coolest person in the world?"

"Morgan Freeman."

"What's the best sport?"

"Football."

"Who's the coolest woman?"

"None. I don't know."

"What's the most important thing in the world?"

"Game Boy." Pause. "No, the world. The world is the most important thing in the world."

Danny's pizzeria is a dark little shop next door to the Montclair Cooperative School. It is not much to look at. Outside, the brick facing is painted muddy brown. Inside, there are some saggy counters, a splintered bench, and enough room for either six teenagers or about a dozen ten-year-olds who happen to be getting along well. The light is low. The air is oily. At Danny's, you will find pizza, candy, Nintendo, and very few girls. To a ten-year-old boy, it is the most beautiful place in the world.

One afternoon, after class was dismissed, we went to Danny's with Colin's friend Japeth to play Nintendo. Danny's has only one game, Street Fighter II Champion Edition. Some teenage boys from a nearby middle school had gotten there first and were standing in a tall, impenetrable thicket around the machine.

"Next game," Colin said. The teenagers ignored him.

"Hey, we get next game," Japeth said. He is smaller than Colin, scrappy, and, as he explained to me once, famous for wearing his hat backward all the time and having a huge wristwatch and a huge bedroom. He stamped his foot and announced again, "Hey, we get next game."

One of the teenagers turned around and said, "Fuck you, *next game,*" and then turned back to the machine.

"Whoa," Japeth said.

He and Colin went outside, where they felt bigger.

"Which street fighter are you going to be?" Colin asked Japeth.

"Blanka," Japeth said. "I know how to do his head-butt."

"I hate that! I hate the head-butt," Colin said. He dropped his voice a little and growled, "I'm going to be Ken, and I will kill you with my dragon punch."

"Yeah, right, and monkeys will fly out of my butt," Japeth said.

Street Fighter II is a video game in which two characters have an explosive brawl in a scenic international setting. It is currently the most popular video arcade game in America. This is not an insignificant amount of popularity. Most arcade versions of video games, which end up in pizza parlors, malls, and arcades, sell about two thousand units. So far, some fifty thousand Street Fighter II and Street Fighter II Championship Edition arcade games have been sold. Not since Pac-Man, which was released the year before Colin was born, has there been a video game as popular as Street Fighter. The home version of Street Fighter is the most popular home video game in the country, and that, too, is not an insignificant thing. Thirty-two million Nintendo home systems have been sold since 1986, when it was introduced in this country. There is a Nintendo system in seven of every ten homes in America in which a child between the ages of eight and twelve resides. By the time a boy in America turns ten, he will almost certainly have been exposed to Nintendo home games, Nintendo arcade games, and Game Boy, the handheld version. He will probably own a system and dozens of games. By ten, according to Nintendo studies, teachers, and psychologists, game prowess becomes a fundamental, essential male social marker and a schoolyard boast.

The Street Fighter characters are Dhalsim, Ken, Guile, Blanka, E. Honda, Ryu, Zangief, and Chun Li. Each represents a different country, and they each have their own special weapon. Chun Li, for instance, is from China and possesses a devastating whirlwind kick that is triggered if you push the control pad down for two seconds and then up for two seconds, and then you hit the kick button. Chun Li's kick is money in the bank, because most of the other fighters do not have a good defense against it. By the way, Chun Li happens to be a girl—the only female Street Fighter character.

I asked Colin if he was interested in being Chun Li. There was a long pause. "I would rather be Ken," he said.

The girls in Colin's class at school are named Cortnerd, Terror, Spacey, Lizard, Maggot, and Diarrhea. "They do have other names, but that's what we call them," Colin told me. "The girls aren't very popular."

"They are about as popular as a piece of dirt," Japeth said. "Or, you know that couch in the classroom? That couch is more popular than any girl. A thousand times more." They talked for a minute about one of the girls in their class, a tall blonde with cheerleader genetic material, who they allowed was not quite as gross as some of the other girls. Japeth said that a chubby, awkward boy in their class was boasting that this girl liked him.

"No way," Colin said. "She would never like him. I mean, not that he's so... I don't know. I don't hate him because he's fat, anyway. I hate him because he's nasty."

"Well, she doesn't like him," Japeth said. "She's been really mean to me lately, so I'm pretty sure she likes me."

"Girls are different," Colin said. He hopped up and down on the balls of his feet, wrinkling his nose. "Girls are stupid and weird."

"I have a lot of girlfriends, about six or so," Japeth said, turning contemplative. "I don't exactly remember their names, though."

The teenagers came crashing out of Danny's and jostled past us, so we went inside. The man who runs Danny's, whose name is Tom, was leaning across the counter on his elbows, looking exhausted. Two little boys, holding Slush Puppies, shuffled toward the Nintendo, but Colin and Japeth elbowed them aside and slammed their quarters down on the machine. The little boys shuffled back toward the counter and stood gawking at them, sucking on their drinks.

"You want to know how to tell if a girl likes you?" Japeth said. "She'll act really mean to you. That's a sure sign. I don't know why they do it, but it's always a sure sign. It gets your attention. You know how I show a girl I like her? I steal something from her and then run away. I do it to get their attention, and it works."

They played four quarters' worth of games. During the last one, a teenager with a quilted leather jacket and a fade haircut came in, pushed his arm between them, and put a quarter down on the deck of the machine.

Japeth said, "Hey, what's that?"

The teenager said, "I get next game. I've marked it now. Everyone knows this secret sign for next game. It's a universal thing."

"So now we know," Japeth said. "Colin, let's get out of here and go bother Maggie. I mean Maggot. Okay?" They picked up their backpacks and headed out the door.

Psychologists identify ten as roughly the age at which many boys experience the gender-linked normative developmental trauma that leaves them, as adult men, at risk for specific psychological sequelae often manifest as deficits in the arenas of intimacy, empathy, and struggles with commitment in relationships. In other words, this is around the age when guys get screwed up about girls. Elaine and Jim Duffy, and probably most of the parents who send their kids to Montclair Cooperative School, have done a lot of stuff to try to avoid this. They gave Colin dolls as well as guns. (He preferred guns.) Japeth's father has three motorcycles and two dirt bikes but does most of the cooking and cleaning in their home. Suzanne, Colin's teacher, is careful to avoid sexist references in her presentations. After school, the yard at Montclair Cooperative is filled with as many fathers as mothers—fathers who hug their kids when they come prancing out of the building and are dismayed when their sons clamor for Supersoaker water guns and war toys or take pleasure in beating up girls.

In a study of adolescents conducted by the Gesell Institute of Human Development, nearly half the ten-year-old boys questioned said they thought they had adequate information about sex. Nevertheless, most ten-year-old boys across the country are subjected to a few months of sex education in school. Colin and his class will get their dose next spring. It is yet another installment in a plan to make them into new, improved men with reconstructed notions of sex and male-female relationships. One afternoon I asked Philip, a schoolmate of Colin's, whether he was looking forward to sex education, and he said, "No, because I think it'll probably make me really, really hyper. I have a feeling it's going to be just like what it was like when some television reporters came to school last year and filmed us in class and I got really hyper. They stood around with all these cameras and asked us questions. I think that's what sex education is probably like."

At a class meeting earlier in the day:

Colin's teacher, SUZANNE: Today was our first day of swimming class, and I have one observation to make. The girls went into their locker room, got dressed without a lot of fuss, and came into the pool area. The boys, on the other hand, the *boys* had some sort of problem doing that rather simple task. Can someone tell me what exactly went on in the locker room?

KEITH: There was a lot of shouting.

SUZANNE: Okay, I hear you saying that people were being noisy and shouting. Anything else?

CHRISTIAN: Some people were screaming so much that my ears were killing me. It gave me, like, a huge headache. Also, some of the boys were taking their towels, I mean, after they had taken their clothes off, they had their towels around their waists and then they would drop them really fast and then pull them back up, really fast.

SUZANNE: Okay, you're saying some people were being silly about their bodies.

CHRISTIAN: Well, yeah, but it was more like they were being silly about their pants.

Colin's bedroom is decorated simply. He has a cage with his pet parakeet, Dude, on his dresser, a lot of recently worn clothing piled haphazardly on the floor, and a husky brown teddy bear sitting upright in a chair near the foot of his bed. The walls are mostly bare, except for a Spiderman poster and a few ads torn out of magazines he has thumbtacked up. One of the ads is for a cologne, illustrated with several small photographs of cowboy hats; another, a feverish portrait of a woman on a horse, is an ad for blue jeans. These inspire him sometimes when he lies in bed and makes plans for the move to Wyoming. Also, he happens to like ads. He also likes television commercials. Generally speaking, he likes consumer products and popular culture. He partakes avidly but not indiscriminately. In fact, during the time we spent together, he provided a running commentary on merchandise, media, and entertainment:

"The only shoes anyone will wear are Reebok Pumps. Big T-shirts are cool, not the kind that are sticky and close to you, but big and baggy and long, not the kind that stop at your stomach."

"The best food is Chicken McNuggets and Life cereal and Frosted Flakes."

"Don't go to Blimpie's. They have the worst service."

"I'm not into Teenage Mutant Ninja Turtles anymore. I grew out of that. I like Donatello, but I'm not a fan. I don't buy the figures anymore."

"The best television shows are on Friday night on ABC. It's called TGIF, and it's *Family Matters, Step by Step, Dinosaurs*, and *Perfect Strangers*, where the guy has a funny accent."

"The best candy is Skittles and Symphony bars and Crybabies and Warheads. Crybabies are great because if you eat a lot of them at once you feel so sour."

"Hyundais are Korean cars. It's the only Korean car. They're not that good because Koreans don't have a lot of experience building cars."

"The best movie is *City Slickers*, and the best part was when he saved his little cow in the river."

"The Giants really need to get rid of Ray Handley. They have to get somebody who has real coaching experience. He's just no good."

"My dog, Sally, costs seventy-two dollars. That sounds like a lot of money but it's a really good price because you get a flea bath with your dog."

"The best magazines are *Nintendo Power*, because they tell you how to do the secret moves in the video games, and also *Mad magazine* and *Money Guide*—I really like that one."

"The best artist in the world is Jim Davis."

"The most beautiful woman in the world is not Madonna! Only Wayne and Garth think that! She looks like maybe a...a...slut or something. Cindy Crawford looks like she would look good, but if you see her on an awards program on TV she doesn't look that good. I think the most beautiful woman in the world probably is my mom."

Colin thinks a lot about money. This started when he was about nine and a half, which is when a lot of other things started—a new way of walking that has a little macho hitch and swagger, a decision about the Teenage Mutant Ninja Turtles (con) and Eurythmics (pro), and a persistent curiosity about a certain girl whose name he will not reveal. He knows the price of everything he encounters. He knows how much college costs and what someone might earn performing different jobs. Once, he asked me what my husband did; when I answered that he was a lawyer, he snapped, "You must be a rich family. Lawyers make $400,000 a year." His preoccupation with money baffles his family. They are not struggling, so this is not the anxiety of deprivation; they are not rich, so he is not responding to an elegant, advantaged world. His allowance is five dollars a week. It seems sufficient for his needs, which consist chiefly of quarters for Nintendo and candy money. The remainder is put into his Wyoming fund. His fascination is not just specific to needing money or having plans for money: It is as if money itself, and the way it makes the world work, and the realization that almost everything in the world can be assigned a price, has possessed him. "I just pay attention to things like that," Colin says. "It's really very interesting."

He is looking for a windfall. He tells me his mother has been notified that she is in the fourth and final round of the Publisher's Clearinghouse

Sweepstakes. This is not an ironic observation. He plays the New Jersey lottery every Thursday night. He knows the weekly jackpot; he knows the number to call to find out if he has won. I do not think this presages a future for Colin as a high-stakes gambler; I think it says more about the powerful grasp that money has on imagination and what a large percentage of a ten-year-old's mind is made up of imaginings. One Friday, we were at school together, and one of his friends was asking him about the lottery, and he said, "This week it was $4 million. That would be I forget how much every year for the rest of your life. It's a lot, I think. You should play. All it takes is a dollar and a dream."

Until the lottery comes through and he starts putting together the Wyoming land deal, Colin can be found most of the time in the backyard. Often, he will have friends come over. Regularly, children from the neighborhood will gravitate to the backyard, too. As a technical matter of real-property law, title to the house and yard belongs to Jim and Elaine Duffy, but Colin adversely possesses the backyard, at least from 4:00 each afternoon until it gets dark. As yet, the fixtures of teenage life—malls, video arcades, friends' basements, automobiles—either hold little interest for him or are not his to have.

He is, at the moment, very content with his backyard. For most intents and purposes, it is as big as Wyoming. One day, certainly, he will grow and it will shrink, and it will become simply a suburban backyard and it won't be big enough for him anymore. This will happen so fast that one night he will be in the backyard, believing it a perfect place, and by the next night he will have changed and the yard as he imagined it will be gone, and this era of his life will be behind him forever.

Most days, he spends his hours in the backyard building an Evil Spider-Web Trap. This entails running a spool of Jim's fishing line from every surface in the yard until it forms a huge web. Once a garbageman picking up the Duffys' trash got caught in the trap. Otherwise, the Evil Spider-Web Trap mostly has a deterrent effect, because the kids in the neighborhood who might roam over know that Colin builds it back there. "I do it all the time," he says, "First I plan who I'd like to catch in it, and then we get started. Trespassers have to beware."

One afternoon when I came over, after a few rounds of Street Fighter at Danny's, Colin started building a trap. He selected a victim for inspiration—a boy in his class who had been pestering him—and began wrapping. He was entirely absorbed. He moved from tree to tree, wrapping; he laced fishing line through the railing of the deck and then back to the shed; he circled an old jungle gym, something he'd outgrown and abandoned a few years ago, and then crossed over to a bush at the back of the yard. Briefly, he contemplated making his dog, Sally, part of the web. Dusk fell. He kept wrapping, paying out fishing line an inch at a time. We could hear mothers up and down the block hooting for their kids; two tiny children from next door stood transfixed at the edge of the yard, uncertain whether they would end up inside or outside the web. After a while, the spool spun around in Colin's hands one more time and then stopped; he was out of line.

It was almost too dark to see much of anything, although now and again the light from the deck would glance off a length of line, and it would glint and sparkle. "That's the point," he said. "You could do it with thread, but the fishing line is invisible. Now I have this perfect thing and the only one who knows about it is me." With that, he dropped the spool, skipped up the stairs of the deck, threw open the screen door, and then bounded into the house, leaving me and Sally the dog trapped in his web.

APPENDIX

The Literary Landscape of Creative Nonfiction

∽

What do you do when you have written a piece of creative nonfiction and want to share it? One place to start is to research literary journals. There are a lot of literary journals, and most contain a mixture of fiction, poetry, and nonfiction—very few publish nonfiction exclusively. Two good places to begin your research are newpages.com (a database of literary journals) and the Web site of the magazine *Poets & Writers* (www.pw.com).

Before submitting your piece to literary journals, here are some questions to consider:

- Do they accept electronic submissions or hard copy submissions or both? Keep in mind that some journals require a nominal fee for online submissions.

- Do they accept simultaneous submissions or allow you to submit a single piece to multiple publications at the same time? If they do, this is a huge advantage to writers because they don't have to rest their hopes on one journal over the six months to a year it takes to get a response.

- When do they accept submissions? Some journals only accept submissions during certain months and don't accept submissions the rest of the year—be cautious of this.

- Is the content of the journal you are submitting to similar to what you are writing? Some journals are specifically geared toward a certain type of nonfiction (i.e., lyric essay, literary journalism, or memoir). It's always good practice to read back issues of journals to make sure you find a good fit for you and your writing. Better yet, subscribe!

- Do they have a page limit or word limit on submissions?

- Do they have formatting requirements? For example, sometimes journals only accept pieces in particular fonts and font sizes, or they only accept submissions with certain margins (perhaps 1" all around). Some journals have stipulations regarding title pages—some like them, some don't. Also, some have specific requirements for having author names on the manuscript or leaving them off, as sometimes editors and their staff do

---

This appendix was written by Andrea Oyarzabal.

blind readings (the author remains anonymous to the staff so his or her name doesn't influence the decision).

- Will you receive any sort of compensation for your submission if it is chosen and printed? Oftentimes, journals do not pay; however, they often will give you some free copies of the journal and sometimes give you a free year's subscription.

Consider making yourself a spreadsheet to track submissions. Some good information to include in your spreadsheet is publication name, submission date, contact name, acceptance/rejection, and the date you get your acceptance or rejection. There's actually software available online to help you with this.

Keep in mind that hundreds if not thousands of people are submitting their pieces to journals each day. The editors of these journals are usually looking for reasons to reject submissions to make their jobs easier, because reading through hundreds of submissions can be a tedious task and a lot of journals have small staffs. When reading through submission requirements, go slowly and read all of the fine print to ensure that you are giving yourself a good chance and that your piece won't be rejected because of a mistake.

The lists that follow will help you explore venues for publishing and reading creative nonfiction. Along with each suggested journal is a brief summary of the publication from its Web site.

Literary Journals That Publish Exclusively Nonfiction

1. *Brevity*

"For more than a decade now, *Brevity* has published well-known and emerging writers working in the extremely brief (750 words or less) essay form. Though still committed to the mission of publishing new writers, *Brevity* has enjoyed an embarrassment of recent riches, including the work of two Pulitzer prize finalists, numerous NEA fellows, Pushcart winners, Best American authors, and writers from India, Egypt, Ireland, Spain, and Japan. Authors published in *Brevity* include Sherman Alexie, Lia Purpura, Terese Svoboda, John Calderazzo, Brenda Miller, Aimee Nezhukumatathil, Robin Hemley, Lee Martin, Rebecca McClanahan, Robin Behn, Abby Frucht, Barbara Hurd, Bret Lott, Ira Sukrungruang, Rigoberto González, Judith Kitchen, and Diana Hume George."

Electronic submissions? Yes. Hard copy? No.

2. *Creative Nonfiction*

"*Creative Nonfiction* was the first and is still the largest literary magazine to exclusively publish high quality nonfiction prose. The journal has consistently featured prominent authors from the United States and around the world and has helped launch the careers of some of the genre's most exciting emerging writers, as well as helping establish the creative nonfiction genre as a worthy academic pursuit."

Electronic submissions? No. Hard copy? Yes.

3. *Fourth Genre*

"...*Fourth Genre: Explorations in Nonfiction* [is] a journal devoted to publishing notable, innovative work in nonfiction. The title reflects our intention to give nonfiction its due as a literary genre—to give writers of the fourth genre a showcase for their work and to give our readers a place to find the liveliest and most creative works in the form.

Given the genre's flexibility and expansiveness, we welcome a variety of works—ranging from personal essays and memoirs to literary journalism and personal criticism. The editors invite works that are lyrical, self-interrogative, meditative, and reflective, as well as expository, analytical, exploratory, or whimsical. In short, we encourage submissions across the full spectrum of the fourth genre. The journal encourages a writer-to-reader conversation, one that explores the markers and boundaries of literary/creative nonfiction."

Electronic submissions? No. Hard copy? Yes.

4. *River Teeth*

"*River Teeth* is a biannual journal combining the best of creative nonfiction, including narrative reportage, essays and memoir, with critical essays that examine the emerging genre and that explore the impact of nonfiction narrative on the lives of its writers, subjects, and readers."

Electronic submissions? Yes. Hard copy? No.

Top Ten Literary Journals Reprinted in The Best American Essays Series *(2004–2010)*

The Best American Essays, published annually, is probably the most widely recognized anthology featuring nonfiction pieces, particularly in the essay genre. Following are some of the journals that are most represented within the series and brief descriptions from each publication's Web site.

1. *The American Scholar*

"*The American Scholar* is a magazine of articles and essays covering the humanities, science, and current events, plus works of fiction and poetry. Published quarterly for the general reader by the Phi Beta Kappa Society, the *Scholar* considers nonfiction by known and unknown writers; unsolicited fiction and poetry are not encouraged."

Electronic submissions? No. Hard copy? Yes.

2. *The Georgia Review*

"Published quarterly by The University of Georgia since 1947, *The Georgia Review* features an eclectic blend of essays, fiction, poetry, graphics, and book reviews. Appealing across disciplinary lines, *The Review* draws its material from a wide range of cultural interests—including, but not limited to, literature, history, philosophy, anthropology, politics, film, music, and the visual arts....We are seeking informed essays that attempt to place their subjects against a broad perspective. For the most part we are not interested in scholarly articles that are narrow in focus and/or overly burdened with footnotes. The ideal essay for *The Georgia Review* is a provocative, thesis-oriented work that can engage both the intelligent general reader and the specialist."

Electronic submissions? No. Hard copy? Yes.

3. *Granta*

"*Granta* does not have a political or literary manifesto, but it does have a belief in the power and urgency of the story, both in fiction and non-fiction, and the story's supreme ability to describe, illuminate and make real. As *The Observer* wrote of *Granta*: 'In its blend of memoirs and photojournalism, and in its championing of contemporary realist fiction, *Granta* has its face pressed firmly against the window, determined to witness the world.'"

Electronic submissions? No. Hard copy? Yes.

4. *Harvard Review*

"In the nearly two decades since it was launched, *Harvard Review* has emerged as a major American literary journal with an eclectic mix of contributors in a wide variety of genres and styles. Contributors to the journal include: Arthur Miller, Joyce Carol Oates, Seamus Heaney, Jorie Graham, John Updike, John Ashbery, Alice Hoffman, and Gore Vidal, as well as those who are making their literary debut."

Electronic submissions? Yes. Hard copy? Yes.

5. *The Iowa Review*

"With 2010, *The Iowa Review* enters its 40th year of continuous publication. We select most of our content from the several thousand unsolicited manuscripts that arrive each year from throughout the country and abroad. We take our mission to be nudging along American literature, to be local but not provincial, to be experimental but not without love for our literary traditions. Although you may find writers already familiar to you in most of our issues, you will surely find others who are not. Discovering a new and compelling writer, one we'd never heard of before but whose writing comes through to us—that still seems the magic of our work."

Electronic submissions? No. Hard copy? Yes.

6. *The Missouri Review*

"*The Missouri Review*, founded in 1978, is one of the most highly-regarded literary magazines in the United States and for the past twenty-five years we've upheld a reputation for finding and publishing the very best writers first. We are based at the University of Missouri and publish four issues each year. Each issue contains new fiction, poetry and essays. We also run interviews with famous authors and found-text features where we print never before published works such as a short story by William Faulkner or one of Tennessee Williams' plays. Recently we did a feature on famous rejection letters of novels such as *Lolita* and *The Bell Jar*."

Electronic submissions? Yes. Hard copy? Yes.

7. *n+1*

"We are a literary magazine but we are interested above all in reports from all the various fields of human endeavor: medicine, computing, the law, sports, crime, art, finance, engineering, construction, music, etc. Please tell us and our readers what we do not know. We do not publish interviews with living authors or appreciations of dead authors, filmmakers, artists, etc."

Online submissions? Yes. Hard copy? No.

8. *PMS*

"*PMS poemmemoirstory* is a 140-page, perfect-bound, all-women's literary journal published annually by the University of Alabama at Birmingham. While we proudly publish the best work of the best women writers in the nation (i.e., Maxine Chernoff, Elaine Equi, Amy Gerstler, Honorée Fanonne Jeffers, Molly Peacock, Lucia Perillo, Sonia Sanchez, Ruth Stone, and Natasha Trethewey, among others) we also solicit a memoir for each issue written by a woman who may not be a writer, but who has experienced something of historic significance. Emily Lyons, the nurse who survived the 1998 New Woman All Women Birmingham clinic bombing by Eric Rudolph, wrote the first of these; women who experienced the World Trade Center on September 11th, the Civil Rights Movement in Birmingham, the war in Iraq, and Hurricane Katrina have also lent us their stories."

Electronic submissions? No. Hard copy? Yes.

9. *The Sun*

"We publish essays, interviews, fiction, and poetry. We tend to favor personal writing, but we're also looking for thoughtful, well-written essays on political, cultural, and philosophical themes. Please, no journalistic features, academic works, or opinion pieces. Other than that, we're open to just about anything. Surprise us; we often don't know what we'll like until we read it."

Electronic submissions? No. Hard copy? Yes.

10. *The Threepenny Review*

"*The Threepenny Review* is a quarterly review of the arts and society. Its consulting editors include Jonathan Franzen, Louise Glück, Ian McEwan, and Tobias Wolff; among its writers are Wendell Berry, Geoff Dyer, Phillip Lopate, Greil Marcus, Javier Marías, Robert Pinsky, Kay Ryan, Oliver Sacks, Amy Tan, and C. K. Williams. Each issue contains new poetry, short fiction, personal memoirs, and essays on books, film, theater, dance, music, architecture, visual arts, television, and politics. Of the total 8,000+ circulation, over 6,500 are long-term paid subscribers, making *The Threepenny Review* one of the largest quarterly magazines in the country."

Electronic submissions? No. Hard copy? Yes.

Top Ten Literary Journals
Receiving "Notable Essay" Status
in The Best American Essays
Series *(2004–2010)*

1. *AGNI*

"Literature for literature's sake is not what *AGNI* is about. Rather, we see literature and the arts as part of a broad, ongoing cultural conversation that every society needs to remain vibrant and alive. What we print requires concentration and takes some time to digest, but it's worth that time and effort: writers and artists hold a mirror up to nature, mankind, the world; they courageously reflect their age, for better or worse; and their best works provoke perceptions and thoughts that help us understand and respond to our age."

Electronic submissions? Yes. Hard copy? No.

2. *Alaska Quarterly Review*

"*Alaska Quarterly Review* is a literary journal devoted to contemporary literary art, publishing fiction, short plays, poetry, photo essays, and literary non-fiction in traditional and experimental styles. The editors encourage new and emerging writers, while continuing to publish award-winning and established writers."

Electronic submissions? No. Hard copy? Yes.

3. *Antioch Review*

"The *Antioch Review*, founded in 1941, is one of the oldest, continuously publishing literary magazines in America. We publish fiction, essays, and poetry from both emerging as well as established authors. Authors published in our pages are consistently included in *Best American* anthologies and *Pushcart* prizes. We continue to serve our readers and our authors and to encourage others to publish the 'best words in the best order.'"

Electronic submissions? No. Hard copy? Yes.

4. *Ascent*

Ascent is an online magazine featuring essays, fiction, and poetry.

Electronic submissions? Yes. Hard copy? No.

5. *Dædalus*

"*Dædalus* was founded in 1955 as the *Journal of the American Academy of Arts and Sciences*.... It draws on the enormous intellectual capacity of the American Academy, whose members are among the nation's most prominent thinkers in the arts, sciences, and humanities.... Each issue addresses a theme with authoritative essays on topics such as judicial independence, reflecting on the humanities, the global nuclear future, the challenge of mass incarceration, the future of news, the economy, the military, and race."

Submission by invitation only.

6. *The Gettysburg Review*

"The editors of *The Gettysburg Review* express their deep commitment to the arts and humanities by seeking out and publishing the very best contemporary poetry, fiction, essays, essay-reviews, and art in issues as physically beautiful as they are intellectually and emotionally stimulating. Our most important criterion is high literary quality; we look for writers who can shape language in thoughtful, surprising, and beautiful ways and who have something unique to say, whatever the subject matter or aesthetic approach. We have very eclectic tastes, but are highly selective, publishing only two percent of manuscripts submitted to us annually."

Electronic submissions? No. Hard copy? Yes.

7. *The Massachusetts Review*

"We seek a balance between established writers and promising new ones. We're interested in material of variety and vitality relevant to the intellectual and aesthetic questions of our time. We aspire to have a broad appeal; our commitment, in part regional, is not provincial."

Electronic submissions? Yes. Hard copy? Yes.

8. *Southwest Review*

"In 1984, for the first time in forty years, editorial responsibility for the magazine was returned to a member of the faculty. Willard Spiegelman, professor of English, was named editor-in-chief, a position he still holds. In 2005, Mr. Spiegelman won the PEN/Nora Magid award for literary editing. PEN stated, 'The *Southwest Review* has emerged in the last twenty years as one of the best literary quarterlies in the United States. Poetry and fiction, memoirs and criticism, appear side by side in its pages, in balanced proportions... It seems impartially welcoming both toward luminous and unfamiliar names, so long as the writing is genuine.'"

Electronic submissions? Yes. Hard copy? Yes.

9. *The Sewanee Review*

The Sewanee Review is "America's oldest continuously published literary quarterly." Only erudite work representing depth of knowledge and skill of expression is published here.

Electronic submissions? No. Hard copy? Yes.

10. *The Virginia Quarterly Review*

"*VQR* strives to publish the freshest, most accomplished writers of our time. We are partial to work that is conscious of language without being self-conscious, that pulls readers in with drama and emotional risk, rather than holding them at arm's length with gimmickry and tricks. In short, we seek writing that uses intensely focused language to affect the way that readers see the world. A well-crafted poem, story, or essay is, at its heart, a statement of refusal to accept conventional wisdom and instead study the world for oneself. We seek that writing which illuminates what we, as a culture, may learn from such close inspection."

Electronic submissions? Yes. Hard copy? No.

BIBLIOGRAPHY

Primary Works: Sources of the
Crafting Truth *Excerpts in Books
and Anthologies*

Ackerman, Diane. *The Natural History of the Senses.* New York: Random House, 1990.

Agee, James, and Walker Evans. *Let Us Now Praise Famous Men.* Boston: Houghton, 1960.

Baldwin, James. *Notes of a Native Son.* 1955. Boston: Beacon Press, 1984.

Bissinger, H. G. *Friday Night Lights.* Cambridge, MA: Da Capo Press, 1990.

Blew, Mary Clearman. *All But the Waltz.* New York: Penguin, 1991.

Capote, Truman. *In Cold Blood.* 1965. New York: Vintage, 1993.

Didion, Joan. *Slouching Towards Bethlehem.* New York: Noonday Press, 1992.

Dubus, Andre. *Broken Vessels.* Boston: Godine, 1991.

Eggers, Dave. *A Heartbreaking Work of Staggering Genius.* New York: Vintage, 2001.

Ehrlich, Gretel. *The Solace of Open Spaces.* New York: Penguin, 1986.

Kingston, Maxine Hong. *The Woman Warrior.* New York: Vintage, 1976.

Kramer, Jane. *The Last Cowboy.* 1977. London: Pimlico, 1998.

Larson, Erik. *The Devil in the White City.* New York: Vintage, 2003.

Mailer, Norman. *The Armies of the Night.* New York: Plume, 1968.

Mairs, Nancy. *Plaintext.* Tucson: University of Arizona Press, 1992.

McCourt, Frank. *Angela's Ashes.* New York: Scribner, 1996.

Mitchell, Joseph. *Up in the Old Hotel.* New York: Vintage, 1993.

Momaday, N. Scott. *The Way to Rainy Mountain.* Albuquerque: University of New Mexico Press, 1969.

Monson, Ander. *Neck Deep and Other Predicaments.* Saint Paul, MN: Graywolf Press, 2007.

Orlean, Susan. *The Bullfighter Checks Her Makeup.* New York: Random House, 2002.

Purpura, Lia. *On Looking.* Louiville, KY: Sarabande Books, 2006.

Sanders, Scott Russell. *The Paradise of Bombs.* Boston: Beacon Press, 1987.

Sedaris, David. *Holidays on Ice.* New York: Back Bay Books, 1997.

Slater, Lauren. *Lying.* New York: Penguin, 2000.

Vowell, Sarah. *Take the Cannoli.* New York: Simon & Schuster, 2000.

Walker, Alice. *In Search of Our Mother's Gardens.* San Diego: Harcourt Brace, 1983.

White, E. B. *The Essays of E. B. White.* New York: First Perennial Classics, 1999.

Wideman, John Edgar. *Brothers and Keepers.* 1984. Boston: Mariner Books, 2005.

Williams, Terry Tempest. *Refuge.* New York: Vintage, 1991.

Wolfe, Tom. *The Electric Kool-Aid Acid Test.* New York: Bantam, 1969.

Wolff, Tobias. *This Boy's Life.* 1977. New York: Harper & Row, 1989.

Secondary Works: Articles and Books About Creative Nonfiction

Birkerts, Sven. *The Art of Time in Memoir*. Minneapolis: Graywolf Press, 2008.

Boynton, Robert S. *The New New Journalism: Conversations with America's Best Nonfiction Writers on Their Craft*. New York: Vintage Press, 2005.

Eakin, Paul J. *The Ethics of Life Writing*. Ithaca: Cornell University Press, 2004.

Gerard, Philip. *Creative Nonfiction*. Cincinnati: Story Press, 1996.

Goldberg, Natalie. *Old Friend from Far Away: The Practice of Writing Memoir*. New York: Simon & Schuster, 2007.

Gornick, Vivian. *The Situation and the Story: The Art of Personal Narrative*. New York: Farrar, Straus and Giroux, 2001.

Gutkind, Lee, ed. *In Fact: The Best of Creative Nonfiction*. New York: W.W. Norton & Company, 2005.

Hartsock, John C. *A History of American Literary Journalism*. Amherst: University of Massachusetts Press, 2000.

Hesse, Douglas. "A Boundary Zone: First Person Short Stories and Narrative Essays." *Short Story Theory at a Crossroads*. Edited by Susan Lohafer and Jo Ellyn Clarey. Baton Rouge, LA: LSU Press, 1989.

Hoagland, Edward. "What I Think, What I Am." *Tugman's Passage*. New York: Random House, 1982.

Kidder, Tracy. "Courting the Approval of the Dead." *Tri-Quarterly* 97 (Fall 1997): 43–59.

King, Stephen. *On Writing: A Memoir of Craft*. New York: Simon & Schuster, 2000.

Kramer, Mark, and Wendy Call, eds. *Telling True Stories: A Nonfiction Writer's Guide*. New York: Plume, 2007.

Larson, Thomas. *The Memoir and the Memoirist: Reading and Writing Personal Narrative*. Athens, OH: Swallow Press, 2007.

Lehman, David W. *Matters of Fact: Reading Nonfiction Over the Edge*. Columbus: Ohio State University Press, 1997.

Literary Journalism in the Twentieth Century. Edited by Norman Sims. New York: Oxford University Press, 1990.

Lopate, Phillip. *The Art of the Personal Essay*. New York: Anchor, 1994.

—. "Reflection and Retrospection: A Pedagogic Mystery Story." *The Fourth Genre* 7.1 (Spring 2005): 143–156.

—. "What Happened to the Personal Essay?" *Against Joie de Vivre*. New York: Poseidon, 1989.

Mailer, Norman. *The Spooky Art: Thoughts on Writing*. New York: Random House, 2003.

Mairs, Nancy. *Voice Lessons: On Becoming a (Woman) Writer*. Boston: Beacon Pess, 1994.

Malcom, Janet. *The Journalist and the Murderer*. New York: Vintage, 1990.

Ozick, Cynthia. "She: Portrait of the Essay as a Warm Body." *Atlantic Monthly* (September 1998): 114–118.

Roorbach, Bill. *Contemporary Creative Nonfiction: The Art of Truth*. New York: Oxford University Press, 2001.

Root, Robert L. *E. B. White: The Emergence of an Essayist*. Iowa City: University of Iowa Press, 1999.

Root, Robert L., and Michael Steinberg. *The Fourth Genre*, 3rd ed. New York: Pearson/Longman, 2005.

Sanders, Scott Russell. "First Person Singular." *Secrets of the Universe*. Boston: Beacon, 1991. 187–204.

Shields, David. *Reality Hunger: A Manifesto*. New York: Knopf, 2010.

Traig, Jennifer, ed. *The Autobiographer's Handbook*. New York: Holt, 2008.

Wolfe, Tom. *The New Journalism*. New York: Harper & Row, 1973.

Yagoda, Ben. *Memoir: A History*. New York: Riverhead, 2009.

Zinsser, William. *Inventing Truth: The Art and Craft of Memoir*. Boston: Houghton, 1998.

—. *Writing About Your Life: A Journey into the Past*. New York: Marlowe & Company, 2004.

CREDITS

Photo Credits

Text Credits

INDEX